PUCKLER'S PROGRESS

Prince Hermann Pückler-Muskau

PUCKLER'S PROGRESS

The Adventures of
Prince Pückler-Muskau in England,
Wales and Ireland as told in letters
to his former wife, 1826–9

Translated by
FLORA BRENNAN

COLLINS
8 Grafton Street, London W1
1987

William Collins Sons & Co. Ltd
London · Glasgow · Sydney · Auckland
Toronto · Johannesburg

BRITISH LIBRARY CATALOGUING IN PUBLICATION DATA

Pückler-Muskau, Hermann, Fürst von
Pückler's progress: the adventures of
Prince Pückler-Muskau in England, Wales
and Ireland as told in letters to his
former wife.
1. Great Britain – Social life and customs
– 19th century
I. Title   II. Prinz Pückler reisst nach
England. *English*
941.07′4′0924   DA533

ISBN 0-00-217631-9

First published 1987

Photoset by Rowland Phototypesetting Ltd
Bury St Edmunds, Suffolk
**Printed and Bound in Great Britain by
T. J. Press (Padstow) Ltd, Padstow, Cornwall**

To Barbara Janet Lindsay Spens
with love

Princess Lucie Pückler-Muskau

TRANSLATOR'S INTRODUCTION

In 1826 those two perfect Elective Affinities, the Prince and Princess Pückler-Muskau, obtained a divorce *invitus invita*. The reason they gave to the Court of Prussia was that the marriage had produced no heir, but in reality they had decided that the only way to stave off imminent financial ruin was for Pückler to marry another and wealthy wife; not a particularly unusual solution for the time, except that Lucie and Hermann still adored each other and had not faced up to the prospect of a permanent separation.

A former soldier and diplomat, the Prince was a talented landscape gardener, a gifted writer, a great traveller and reputed to enjoy sowing wild oats. Lucie, his wife, was nine years his senior; she was the daughter of the Chancellor of Prussia, Prince von Hardenberg, and widow of the wealthy Count von Pappenheim. She had married Pückler in 1817 and the only unhappiness in an otherwise perfectly happy marriage was their desperate need of money. The Prince had inherited from his father the small absolute principality of Muskau and an enormous debt. He had also inherited his extravagant tastes: during their engagement he spent most of Lucie's considerable dowry planting a million trees. Then disaster struck: Muskau was absorbed into the Kingdom of Prussia along with all its revenues, and the Prince's father-in-law died, leaving his entire fortune to his rapacious mistresses.

This desperate situation called for a desperate remedy; the difficulties of obtaining a divorce surmounted, Pückler set out in 1826 for England, the richest country in Europe and so the most fertile garden of heiresses.

During the two years of his stay he wrote to Lucie every day, and sometimes more than once a day, describing everything he saw with the skill of a born writer and through the eyes of a man of catholic tastes and lively interests. She had asked for the small details of everyday life 'since nothing gives a livelier picture of a foreign land', and he has given them to her; no painter of seventeenth-century

Holland could have depicted more faithfully the life of the great country houses, the varying degrees of comfort to be found in the roadside inns at greater or lesser distance from the capital, Donnybrook Fair in rural Ireland and the hardships of travel in Wales on the way to his triumphant conquest of Mount Snowdon. His rank opened doors usually firmly closed, and his descriptions of the life of the royal family are very interesting and very sympathetic – probably because of royalty's liking for all things German. His accounts of race meetings, balls, the social life of Brighton, make splendid reading, and we can compare his account of the English theatre with that of Hazlitt. The stage in the early nineteenth century must have been as glorious as that of the mid-twentieth; the same subtlety and understanding of the dramatist. Pückler relished the gifts of Kean, Kemble and Young, and his detailed accounts of their performances brings some of his delight to his readers. He also enjoyed humbler forms of entertainment; it was at Vauxhall that Keats caught his fleeting glimpse of that 'fair creature of an hour', and we can be grateful to Pückler for filling in the background. In his description of the Battle of Waterloo, we learn that the trees of the park were festooned with coloured lamps, and we are free to wonder how on earth the management got them lighted; we are also told of the realism of the sets – a reconstruction of the hill of Huguemont and the engagement of whole armies of extras.

The result is an incomparable social document, a vivid portrait of an age when England's wealth and progressiveness were the envy of Europe, reflected in such triumphant inventions as the tunnel under the Thames and the new steam engine, in Nash's great 'royal mile' in central London.

Pückler, that faithful Liberal, was naturally interested in the world's unfortunates; taking our account of Bedlam, as most of us do, from Hogarth and Goya, it is reassuring to discover that we were, in the early nineteenth century, neither as foolish nor as heartless in our treatment of lunatics as we had believed. At the same time, however, it seems that the fantastic world of Dickens' Marshalsea was the real thing, as is borne out by Pückler's description of King's Bench prison, and the Prince was moved by the Newgate villain who filled in the time before execution studying French. One distinguished parallel between Pückler and his English contemporaries is to be found in the *Pickwick Papers* – Count

8

Smorltork, gathering material for his great work on England, must be none other than Pückler himself.

Pückler's quest for a rich wife was not successful and in February 1829 he returned to Muskau as poor as when he had left it. However, that was not the end of the story. Lucie had preserved his letters and apparently they decided, on reading them over, that they were worth something. Even after careful pruning there was still enough material for four volumes. They came out in 1830 under the anonymous title *Briefes Eines Verstorbenen* (Letters from a Dead Man).

Like Byron, Pückler woke one morning to find himself famous. The reception of the book was certainly mixed, but it was read in Europe, America and the Near East. Goethe himself rumbled his praises of it – of course he was very anglophobe and perceptive enough to recognize the book's merits. The reception of Sarah Austin's English translation *The Tour of a German Prince*, which was published in 1832, was just as mixed. A highly respected, very cultured woman, Mrs Austin's translation was rightly praised, but its German author, whose identity was at once guessed, was pilloried for his presumption and arrogance. Britannia, who ruled the waves, was not likely to take kindly to criticism or mockery from a mere foreigner – to whom was given the subtle soubriquet of 'Pickling Mustard'.

Recipient of the biggest publisher's cheque yet drawn in Europe, Pückler could now turn to the maintenance and embellishment of Muskau, although in 1845 he sold it and moved, with Lucie, to the smaller family estate of Branitz. He travelled a great deal and wrote of his experiences. Lucie never again suffered a permanent separation from Hermann and she remained his devoted companion until her death in 1854. They had achieved their ambition of life together in their own home and we may assume that they enjoyed as much happiness as this uncertain world affords. Pückler himself died in 1871. He is buried at Branitz, under the great pyramid he had designed as his tomb, on which is an inscription from the Koran 'Graves are the mountain tops of a distant, lovely land'.

Like all correspondences, the Prince's letters give us an immediate and vivid picture of both writer and recipient, and also of the relationship between them. We have none of Lucie's letters, but her character emerges in the account of her actions over this period. It was she who brought the affairs of Muskau into as much order as possible; who recognized the impracticality of their ever setting up a *ménage à trois*. She anticipated his pecuniary needs; she sent him a carriage and coachman and a fur wrap for his journey through the wintry landscape on his return to Muskau. He confided to her his every adventure, great and small, in the obvious certainty that he would find a sympathetic listener, and he repeatedly assured her that, if he was certain of one thing upon this earth, it was her unchanging love. Such general character lines require very little filling in.

Pückler himself, of course, appears in much greater depth and detail. He would be on the short list of any quest for Man of the Romantic Movement. The Beautiful and the Noble were written for him with capital letters; he was a worshipper of Nature, who saw the mountains of Wales through the eyes of Salvator Rosa and invested Brighton beach with all the terrors of the deep; he looked back with longing to the romance of the Middle Ages; he took real interest in the plight of prisoners and miners, and the conditions of factory workers. Like his contemporary, fellow German traveller, Heinrich Heine (whose *English Fragments* was published in 1831), he was a Liberal, a Canningite, a constant champion of the, in his opinion, sadly neglected Byron; and his epic journey to the castle of the great Daniel O'Connell in Ireland was more in the nature of a pilgrimage than a social visit. Pückler was brave and capable of physical exertion; he was also a bellicose patriot, bigoted and a terrible hypochondriac.

For all the generations that have rolled since Adam, and for all the speed of mankind across the globe, the relationship between these two may well be unique. They decided together to resolve their difficulties by the traditional means of acquiring a wealthy wife. This did not mean to either Lucie or Hermann that they would cease to be all in all to each other. Pückler had always been a great womaniser, and this for him, and for those who knew him, had devalued the currency of sex. Lucie was Hermann's closest confidante in his search for a wife. Whether expressing his horror at the impossible bourgeois vulgarity of the Gibbins family in Brighton, or his distaste for the self-willed little redhead in the same town; lamenting the immovable religious prejudices of the beautiful and wealthy jeweller's daughter, Harriet Hamlet, or even hymning the charms of Lady Garvagh, it was to Lucie that he voiced his views and from Lucie that he sought advice. And when he finally admitted that 'The whole idea of marriage is repugnant to me', there was undoubtedly an element, combined with frustration and pique, of relief at his repeated matrimonial disasters because, after Lucie, anyone else was second best.

This translation is from the 1965 Taschenbuch edition, titled *Furst Pückler Reisst Nach England* (Prince Pückler Travels to England). The story of his increasingly desperate search for a suitable wife, his money troubles, his dependence on Lucie for comfort, financial and emotional, is told by Pückler himself for the first time in English. However, even this edition is not complete, and several episodes which have perhaps less appeal for a German readership than an English one were omitted. In such cases we have borrowed from Sarah Austin's translation (indicated by square brackets in the text). We are indebted to the late E. M. Butler's introduction and admirable biographical index to her edition of Mrs Austin's translation *A Regency Visitor* (Collins 1957) in compiling our own introduction, footnotes and index, and to Dr Rosemary Ashton of the University of London, who gave us advice, information and editorial help.

FLORA BRENNAN
London, July 1986.

FIRST LETTER

My true love,

Your sweet affection at our parting in Bautzen has given me such mingled joy and woe that I cannot put it from me. Your sad face is always before me; I still read the deep sorrow in your looks and tears, and my own heart tells me only too well what you must have been feeling. God give us soon a reunion as joyful as the parting was sad! It is already a real consolation to me to have written a few lines to you. I cannot tell you any travellers' tales; I was so preoccupied with my inner feelings that I scarcely know what places I have passed through. Dresden seemed to me less friendly than usual, and I thanked God when I found myself once more comfortably settled in my room at the inn. Moreover the storm, which has been blowing straight into my face all day, has made me very feverish and tired. May Heaven grant you, in Muskau, a restful night and a loving dream of your friend.

September 10th, early

As I opened my eyes, they fell upon a note from you which the worthy B. had laid upon the bedclothes, well knowing that I could not begin the day more happily. Indeed, after the pleasure of hearing from you there is only one other for me to enjoy – that of writing to you. Just go on expressing your feelings as they come, and do not spare mine. I know well that your letters must, for a long time to come, be like a sombre, sorrowful landscape. I shall feel easier if only I sometimes see a sweet sunbeam throw its rays upon it!

Leipzig, September 11th

I left Dresden today, early, in pretty good spirits as I painted bright fancies for the future. Only the longing for you, dear Lucie, and the contrast between my dull and friendless solitude and the splendid joy it would be to make this journey with you, in happier circumstances, often gripped sorely at my heart.

I pride myself on understanding certain aspects of travel better than most: especially on how to combine the greatest possible comfort – which includes taking along as many things as possible, for in foreign lands they are often dear and familiar – with the least expenditure of money and time. In my room in Dresden you would have thought you were looking at a warehouse. Now everything has disappeared into the multiple compartments of the carriage, without giving it that heavy, overladen appearance that horrifies postilions and betrays to innkeepers those making the Grand Tour. Every article is to hand and yet in its own place, so that when you arrive at your night quarters it takes only a few minutes to set up a homely habitat in a foreign place. On the road the large clear glass windows, unobscured by luggage or the box seat, give as free a view as an open calèche, but at the same time allow me to control the temperature as I wish. The servants on their high seats behind the carriage keep an eye on all the luggage and the horse without being able to peer in, or eavesdrop on a conversation.

I could write a dissertation on the theme that to the traveller nothing is unimportant, but I have only been as long-winded as this to give you a complete picture of the moving dwelling which our succession of post horses draws every day further from your skies.

Weimar, September 13th, evening

Yesterday I presented myself before my old master.[1] They extend here a politeness towards strangers elsewhere quite out of fashion. No sooner was I announced than a court lackey immediately appeared at my side to place himself and a court equipage at my disposal for the duration of my stay.

This morning the Grand Duke was so good as to show me his

---

[1] The Grand Duke of Weimar to whom Pückler had once been adjutant.

private library, which is elegantly arranged and rich in splendid English engravings. He laughed heartily when I told him I had read recently in a Paris newspaper that, on his orders, Schiller[1] had been exhumed so that his skeleton might be set up in the Grand Ducal library in natura. The truth is that only his bust, among others, adorns the apartment though his skull, if I am correctly informed, is preserved inside the pedestal – a strange mark of honour.

Since they eat very early at the court I had scarcely time to change and found, coming in rather late, a large company assembled among whom I noticed several Englishmen. They are now very sensibly studying German here instead of, as in the past, learning the ugly Dresden dialect, and are most hospitably received.

September 14th

This evening I paid my visit to Goethe.[2] He received me in a dimly-lit room, the *clair-obscur* of which was arranged not without a certain artistic coquetry. Indeed the handsome old man with his Jove-like countenance looked very majestic. Old age has only altered him, hardly weakened him. He is perhaps less lively than in other days, but more composed and milder, and the lightning that often used to flash through his sententiousness has been replaced by a more dignified serenity.

I heartily rejoiced over his health and remarked in jest how happy it made me to find our spiritual king as robust as ever.

'Oh, you are too kind to give me such a name,' said he, in the south German manner he has never quite lost.

'No,' I returned, 'truly, with all my heart, not only king but even dictator, since you carry all Europe forcibly with you.'

He bowed politely, and asked me about several things concerning my earlier stay in Weimar, then made many kind remarks about Muskau and my ambitions for it, remarking mildly how good it is to cultivate a feeling for Beauty in whatever form it takes, since it is from the Beautiful that the Good and Noble develop of themselves. He even, at my request, gave good reason to hope that he would visit

[1] Dramatist, historian and aesthetic philosopher.
[2] Goethe had been living in Weimar since 1775, and Pückler had been his pupil.

us there one day. You can imagine, dearest, with what joy I snatched at this, even if it was merely a *façon de parler*.

In the last part of the conversation we came to Sir Walter Scott. Goethe was not very enthusiastic about accepting the Great Unknown.[1] He had no doubt, he said, that Scott wrote his novels in the same way that old painters worked in conjunction with their pupils; that is, he provided the plan, the main ideas and the skeleton of the scenes, but left their final execution to his assistants. 'If I,' he added, 'had been inclined to write merely for gain, I could have done it before this with Lenz[2] and others. Even now I could turn out works which would astonish the public as well as have them breaking their heads over the identity of the author, but they would, in the end, remain mere mass-produced articles.'

I suggested that it would be beneficial to see how our literature now overtopped that of other nations, and in this I asserted that our Napoleon would meet no Waterloo.

'Certainly,' he answered, passing over my rather commonplace compliment, 'quite apart from our own creations, we stand on the highest rung of culture through our taking over and complete adoption of foreign writers. Because of this the other nations will soon realize that, by learning German, they can to a certain extent save themselves the trouble of learning all the other languages. For have we not the original works in excellent German translation? The ancient classics, the masterpieces of modern Europe, Indian and oriental literature, have they not all been better rendered in the rich and versatile German language, with true German industry and deep-seated genius, than is the case in other languages? France,' he continued, 'certainly owes much of its former superiority in literature to the fact that it was the first to produce tolerable translations from the Greek and Latin, but how completely since then has Germany overtaken her!'

In the political field, he did not have much to say about the present popular constitutional theories. I defended myself and my opinions pretty warmly. He several times repeated his favourite ideas, especially that every man should concern himself

[1] Sir Walter Scott, whose novels were very popular in Germany, was long referred to as 'The Great Unknown' because he published anonymously.
[2] German dramatist, contemporary with Goethe.

16

only with his own affairs, great or small, faithfully and with love: in this way the general good cannot fail to be served under any form of government. He, for his part, had done nothing else and I, he added good-humouredly, was doing the same in Muskau.

I then said frankly that, with all respect, however true and noble this principle might be, it must first be called into being by a constitutional government, because this establishes in every individual the conviction of greater security of life and property, and consequently the most cheerful energy and an unshakeable love of country. Moreover, through its silent working in every community a much solider basis would be provided, and I concluded perhaps tactlessly by citing England as a proof of my contention. He rejoined at once that the example was not the most fortunate choice, since in no country was selfishness more prevalent, perhaps no people today more inhuman in political and private relations. Salvation comes, not from without through forms of government, but from within through wise restraint and modest activity, each one in his own circle. This remains the chief ingredient of human happiness, and is the easiest and simplest to achieve.

Later he spoke of Lord Byron with great affection, almost like a father of his son, which was very gratifying to my warm enthusiasm for this great poet. He deeply regretted never having met the lord personally, and with good reason castigated the English for judging their great countryman so meanly, and in general having understood him so little. [1]

Finally I mentioned the production of *Faust* in a private theatre in Berlin with music by Prince Radziwill, and praised the gripping effect of certain parts of this performance. 'Well,' said Goethe gravely, 'it's a strange undertaking but all views and endeavours should be respected.' I feel resentful of my bad memory that I cannot remember more of our quite lively conversation. It was with the highest veneration and love that I left the great man, the third in a constellation with Homer and Shakespeare, whose name will shine immortal as long as the German tongue endures. And had there been

[1] Goethe had become a great admirer of Lord Byron in his old age and did much to spread his fame in Germany.

anything of Mephistopheles in me, I too would certainly have called out from the staircase:

> *It is really good of a great gentleman*
> *To speak so kindly with a poor devil.*[1]

Your faithful Lou[2]

---

[1] Pückler is quoting from Goethe's *Faust*.
[2] Short for 'filou' (thief), a reference to his having stolen Lucie's heart.

SECOND LETTER

Beloved friend,

After I had taken leave of Goethe and his family, and visited a distinguished and charming artist for the last time in her studio, I left the German Athens full of happy memories.

It was already dark when I reached Eisenach, where I had a commission of the Grand Duke's to one of my former comrades. I saw his house brightly lit up, heard dance music and walked right into the midst of a large gathering, which was surprised by my travelling costume and stared at my hunting cap. They were celebrating the wedding of the daughter of the house, and the father heartily welcomed me to it. I apologized to the bride for not being dressed for a wedding, drank a glass of iced punch to her health and another to that of her father, danced a polonaise and disappeared *à la française*. I made my preparations for the night straightaway and laid myself comfortably to rest in the carriage.

When I awoke, I found myself already a stage before Kassel. I pressed on [all day] through monotonous surroundings to arrive at the dinner hour in the ancient bishop's seat of Osnabruck.

One always sleeps even better on the second night than on the first in the carriage, whose movement works, on me at least, like a cradle on children. I felt very well and cheerful the next morning and noticed that the country was gradually beginning to take on a Dutch character. Old-fashioned houses, with many gables and sash windows, better furnished rooms, tea instead of coffee, splendid fresh butter and cream along with larger scale everything led us into this bright world. Every village stands in a grove of trees in lovely leaf and nothing can exceed the luxuriance of the meadows through which the Ruhr winds in strangely shaped bends. I reflected in amusement that, if it were foretold to someone that he would die in the Ruhr, he would have to settle down here so that he might at once fulfil and disarm the prophecy.

I came unfortunately a day too late to connect directly with the steamer which leaves from [Wesel], otherwise I should, counting from Weimar, have reached London in four and a half days. Now I shall travel by land to Rotterdam and must there await the departure of the next ship.

London, October 5th

I have had a most unlucky crossing, forty hours instead of twenty. I was pretty seasick, and to crown everything we were stuck on a sandbank in the Thames, where we had to remain for six hours before the tide floated us off again.

It is ten years since I last left England, and I do not know whether in those days I saw beauty wherever I looked, or whether my imagination has since then without my knowing it painted everything in more attractive colours, but this time I found the views from both sides of the river neither so fresh nor so picturesque as before, although from time to time magnificent groups of trees and friendly country houses came into view. Here, as in Northern Germany, the foliage of the trees veils the landscape; only their numbers, in the many hedges which surround all the fields, and the fact that their topmost branches are preserved, make the prospect less comfortless than in otherwise so beautiful Silesia.

Among the passengers was an Englishman who has quite recently returned from Herrnhut and had also visited the baths at Muskau. It amused me very much, unknown to him as I was, to hear his opinion of the grounds there. How tastes differ and how, therefore, one should despair of nothing, you can gather from the fact that this man felt uncommon admiration for that gloomy region solely because of the immensity of its *evergreen woods*, by which he meant the endless monotony of pinewoods which to us seem so unbearable, but which, in England, where pines are carefully planted in the parks and as a rule fare badly, are a highly prized rarity.

In the middle of the second night we anchored at London Bridge, the most fatal circumstance which anyone can encounter here. Because of the strictness of the Customs, no one can bring anything with him from the ship before his things have been searched, and the offices do not open until ten in the morning. Since I did not want to leave my German servant alone with the carriage and effects, and had neither arranged with the ambassador for an exemption from search nor ordered lodging for myself, I was obliged to pass the night with little more than what I stood up in, in a miserable sailors' inn on the waterfront. In the morning, however, when I went to assist at the examination of my effects, I found that the golden key which seldom fails proved very efficacious here, too, in sparing me a long wait and a lot of wearisome detail. Even a couple of dozen French gloves, which were lying quite innocently on top of my linen, seemed, through the operation of my guineas, to have become invisible.

I hurried as fast as possible out of the dirty City, with its unending bustle, but had to make a half-stage with posthorses before I reached the west end of the town where I alighted at my former lodgings in the Clarendon Hotel. My old landlord, a Swiss, had by this time exchanged England for another land, but his son had taken his place and he welcomed me with all the respectful attention which distinguishes the English land-lord, and indeed everyone in this country who lives on others' money.

London is now so dead, without elegant and fashionable people, that one hardly sees a single equipage driving by, and of all the *beau monde* there are only a few ambassadors about. Moreover the huge town is full of dirt and fog, the streets are like rutted country roads, and the old road surface has been torn up and replaced with chips of granite mixed with gravel, which in fact gives a softer ride and deadens the noise. However, in winter, the town practically changes into a swamp. But for the splendid footpaths one would have to go on stilts, as they do in the *landes* near Bordeaux. In fact lower-class Englishwomen do wear something like them made of iron on their big feet.

The town has, however, greatly gained from the new Regent Street, Portland Place and the Regent's Park. For the first time it seems like a royal residence, and no longer simply a boundless capital for shopkeepers – in Napoleon's immortal words. Although poor Mr Nash,[1] an influential architect of the King's from whom these improvements stem, is badly regarded by many art connoisseurs – and indeed it cannot be denied that in his buildings all styles have been thrown together and that the mixture often seems more baroque than *genial* – still, in my view, the nation owes him a great debt for having conceived and carried through such ambitious plan for the beautification of their capital. Most of it, by the way, is still *in petto*, but with the Englishman's mania for building and abundance of money it will certainly soon be brought to life. It is true one must not look too closely at the details – the spire serving as a *point de vue* to Regent Street, for instance, which ends in a needle point, and in which the main building and roof from beginning to end seem at odds, is a strange architectural abortion, and there is nothing funnier than the caricature they made of it in which Mr Nash (a very small, shrivelled-looking man) is well represented booted and spurred, riding upon the aforesaid spire as if spitted upon it, over the caption 'National Taste'.

One could instance many similar abnormalities. Faultless, on the other hand, is the plan of the country style lay-out in this park, also by Mr Nash, the waterway being especially excellent. Here Art has completely solved the difficult problem of concealing her operations in apparently freely growing Nature. You would think that a broad river was flowing far into the distance between luxuriantly wooded banks and there dividing into several branches, while in fact all you have before you is a laboriously excavated, shored up and confined, though clear piece of water. So charming a landscape as this, with commanding hills in the distance and surrounded by a mile-long circus of splendid buildings, is certainly a design worthy of one of the capitals of the world, and will, when the young trees have become old giants, scarcely find an equal anywhere.

Many old streets have been demolished to create all this and, in the last ten years, more than 60,000 new houses have been built in this part of the town. It is, I think, a special beauty of the new streets that they are quite broad, but not as straight as a string throughout their entire length; rather they are like the paths in a park, occa-

---

[1] John Nash had been commissioned to create a 'royal mile' from Regent's Park to St James's Park; he was also responsible for the Royal Pavilion at Brighton.

sionally describing bends which break up their former oppressive monotony. If London also possessed quays, and if St Paul's Church were set in open ground, as the plan of the talented Colonel Trench[1] suggests, then no town could compete with her in splendour as she already surpasses all others in size.

Among the new bridges, Waterloo Bridge stands in the first rank, though its promoters must have lost £300,000 in the undertaking. 1,200 feet long, and furnished with a solid granite balustrade, even so it is almost always comparatively deserted and affords a charming walk with the most beautiful river views – a stately mingling of palaces, bridges, ships and towers – as far as the fog allows them to be seen.

October 7th

What would please you very much here is the outstanding cleanliness in all the houses, the great comfort of the furniture, and the respect and politeness of the servants. It is true that you pay six times more for everything pertaining to luxury (for the bare necessities are, in fact, no dearer than with us), but you also get six times as much comfort. In the inns everything is much richer and in greater abundance than on the Continent. The bed, for instance, has three mattresses, one on top of another, and the bed is big enough to accommodate two or three people; when the curtains of the rectangular canopy, which rests on stout mahogany pillars, are pulled to, you find yourself in a little cabinet, a space in which any Frenchman would quite comfortably dwell. On your washstand you find not a miserable water bottle, with a single china or silver jug and basin and streeling towels, such as are provided in German and French hotels and even in some private houses, but instead real tubs of Chinese porcelain in which one can plunge half one's body without trouble; taps which in an instant provide just the flow of water one desires; half a dozen large towels, a crowd of crystal bottles, large and small, a tall pier glass, foot baths and so on, not to mention other nameless little comforts for the toilet, all of equal elegance.

[1] Planner of the Thames Embankment.

23

Everything is so conveniently to hand that, as you are washing yourself, you experience straightaway a real delight in bathing. If you need anything else, at the sound of the bell there appears either a neatly clad girl, with a very deep curtsy, or a waiter who receives your orders in the costume and with the correctness of a well-trained valet, instead of an uncombed lout in a ragged jacket and green apron who with stupid impudence asks you: 'What's up, Your Grice?' or 'Did anyone ring here?' and then runs out again before he has really taken in what you actually want of him. Good carpets cover all the floors, and in the brightly polished iron fireplace burns a cheerful fire, instead of the dirty boards and smoky, evil-smelling stoves of so many of our inns at home.

If you go out, you never find a dirty staircase nor one so dimly lit that only the darkness is really visible. Throughout the whole house, day and night, reign the greatest peace and order, and in many hotels each roomy lodging even has its own staircase, so that you need not come in contact with anyone else. At table, the guest is confronted with a profusion of white table linen and shining polished cutlery, and a choice of either a *plat de ménage* or an elegant buffet which, from the point of view of price, leaves nothing to be desired. The servants are always there when you need them, and yet are not obtrusive, while the landlord usually appears at the beginning of the dinner in order to satisfy himself that everyone is content; in a word, you lack for nothing in a good inn here which the wealthy, well-travelled private person would not have in his own home, and perhaps more attentively served. Of course, the bill is commensurate with all this, and the waiters must be tipped nearly as lavishly as the valets. In the best hotels, a waiter is not really content with less than two pounds a week in personal fees. Tips in England are even more the order of the day than elsewhere, and are pursued with singular shamelessness even in the churches.

I finished this day with a walk to Chelsea, to the barracks of the invalids of the infantry, where it makes one happy to see the old warriors well-cared for, living in a palace, in carefully maintained gardens with the most beautifully close-mown bowling greens and lofty chestnut alleys of which a minor ruler would not be ashamed. I then dined at eight o'clock with the [Austrian] ambassador, a dinner which, apart from the amiability of my host, was memorable for the genuine Metternich-Johannisberg, for which nectar the liberality of the great minister[1] must be given its due.

October 10th

A few days ago I made use of somewhat clearer weather to visit Chiswick, a villa of the Duke of Devonshire, which is considered to have the most elegant grounds of its kind in England, and which I had seen only superficially some years ago at a party given by the Duke. I could not examine the paintings this time either, because there was a visitor living in the house. The garden I found much altered, but hardly to its advantage, since there is now a mixture of the regular and the irregular which produces an unfavourable effect. Above all the ugly fashion, now prevalent in England, of planting pleasure grounds with thinly spaced, almost militarily arranged trees has given the lawns the appearance of tree nurseries. In the shrubberies they prune the bushes all over so that they cannot touch the neighbouring shrubs, carefully clear the earth around them every day, and arrange the borders of the lawns in stiff lines so that you see more black earth than green, and the unfettered beauties of Nature's forms are altogether suppressed.

[Mr Nash, however, adheres to a very different principle, and the new gardens of Buckingham Palace are models to all planters. The most favourable circumstance to English gardeners is the mildness of the climate. Laurels, azaleas and rhododendrons are not injured by the frost, and afford the most beautiful luxuriant thickets, summer and winter, and, in their respective seasons, the richest blossoms and berries. Magnolias are seldom covered, and even camellias stand abroad in peculiarly sheltered spots, with only the protection of a matting. The turf preserves its beautiful freshness all winter, indeed in that season it is usually thicker and more beautiful than in summer. The present is just the season in which the whole vegetation is at its most magnificent.]

A beautiful effect is made in Chiswick by a single great tree in front of the house, the trunk of which has been trimmed right up to the crown and under which you can look over the whole garden and

---

[1] Prince Metternich, foreign minister and chancellor of Austria.

a portion of the park. A good hint for landscape gardeners, which I advise you to use in Muskau.

[There is a menagerie attached to the garden, in which a tame elephant performs all sorts of feats, and very quietly suffers anybody to ride him about a large lawn. His neighbour is a lama, of a much less gentle nature; his weapon is a most offensive saliva, which he spits out to a distance of some yards at anyone who irritates him; he takes such good aim, and fires so suddenly that it is extremely difficult to avoid his charge.]

Through a succession of charming villas and country houses of all kinds, amongst the press of horsemen, country coaches, travelling carriages and coal drays drawn by mighty horses, varied by occasional lovely views across the Thames, after an hour's rapid journey I arrived at Hyde Park Corner and betook myself once more into the labyrinth of the boundless town.

The next day I visited the City with my guide, a Swiss who has travelled in Egypt, Syria, Siberia and America, published a Russian newsletter, brought to London the first news of the taking of Hamburg by Tettenborn, purchased Napoleon's coronation robe in Paris and showed it here for a five shilling entrance fee. In addition, he speaks most European languages fluently and so is not dear at half a guinea a day. He can also serve as a doctor, because he has amassed so many pills and prescriptions on his travels that he has wonderful home remedies for every ill and, moreover, possesses a thousand different recipes for punch. Conducted by this universal genius, I entered the Royal Exchange for the first time.

In other places the Exchange has as a rule only a mercantile appearance; here, a thoroughly historical one. The imposing statues of English rulers around it (among which Henry VIII and Elizabeth are especially prominent), as well as the ancient and venerable architecture, awaken poetic feelings, to which the thought of the world market, of which London is the centre, lends an even deeper significance. However, the people who enliven this picture soon draw one back again into the realm of the everyday, for here self-interest and greed gleam in every eye, so that in this respect this place, like the whole City, offers an almost uncanny spectacle, not unlike that of the restless, comfortless throng of damned souls.

The great court of the Exchange is surrounded by covered arcades, where inscriptions indicate their gathering-point to merchants of all nations. In the centre of the court is a statue of Charles II, who built the palace. It expresses perfectly in bearing and gesture the man as history depicts him: not handsome, but yet not without grace, and with a deep-rooted frivolity in those half-mocking, half-pompous features; a frivolity which, springing as it does from mediocrity, nothing can cure, and which made of this king as amiable and carefree a roué as he was a bad ruler. In niches which have been placed around the second storey stand the busts of other English rulers. I have already mentioned Henry VIII and Queen Elizabeth. They would be striking even without the memories associated with them: Henry, appearing fat and comfortable and, so to speak, cosily cruel, Elizabeth, masculine and magnificent and yet femininely malicious. The busts were certainly executed after the best Holbein paintings. On this storey is found the famous Lloyd's Coffee House, the grubbiest locale of this kind in London. No one would think that millions and more are handled here every day, although more paper and pens than refreshments are to be seen.

Nearby is the beautiful, gigantic building of the Bank of England, with a maze of large and small rooms lit from above, which are allocated to the various counting houses. Hundreds of clerks work here, crowded together, and mechanically transact the colossal business which makes *nil admirari* difficult for the poor German who is anyway all too ready to admire, especially if he is in the bullion office where the ingots are kept, and gaping at the heaps of gold and casks of silver which seem to him to bring to life the treasures of the Arabian Nights.

From there I proceeded to the Guildhall, where the Lord Mayor of the day, a bookseller, was just then speaking; in his blue robe and gold chain he did not look at all bad and was able to give quite a regal impression. I thought that he acquitted himself no worse than an official of the court; ever since the days of Sancho Panza it has been accepted that sound commonsense quite often recognizes the rights of a case better than the sage who cannot see what is under his nose owing to too much peering through highly polished spectacles.

Then we wandered into the tumultuous City where you can get lost like an atom [if you do not know where you are going,] and where, if you are not careful to look to right and left, you are in constant danger of being spitted by the shaft of a cabriolet which comes too near the footpath, or crushed to death by some diligence which has broken down and overturned. We arrived at last at an extremely dark and insignificant café called Garroway's Coffee House, where, in a miserable setting, estates and palaces often worth hundreds of thousands of pounds are auctioned off every day. We sat down very seriously, as if we were most desirous of making such an acquisition, and admired the uncommon amiability and address of the auctioneer in arousing a lust for purchase in his audience. He appeared in a becoming black apparel and wig and stood like a professor on a high podium. He made a charming speech about each property which he did not fail to spice with many a jest, and he praised every object so unanswerably that even the disinterested would have been inclined to swear that everything was going for an outrageously low price.

My guide told me that this famous auctioneer had recently been involved in an unpleasant lawsuit. He had extravagantly praised an estate because of the romantic hanging wood in its vicinity, a kind of wood greatly prized in England and in which weeping willows, weeping birches, hanging ashes, pines and so on are to be found. On account of this, a purchaser let himself be tempted into buying, since it is an English peculiarity that almost all sales that take place here go through without personal inspection of the site. When he arrived at his newly acquired property, he found the place almost entirely denuded of trees, and no hanging wood in the vicinity other than a neighbouring gallows. So much for English humour and fair play.

How could I leave the City without first having visited its real lion (the English expression for the most outstanding man in his own field), its ruler – in a word, Rothschild?[1] In fact he occupies here only an insignificant location (his townhouse is in the west end of the town) and in the little courtyard of the counting house my access to this best-connected member of the Holy Alliance was impeded by a van loaded with silver ingots. I found the Russian consul there, engaged in paying his court. He was a distinguished and intelligent man, who knew perfectly how to play the role of the humble debtor, while retaining the proper air of dignity. This was made the more difficult since the guiding genius of the City did not stand on

[1] Baron Nathan Rothschild was head of the London branch of the House of Rothschild, founded by his father; under Nathan it became one of the world's leading banks. He and his four brothers were made Barons of the Austrian Empire in 1822.

ceremony. When I had handed him my letter of credit, he remarked ironically that we rich people were fortunate in being able to travel about and amuse ourselves; while on him, poor man, there rested the cares of the world, and, he went on, bitterly bewailing his lot, no poor devil came to England without wanting something from him.

['Yesterday,' he said, 'there was a Russian begging of me' (an episode which threw a bittersweet expression over the consul's face) 'and,' he added, 'the Germans here don't give me a moment's peace.' Now it was my turn to put a good face on the matter. After this the conversation took a political turn, and we both of course agreed that Europe could not subsist without him; he modestly declined our compliment and said, smiling, 'Oh no, you are only jesting; I am but a servant whom people are pleased with because he manages their affairs well, and to whom they let some crumbs fall as an acknowledgement.'] All this in a language peculiarly his own, half English, half German, the English with an entirely German accent, yet all declaimed with an imposing self-possession which seemed to find such trifles beneath his notice. To me this same original style of speech seemed very much in character with a man to whom one cannot deny genius and even, in its way, greatness of character.

[I had begun my day, very appropriately, with the Royal Exchange, the resort of merchants, and now ended it with Exeter 'Change, where I saw – the wild beasts. Here I found another lion, a real one this time, called Nero, who has the rare merit in our northern latitudes of having presented England with six generations of young lions. He is of enormous size and dignified aspect, but now rests on his laurels and sleeps royally nearly all day long. If he wakes in an ill humour, however, he makes the old wooden house and all the herd of subject beasts tremble. These consist of elephants, tigers, leopards, hyaenas, zebras, monkeys, ostriches, condors, parrots, etc. The variety is great and the price moderate. The ambassador of the late King of Würtemburg spent, as I well remember, more time here than in St James's and Downing Street; indeed he was for some considerable time in fear of losing his post on account of a strange enormous dead tortoise.]

October 13th

Tired from yesterday's tour, I spent the next morning in my four-poster, but in the evening visited the English opera in the Strand. The house is neither elegant nor large, but the actors are not at all bad. On this occasion they did not do an opera, but two frightful melodramas: first *Frankenstein*, in which a being is produced by magic without the aid of a woman – an ill-advised procedure; and then *The Vampire*, based on the famous tale wrongly attributed to Lord Byron. In both Mr Cooke[1] played the principal part, and in both distinguished himself by a handsome person, very clever acting and a most refined and noble presence. The acting, indeed, was masterly throughout, but the plays so foolish and rubbishy that one could not sit through to the end. Besides the heat, perspiration and audience were not of the most uplifting. Moreover, the performance went on from seven o'clock until half-past one, which is too long even for the most excellent play.

The next day I went to Hampton Court to pay a visit to the palace, the stud farm and my old friend, Lady Lansdowne.[2] Of all three I found the first the least changed, and the famous vine in the garden weighed down with a hundred or more bunches of grapes. It now has more than a thousand branches and completely covers the hothouse, a good seventy-five feet in length and twenty-five feet in breadth, which has been given over to it. In one corner stood, like the dusky ancestor of a proud race, its brown stem, as lost and invisible as if it no longer belonged to the splendid cloud of leaves and fruit which, nonetheless, owe their being to it alone.

Most of the rooms in the palace are furnished just as they were in the time of William III a hundred and twenty years ago. The tattered chairs and tapestries are carefully preserved. Many interesting and excellent pictures adorn the walls, especially the famous Cartoons of Raphael, which, however, will soon be moving from here to the King's new palace. You have so often read

---

[1] Thomas Cooke had once served in the navy, and was reputed to be 'the best sailor that ever trod the boards'.

[2] Widow since 1805, during Puckler's previous visit to England (1815) Lady Lansdowne had become engaged to him, and only jilted him just before their wedding, probably because of family pressures. They remained good friends and she acted as confidante-in-chief during this visit (especially over his search for a rich wife).

descriptions of them that I shall refrain from reiterating them. Let me mention only two splendid portraits: of Wolsey, the proud builder of this palace, and of Henry VIII, his treacherous master. Both are magnificent, and entirely characteristic. You remember that fat lawyer, whom we had so much trouble in shaking off; his look of a wild beast, sensual, bloodthirsty – so far as one can be today – shrewd, crafty, full of intelligence and slyness, of boundless arrogance, and yet with an overwhelming tendency to baseness, and lastly entirely and frankly devoid of conscience – give the likeness of Henry a green frock coat with mother-of-pearl buttons, and you have his portrait to the life.

Nature keeps repeating herself in different nuances, but ranks are different, and so are the formation and the fate of men and of the world.

Last night I all but stifled to death because Jocrisse, whom I brought with me from home, apparently having been too well entertained earlier by an English comrade, decided to take coals out of the fireplace when I was already asleep, and laid them on a lacquered salver. Fortunately a fearful smoke and an infernal stench woke me, just as I was dreaming that I was one of Henry VIII's courtiers and that I had conquered a French beauty on the *Champ du Drap d'Or*, otherwise I would certainly have kissed my dream bride only in Heaven.

About as far away as that Heaven, and just as lovesome, seems to me the place where you dwell, my beloved, and so I send you the kiss of peace over the sea, and close, wishing you health and blessing. Here endeth the first English letter.

With all my heart, your devoted Lou

THIRD LETTER

London, October 15th, 1826

It seems impossible to deal with the climate here, as I have been constantly unwell since my arrival. However, so long as I am not confined to my room, I do not let myself become depressed, and as a cure I ride a lot in the charmingly cultivated country around London and have not given up my walks in the town.

It was recently the turn of the British Museum, where a strange mishmash of objets d'art, natural exhibits, curiosities, books and models are kept in a pitiful condition. At the top of the steps, as you enter, stand two enormous giraffes, at once guards and emblems of English artistic taste. There are undoubtedly many interesting things in the various rooms; however, I must to my shame confess that from seeing too many similar remarkable things, I am in the mood to feel a kind of indigestion at the sight of them. Among the antediluvian remains was a monstrous stag's head, extremely well preserved, which was at least six times as large as the biggest which my friend C. has hanging in the stag gallery in his castle. In the antiques room, which is in fact like a barn, you can enjoy the splendid Elgin Marbles as they are called here. If one could only, just once, see this ruined world of art in all the splendour and perfection of its monuments, that would indeed be well worth the trouble – the single torsos with which we must be content give only (*déclamation à part*) about the same amount of pleasure as, for instance, a lovely woman with one leg, amputated arms and blinded eyes.

A bust of Hippocrates appealed to me because it represented so perfectly the professional medical man that, at the very sight of him, one automatically puts one's hand in one's pocket. English doctors are so renowned for their practice of getting a guinea for every visit that, if one of their number should be sick and write a prescription for himself, he would undoubtedly take a guinea out of his left pocket and stick it into his right.

I also looked at the famous Portland Vase with guilty enthusiasm; I shall send you by a later mail two special works on the Vase and the Elgin antiquities, tolerably illustrated, but now I must say goodbye, so as to get my packing done, for tomorrow I intend to go to Newmarket to spend a few days at the races.

Newmarket, October 19th

The beauty of the country and uncommon charm of all the places through which my way today took me, struck me anew in the most delightful manner. These stretches of country, as fertile as they are well-ordered, these thousands of snug, charming farmhouses scattered through all parts of the region, this continual throng of elegant carriages, riders, and well-dressed pedestrians, are peculiar only to England. There is, however, one blemish on this beautiful whole: everything is too cultivated, too complete, and so in the end wearisome; indeed it even occurs to me that it must in the end be repellent, just as a surfeit of a fragrant dish full of delicacies nauseates one. This may also explain, to some extent, the great wanderlust of the English. It is exactly the same in life; men find it most difficult to put up with undisturbed bliss, which is perhaps why the dear Lord drove our ancestor Adam out of Paradise so that he would not die of boredom in the place.

Today, however, was provided with a few shadows. Because of the great crowd at the races, at every staging post I found only worn-out horses and often could get none, so that, at least by English standards, I had a pitiful drive and only reached Newmarket late at night.

There was no vacancy to be found in any of the inns, and at last I had to consider myself very lucky to rent a small room in a private house at three guineas a week. Fortunately I ran into a kindly acquaintance in the same house, the young son of a Hungarian grandee who, from his unassuming ways and irrepressible *joie de vivre*, seems to have been put into the world to please himself and others; I honour such natures because they possess absolutely everything that I lack.

The next morning I went riding with him, so that we could orientate ourselves. One day resembles another here, much as one egg is like another. Early, at half-past eight in the morning, you see a few hundred racehorses, draped in rugs, taking their morning exercise. The wide, treeless, grassy hill is everywhere covered with them, as if with a herd; some are walking, others galloping, now slower now faster, but never flat out. As a rule, an overseer on a little pony accompanies the horses which belong to the same owner, or are being fed and lodged by the same trainer. The racehorses here are all ridden only with saddlecloths by half-grown boys, one of whom is occasionally thrown, to the delight of the onlookers. When this spectacle, so interesting for horse lovers, is finished, you have your breakfast and then spend a good half-hour at the horse auctions, which are conducted by the famous Mr Tattersall[1] and take place almost all day on the open road; then you ride or drive to the races.

These begin pretty punctually at twelve o'clock. The course is an unimaginably smooth sward, sown with fine, thick meadow grass, and here different distances – from a complete German mile as maximum to an eighth or a tenth as minimum – are run as a handicap. Towards its end, the course is railed in with ropes on the outside of which stand rows of unharnessed carriages three and four deep, which are crammed from top to bottom, inside and outside, with spectators. At the winning post itself is a little wooden hut, rather like the ones used by shepherds in many parts of Germany, raised on wheels so that it can be pushed in any direction if the winning post has to be moved forward or back. Here sits the steward, so that he can see from a pole planted opposite him exactly which horse's nose appears first on the line. For there is often an inch of difference, and it is skilful policy on the part of the jockeys here to reveal the real speed of their mounts as little as possible, but to show only as much as is absolutely necessary to win. If it is obvious that they have no chance, they prefer to remain right at the back, whereas the others, who are contesting the lead, are usually a very short distance apart at the winning post. It is only in Germany and France that you see the grotesque spectacle of a rider a thousand strides behind the field exhausting himself and his horse with whip and spur. If two horses reach the winning post exactly together, they have to run it off, which often occurs.

[1] Richard Tattersall founded 'Tattersalls', market for high-class horses and a great racing centre. He died in 1795, so this may be his son.

34

English jockeys (not little boys, as foreigners often think, but frequently old midgets, of sixty years of age) have formed a guild of their own, and are the best riders I know. They are always men, as small and slender as possible, who constantly reduce themselves with Turkish baths, purges and so on. You will remember that I once kept racehorses myself and, for a time, had in my employ a Newmarket jockey who won a considerable bet for me in Vienna. It amused me very much to see this man when he put himself in training. After strengthening himself with several purges, he would set off at a trot in the heat of the day over set distances, swaddled in three or four pelts, until the sweat ran down him like rivers and he was nearly ready to drop with fatigue. *Mais tel était son plaisir* – and the more miserable he felt, the better pleased he was.

At a certain distance from the winning post, about a hundred paces to the side, there is another white post called the betting post. Here gather the bettors, after they have seen the horses saddled in their stalls and satisfied themselves as to all the prevailing conditions, and perhaps, too, given a hint to the accommodating jockey. To many what goes on here might seem the most repellent of spectacles. With its noise and confused cries it is very like a school for Jews, except that you see more passionate feeling here, and the cast of actors is made up of the first peers of England as well as liveried servants, and the lowest 'sharpers and blacklegs' (cheats and confidence men) – in a word, of everybody who has money to bet with. Most of them have their pocketbooks in their hands as they call out their odds, and when their bet is accepted, each party notes it down in his book. Dukes, lords, stable hands, rogues all yell at each other, and bet with each other, with a skill and in a technical language of which no foreigner, without long study, could make any sense, until suddenly the cry goes up: 'They're off!'

Now the crowd quickly disperses, though the bettors seek each other out again at the ropes which fence in the course. From carriages and horseback, countless binoculars, opera glasses and lorgnettes are trained on the distant, oncoming jockeys. Swift as the wind these sweep ever closer and for several moments an anxious silence hangs over the colourful crowd, whilst a marshal on horseback keeps the course clear and drives back intruders without ceremony, with his whip. The silence lasts only moments; soon the wildest tumult breaks out: loud shouts of joy and lamentation, oaths and acclamations, from all sides, from gentlemen and ladies, from above and below. 'Ten to four on the Admiral!' 'A hundred to one on Putana!' 'Smallbeer against the field!' 'Diamond Boy to win!' and so on, are heard from the frantic bettors. And scarcely have you heard, from this side or that, a 'Done!' than the noble animals are already upon us, in a second past us, in two seconds at the winning post, and fate, or skill, or dishonesty have decided. The heavy losers stand a moment staring before them, the winners triumph loudly, many make *bonne mine au mauvais jeu*, but all hasten after the jockeys to see them weighed in and the horses unsaddled, in case an irregularity might yet give them a chance. In a quarter of an hour the same game begins again with different players, and repeats itself six or seven times. *Voilà les courses de Newmarket!*

My judgement on the first day was so fortunate that I picked the winner three times in the saddling paddock, purely on opinion and discernment, and so won pretty considerably. Still, as always happens when I gamble, the next day I lost as much again. Anyone who wins here constantly is sure of his business *beforehand*, and it is well known that a great part of the English nobility has very liberal principles in this matter.

On the very first day of my stay in Newmarket, my Hungarian friend introduced me to the family of a rich merchant, well known in the neighbourhood, who with their house party, which included several very pretty girls, come daily to the races, and afterwards return to their property nearby. They invited us to eat there the next day and to spend the following day with them, which we accepted with pleasure.

[At about five o'clock we set out on horseback. A newly planted, broad double avenue of beeches marked the beginning of our host's property, and led us through about half a mile of road to the entrance of his park – a sort of triumphal arch between two lodges. Some of our way led us through a thick plantation, till we reached the lawn, studded with groups of trees, which invariably forms the chief feature of an English park. Some cows lay on the grass just in front of the door of the house, so that we were obliged to ride almost over them – a strange anomaly.

We found a pretty numerous company consisting of the master and mistress of the house, both of middle age, their eldest married daughter with her husband, two younger daughters, a neighbouring

36

baronet with his pretty wife and her very pleasing but very melancholy sister, three gentlemen not remarkable for anything, the son of the house and, lastly, a London beau of the second class – an aspiring City dandy.

The baronet had served in Germany and was a simple, kind-hearted man, who appeared to have been invited to meet us as being well acquainted with the Continent. We, however, preferred taking lessons in English manners from his wife and her sister.

According to this system of manners, a visit from two 'noblemen' (even foreign ones, though these are full fifty percent lower than native ones) was an honour, and we were therefore amazingly fêted; even the dandy was – as far the rules of his *métier* would permit – civil and obliging towards us. It is an almost universal weakness of the unnoble in England to parade an acquaintance with the noble; thus English of the middle class take a great delight in travelling on the Continent, where they can easily meet with people of rank, of whom they talk as of intimate friends when they come home. For instance, a merchant's wife once said to me: 'Do you know the queen of –?' to which I replied that I had had the honour of being presented to her. 'She is a great friend of mine,' she went on, exactly as if she had been talking of her husband's partner's wife.

It requires a considerable fortune to keep up a country house, for custom demands many luxuries: a handsomely fitted house with elegant furniture, plate, servants in new and handsome liveries, a profusion of dishes and foreign wines, and in all things an appearance of superfluity – 'plenty' the English call it. As long as there are visitors in the house this way of life goes on, but many a family atones for it by meagre fare when alone; for which reason nobody here ventures to pay a visit in the country without first being invited. These invitations usually fix the day and the hour, and are generally numerous; as both room and the time allotted for the reception of guests are small, one must give way to another. True hospitality this can hardly be called; it is rather a display of one's possessions, for the purpose of dazzling as many as possible.]

Since you have never been in England, I would like to describe to you, in a few words, the course of an English dinner which, as I have said, is almost the same everywhere. You love the details of everyday life and have often said to me, 'You miss these out in most of your travel descriptions, and yet nothing gives a more lively picture of a foreign land.' Forgive me, then, if you find me going into too trifling detail.

You lead the lady to table not, as in France, holding her hand, but on your arm; however, as there, you are free from the old-fashioned bow and curtsy which even in many of the most distinguished German circles are still exchanged every time you take in a lady. On the other hand, they are very careful here about the observance of rank, though indeed they understand very little of the rank of foreigners. Today I cursed mine, which brought me next to the hostess, while my friend wisely slipped himself in between the lovely sisters.

In the French style you find, when you go in, the whole first course of the meal set out on the table. After the soup is removed, and as soon as the covers have been taken off, every man helps himself from the dish in front of him, and offers it to his neighbour. If he wants something extra, he must either ask across the table for it or send a servant in search of it. Fundamentally a tiresome custom, for which reason several of the most elegant of those who have been abroad have adopted the more convenient German practice of having the dishes handed round by the servants.

It is not usual to drink wine at table without emptying one's glass at the same time as another person, to do which you lift your glass, put on a stuffed look, nod your head and only then gravely take your drink. Certainly many a South Sea Island custom, which we find odd, would be less ridiculous. It is, moreover, a courtesy to call on everyone to drink in this manner, and a command will often be sped from the other end of the table to advise B. that A. wishes to drink a glass of wine with him; whereupon both of them, sometimes with considerable weariness, try to look each other in the eye and then, just like Chinese pagodas, carry out the ceremony of the obligatory nod with the utmost formality. If, however, the company is small, and you have drunk with all your acquaintance but still would like to enjoy more wine, you must wait until dessert, if you can't summon up enough courage to set yourself above convention.

When the second course is finished, as well as an intermediate dessert of cheese, salad, raw celery and the like, they bring in ale that is sometimes twenty or thirty years old, and so strong that if it is thrown on the fire it flares up like spirit. The tablecloth is removed and, in the best houses on a still finer tablecloth lying beneath it, in others on the bare, polished table, the dessert is set out. This consists of all possible hothouse fruits, which here are of the finest quality: Indian and English preserves, stomach-strengthening ginger, ices and so on. Before each guest fresh glasses are placed, and under the dessert plates and cutlery small, fringed napkins are set. Before the host three bottles of wine are laid – usually claret (wine of Bordeaux), port and madeira. The host now pushes these, either on their mats or on a small silver trolley, to his neighbour on the left. Everyone serves himself, and if there is a lady sitting beside him, serves her too with whatever she wants, and so it goes on until it has come back to the starting point, and from there it sets forth again. Several crystal jugs of iced water allow the foreigner, fortunately, to mix an antidote to the spirit which strongly predominates in English wines. All the servants leave the room when the dessert has been served, and if fresh wine is needed the butler is summoned, and he alone brings it in.

The ladies remain for a quarter of an hour, and sweet wine is sometimes specially served, and after that they leave the table. The gentlemen get up with them, one of them opens the door for the ladies, and as soon as they are alone, they draw cosily together; the host takes the seat of the hostess, and a conversation on matters of daily interest begins, during which the foreigner is, for the most part, overlooked, and must content himself with listening. Everyone is free to follow the ladies, if he wants to, a freedom of which Count B. and I availed ourselves as soon as possible today, the more since this is now the mode and heavy drinking is unfashionable. For that reason, the dandy joined us as soon as we reached the ladies, who were waiting for us in the salon, gathered round a large table with coffee and tea.

When the whole company was together again, it divided itself into groups according to preference. Several made music, which the melancholy beauty accompanied on the organ, apparently conse- crated to religious uses here, others played whist, here and there a young couple whispered in window seats, several talked politics and the dandy remained alone, sunk in a deep armchair, his prettily- shod right foot laid over his left knee, and in this attitude was apparently immersed so deeply in Madame de Staël's book *De l'Allemagne*[1] that he took not the least notice of the company round him. *A tout prendre*, I must do the pretty young man the justice of saying that he is not at all a bad copy of more distinguished originals. Perhaps I have arrived at this prejudiced conclusion because at table he spoke a lot of the great Goethe and praised his 'Fost', both of which (Goethe and 'Fost') Lord Byron has made the fashion in England.[2] 'Fost' seemed especially to please him because of what he considered its atheistic tendencies, for he had spent, as he told us, half his time in Paris and declared himself a free spirit.

The next day, after the communal breakfast, we went riding with the ladies in the park, which had nothing worth seeing to offer; and after that were all the better pleased with the hothouses and orchard. The first, a favourite hobby of the owner, were steam-heated in a very inventive manner, contrived by himself; and the warmth, by the simple turning of a cock, can be in an instant raised or lowered to the desired degree. These spacious, elegant houses are filled with twenty-three different sorts of pineapple, over which giant, dark blue grapes hang from the glass roof. In the orchard we admired some espaliered pears which, as well as tasting very good, had reached a size of seven inches long and sixteen inches round.

At one o'clock the postchaise arrived to take us back to Newmarket. At the races we saw the young ladies again, betted with them for gloves until we lost, and then delighted them with dyed black ones from Paris. We declined a second invitation to the country because we were engaged for a stag dinner, and Count B wanted to set out in the evening for Melton to go fox-hunting. Also I want to leave Newmarket and will go on with my letter again in London.

London, October 21st

By midday today I was safely back here again, in the midst of incessant showers. I restored myself in the Club with a good dinner, and at the evening's whist, in a fortunate hour be it said, won my

[1] *De l'Allemagne* (1813) was the main source of information about German culture in England at this time.

[2] The considerable interest in Goethe in England at this time was partly due to *De l'Allemagne* and partly to Lord Byron's influence – he dedicated *Sardanapalus* and *Werner* to 'the illustrious Goethe'.

travelling expenses six times over. I am well and cheerful and feel that I lack nothing but you . . .

Let me under such a good conjunction bring my letter to an end.

Ever your truly devoted Lou

FOURTH LETTER

London, November 20th, 1826

Beloved friend,

I would like to advise travellers in foreign lands never to take servants from the home country with them – at least, if you imagine that you are going to save money by doing so. This economy is one of those that costs more than *four* extravagances, and annoys him many more times over. Such wise reflections were awakened in me by my old valet, who has taken to falling into an English spleen because he finds so many daily difficulties here – above all, in getting for his midday meal the soup which reminds him, with tears in his eyes, of this favourite food at home. He reminds me of the Prussian soldiers who, amid streams of champagne, thrashed the French farmers because they did not produce any Stettin beer.

It is true that the Englishman of the middle class, accustomed to a nourishing meat diet, knows nothing of Northern water-soup and broth, and what goes by that name with them is an expensive witches' brew of all sorts of peppers and spices from the two Indies. The picture of my faithful follower when he got the first spoonful of it into his mouth was worthy of an illustration in Peregrine Pickle's[1] meal of old, and turned my annoyance into loud laughter. Still, I can see that his attachment to me is going to founder on this reef, for we Germans are and will remain peculiar fellows, clinging longer than others to our customs, whether in faith, love or soup.

While there is little society, the various clubs (to which, contrary to former custom, foreigners can now be admitted) are a great comfort. Our ambassador has procured my admission to two of them: the United Service Club, to which, apart from foreign

[1] The hero of Tobias Smollett's novel, *The Adventures of Peregrine Pickle* (1751).

42

ambassadors, only military men of the rank of staff officers are admitted; and the Travellers' Club, to which all educated and well recommended foreigners are admitted, but in a rather humiliating way – they have to ask for re-admission every three months, which is insisted upon with almost impolite strictness and held to the very day.

In Germany we have as little clear idea of the elegance and comfort as of the strict administration of club rules which prevail here. Everything which promotes luxury and comfort without ostentation can be found united as successfully as in the best organized private house. Staircases and rooms are always adorned with fresh carpets, and *rugs* (brightly coloured or of treated sheepskin) are laid before the door to stop the draught; marble fireplaces, beautiful looking glasses (always of one pane – a feature of solid English luxury), rich upholstery on the furniture, and so on – these make every room as comfortable as possible. There are even scales, with which one can easily ascertain one's weight every day (a favourite hobby of the English). You never see the numerous domestic staff without shoes, but clad in plain clothes or livery as clean as can be, and there is always a porter at his post to take the overcoats and umbrellas. These last attract great care in England since umbrellas, which are so necessary, are stolen in a quite shameless fashion if one does not watch very closely after their safety.

The table, by which I mean the food – to most people the principal thing and to me not the least – is for the most part prepared by French cooks, as well and cheaply as is possible in London. Since the club also procures the wines and sells them again to members at cost price, these, too, are very cheap and drinkable. That the gourmet must do without the finest wines in London, even in the best houses, arises from the strange custom of the English (and these people stick to their customs faster than the oyster to his shell) of having their wine provided only by London wine merchants, and never, as we are used to doing, from the countries where they grow. [These wine merchants adulterate the wine to such a degree that one who was lately prosecuted for having some thousand bottles of port and claret in his cellars on which he had not paid duty, proved that all this wine was manufactured by himself in London, and thus escaped the penalty. You may imagine, therefore, what sort of brewage you often get under the high sounding names of Champagne, Lafitte, etc.

Excuse this wine digression which to you, who drink only water, cannot be very interesting; but you know I write for us both and to me the subject is, I confess, not unimportant.]

But back to our clubs; the peculiarity of English customs can be much better observed here, at first glance, than in the great world which is always more or less the same, for the same individuals which in part make it up reveal themselves here entirely without restraint. In the first place, the foreigner must admire the refinement of comfort which the Englishman brings to the art of sitting; I must confess that anyone who does not fully understand that work of genius, the English chair, designed for every grade of fatigue, illness and peculiarity of constitution, has truly missed a great part of the pleasures of earthly life. It is indeed a real pleasure just to *see* an Englishman sit, or rather lie, in one of those bedlike chairs by the fireplace, an arrangement like a writing desk placed on the chair arm and furnished with a light, so that with the slightest pressure he can push it nearer or further away, right or left, as he wishes. Moreover a curious device, of which several stand around the great fireplace, holds up one or both of his feet, and the hat on his head completes the charming picture of ease.

This last is, for those brought up in the old ways, the most difficult to adopt; though he cannot refrain from a provincial shudder when he walks into the brightly lit drawing room of the club, where dukes, ambassadors and lords, elegantly dressed, are sitting at the gaming table, he must, if he is to imitate the fashionables, keep his hat on his head, join a whist party, nod to this or that acquaintance, and then carelessly take up a newspaper as the occasion offers and drop down with it on to a sofa. It is only after a certain time that he can nonchalantly throw down the hat, now become frightfully uncomfortable to him; if he is only staying a few minutes he must not take it off at all.

The custom of half lying instead of sitting, occasionally also lying at full length on the carpet at the feet of the ladies, throwing one leg over the other so that you are holding one foot in your hand, putting your hands into the armholes of your waistcoat, and so on – these are things that are often passed over at the highest society and in the most exclusive circles, so it is quite possible that the keeping on of one's hat will likewise come to be so honoured, since Parisian society is now showing a reaction, that is to say, just as once all Europe copied her, now (often in a pretty grotesque fashion) she does not disdain to make herself the ape of England, and, as commonly happens in such cases, often surpasses the original.

One must be especially careful to avoid as far as possible anything that the English do not do, and at the same time try to imitate them in everything, because no race of men can be more intolerant. Besides, most of them look unfavourably on the admission of foreigners into their closed society, and all consider it an outstanding favour and grace conferred upon us.

Of all the offences that one can commit against English manners and for which, apparently, all further entrance into society would be barred to one, the three following are the greatest: to put a knife into your mouth like a fork; to take sugar or asparagus with your hand; or to spit anywhere in a room. This is certainly praiseworthy, and well-bred people of all countries avoid such practices (though in this, too, manners alter considerably, for the Maréchal de Richelieu knew and recognized someone who set himself up as a fine gentleman merely because he always took olives with a fork and *not with his fingers*); the only ridiculous thing is the extraordinary importance which is attached to these things. The last named crime especially is, in England, so pedantically forbidden that one can seek in vain through the whole of London such an article as a spittoon. A Dutchman, who found himself very uncomfortable here for that reason, declared with great annoyance that the Englishman's spittoon is his stomach.

These are, I repeat, no more than trivial things, but the best rules of life when abroad always concern trivialities. If I, for instance, had to give some general rules to a young traveller, I would advise him very seriously: in Naples, treat the people brutally; in Rome, be natural; in Austria, do not talk politics; in France, do not give yourself airs; in Germany, give yourself plenty, and in England, never spit. With these rules, the young man will get pretty well through the world.

What one must admire, and rightly, is the practical arrangement of the entire economy of life, and of all public establishments in England, as well as the systematic strictness with which regulations, once laid down, are followed without slacking. In Germany all good arrangements soon fall asleep, and only new brooms sweep clean. Things are quite different here; they do not ask everything of a man, but only that which belongs to his job. [None but a nation so entirely commercial as the English could be expected to attain to such perfection of methodizing and arrangement. In no other country are what are here emphatically called 'habits of business' carried so extensively into social and domestic life; the value of time, of order, of despatch nowhere so well understood. This is the great key to the most striking national characteristics. The quantity of material objects produced – *the work done* – in England exceeds all that man ever effected, but the qualities which have produced these results have as certainly given birth to the dullness, the contracted views, the routine habits of thought as well as of action, the inveterate prejudices, the unbounded desire for, and deference to, wealth which characterize the mass of Englishmen.]

If only we, in our German towns, could imitate the organization of English clubs, even if with less luxury because we are not so rich. In essentials it would be quite possible to treat the English as equals, and not always be on our knees before their money and names in childish-slavish admiration; with all humanity and more politeness than they show us in England, we could yet make them feel that we in Germany are the hosts and consequently have more authority to maintain than they, who, in any case only come to us to save money or to raise themselves in the world a little; to make splendid connections which would be denied to their middle-class station at home; or to give themselves the comfortable assurance that, in the matter of physical enjoyment of life, we are half barbarians compared with them.

It is indeed inconceivable and a real sign that it is enough merely to treat us contemptuously in order to obtain our respect, that among us the very name of Englishman serves instead of the highest title. Someone who in England, where society down to the very lowest grades is so ruggedly aristocratic, would scarcely be admitted into the lowest circles, is in German lands fêted at courts and carried shoulder-high by the most distinguished nobles, all his blunders and unhelpfulness regarded as amiable English originality, until by chance a really distinguished Englishman appears on the scene and they learn with astonishment that it is only a half-pay ensign or even a rich tailor or cobbler to whom they have been paying so much honour.

November 21st

Let me lead you today to the Haymarket Theatre, which I visited recently while the renowned Liston[1] was playing for the hundred and second time the character of Paul Prye, a kind of lout who delights the public. This actor, who is said to have an income of six thousand *louis d'or* a year, is one of those whom I would call natural comedians, of the type to which the Berliners Unzelmann[2] and Wurm[3] belonged: people who, without any deep study of their art, in their own droll fashion knew how to release an inexhaustible flood of laughter the moment they walked on, although they themselves are often hypochondriacs in everyday life, as must have been the case with Liston.

The notorious Madame Vestris is also engaged here, she who formerly caused such a *furore* and even now, though somewhat past her prime, appears very fascinating on the stage. She is an excellent singer, an even better actress, and, even more so than Liston, the darling of the English public; but she is especially famous for her beautiful legs which have become almost a permanent feature of the newspaper reviews, and which she often displays in men's clothing. Indeed, they are of such a symmetry, a *moelleux* and a play of muscle, that the mere sight of them is enough for the art lover. Her grace and the inexhaustible wit of her playing are really enchanting, although not infrequently lascivious and too coquettish with the public.

How outstanding she was in her profession and how much the English Croesuses have spoilt her, is proved by the following anecdote from a somewhat earlier time, which was guaranteed to me as authentic. A foreigner had sent Madame Vestris, on the occasion of her benefit, a banknote for £50 with the written request that he be allowed to present his entrance ticket in person that

---

[1] John Liston played comic parts at the Haymarket, Covent Garden and Drury Lane.
[2] German actor; worked under Goethe 1820–1.
[3] Comic actor in Berlin under Iffland.

evening. This request was granted, and the young man appeared at the appointed hour with the confidence and the air of a conqueror, but the outcome was entirely different from what he had expected. Madame Vestris received him with a sedate and very serious air and silently pointed to a chair, which the astonished man took, all the more embarrassed because he saw his banknote openly displayed in her beautiful hand. 'Sir,' said she, 'this morning you sent me this note for a ticket to my benefit performance, and for such a ticket it is *too much*. Should you, however, have laid other hopes in with it, I must have the honour of assuring you that it is more than *too little*. Allow me to light you home with it.' With these words, she stuck the note into a nearby candle and lighted the apologetic, unfortunate suitor down the stairs.

November 23rd

An extraordinary English custom is the constant intrusion of the newspapers into private life. Anyone who is of the slightest importance sees himself not only exposed by name in the most tasteless detail – for example, where he went for dinner, what evening party he attended, and so on (many foreigners read this with great satisfaction) – but also, if he does anything worth recounting, he will be exposed without shame and judged *ad libitum*. Personal enmities can be played off in this way as easily as the requital of friends, indeed many use the newspapers to write articles for their advantage, which they themselves send in, and the foreign embassies cultivate this practice most enthusiastically.

You can see what a dangerous weapon this provides, but fortunately the poison carries its own antidote, and this consists of the indifference with which these matters are generally received by the public. A newspaper article, after which a Continental would not show himself for three months, awakes here at the most a momentary smile of malicious pleasure and is forgotten by the next day. They have tried to deliver a *coup fourré* against me too. The English obstinately and firmly believe that all eligible men who come here do so only to find a rich English wife, and have included in several newspapers a satirical article, borrowed from material which appeared at home. I, however, have long been an old campaigner and, alerted in this matter, had the loudest laugh over it by being lavish in my harmless jokes against myself and others. This is the only sure means of standing up to the absurd in this world, for if one shows oneself to be sensitive or excited then the poison begins to work which would otherwise evaporate, like cold water on a red-hot stone. The English also understand this very well.

The striking thing to a foreigner in the local theatres here is the unheard-of roughness and coarseness of the audience. It means that, apart from the Italian opera where only the best society congregates, the higher classes rarely visit their national theatre, a circumstance which may or may not have a beneficial effect on the stage itself. A second reason for the absence of decent families from the theatre is the attendance of several hundred *filles de joie*, from the kept lady who devours six thousand sterling a year and has her own box, down to those who bivouac on the streets under the open sky. During the intermissions they crowd the large and fairly elaborate foyer, where they put all their effrontery unrestrainedly on show. It is strange that such spectacles are in no country on earth more shamelessly displayed than in pious and decent England. It goes on to such an extent that often in the theatre one can hardly ward off these repellent priestesses of Venus, especially when they are drunk which is not infrequently the case, at which time they also beg in the most shameless fashion; one frequently sees the prettiest and best-dressed young girl, who does not disdain to accept a shilling or sixpence just like the lowest beggar woman, getting herself half a glass of rum or ginger beer at the bar – and such things go on, I repeat, in the national theatre of the English, where their highest dramatic talent is displayed; where immortal artists, like Garrick, Mrs Siddons, Miss O'Neill enchanted by their excellence, and where today heroes such as Kean, Kemble[1] and Young make their appearance! Is not this in the highest degree unworthy and an altogether new and striking proof that Napoleon was not wrong when he called the English a nation of prosaic shopkeepers? At least you cannot, in general, deny outright their genuine love of art, for the vulgarity of which I spoke earlier almost never arises out of anything belonging to the actual performance (generally it is a matter of personal

---

[1] Not the great Shakespearean actor John Kemble (who had died in 1823), but his younger brother, Charles.

intrigue for or against an actor), but is almost always of an entirely unrelated nature that has no connection with the stage.

The Ambassador of . . . accompanied me to the theatre and told me, as we were walking about in the foyer, many not uninteresting details concerning this or that beauty as she swept by. The unbelievable thoughtlessness, levity and wondrous changes of fortune of these creatures were to me the most remarkable things about them.

'That one with the languishing eyes,' said he, 'has just come out of the King's Bench, where she has been for a year because of £8,000 worth of debts, still practising her profession though and, God knows how, finally finding the means of getting free. She has a strange weakness for her station in life, to wit, sentimentality, and has been known to give a lover ten times more than she receives from her protector. I know very distinguished people,' he added, 'who have abused this weakness of hers irresponsibly, and I do not doubt that, at the first opportunity, she will be moving back into her old lodging in the shelter of the King's Bench.

'See that rather overblown beauty,' he went on. 'Ten years ago she was living on a scale of luxury which few of my colleagues could emulate. Far from laying by part of her riches of those days, she had a real passion for throwing everything out of the window, and today will be very grateful if you help her with a shilling.'

In contrast to these poor souls, he showed me later, in one of the best boxes, a charming woman of the highest standing who had married a man with an income of twenty thousand pounds, and yet was only too willing to be all things to all men for just one of those guineas.

These licentious manners extend as far as the stage itself, where you see and hear such gross double meanings in word and even in gesture, that you can no longer feel surprise at reading in the old memoirs of the things in which the Virgin Queen took her pleasure.

Every thy
Lou

FIFTH LETTER

London, November 25th, 1826

Best beloved,

It is an absolute necessity for me to spend a day at home from time to time, quite alone, and to spend it in dreamy introspection, running through what is past and what is new, until, through the mixing of so many bright things, one misty hue spreads over everything, and the dissonances of life melt into a soft, gentle, aimless feeling. This mood is enhanced by what would otherwise be unbearable barrel organs, which play day and night in every street, for they grind in a wild flight through a hundred melodies, until all the music is lost in a dreamy ringing in the ears.

December 1st

A few days ago I was present at the very interesting opening of Parliament by the King in person, a ceremony which had not taken place for several years.

In the centre of the chamber of the Upper House the peers were gathered, their red mantles thrown carelessly over their ordinary morning dress. Against the back wall stood the King's throne, on staging to the left sat many ladies in their jewels and to the right the diplomatic corps and foreigners. In front of the throne was a barrier, and behind it stood the members of the Lower House, in the everyday dress of our day. The outside of the House and the staircases were crowded with servants and heralds in the costume of the fourteenth century. At two o'clock, cannons announced the approach of the King in state. The procession was made up of many splendid carriages and horses, of which I have a sketch in my notebook, and as a contrast I have placed a triumph of Caesar's

51

beside it. Looking at these pictures, one involuntarily asks oneself whether mankind has made any real progress since then – especially when judged in terms of the two most prominent and highly placed persons of the respective ceremonies, namely the royal coachman and Caesar. At about half-past two the King appeared, the only man in full dress, in fact clad from head to foot in the old royal regalia, with the Crown on his head and the Sceptre in his hand.

He looked pale and puffy, and had to sit for some time on his throne before he could get enough breath to read out his speech. In the meantime, he threw loving glances and condescending greetings down to several favoured ladies. Lord Liverpool[1] stood beside him, with the Sword of State and the speech in his hand; on the other side, the Duke of Wellington. All three looked so miserable, so ashen-grey and exhausted that it seemed to me that human greatness had never looked so pitiable. Indeed the tragic side of all the comedies that we play here below fell almost like a weight on my heart. At the same time, the occasion aroused in me a lively sense of the comic, to see how the most powerful monarch on earth had to appear before an audience which in his opinion was so far beneath him! Indeed the whole scene, with its entrances and exits and the King's costume, striking in its way, reminded me of how the History Plays are generally performed here. The only thing lacking was the obligato flourish (fanfare of trumpets) which always accompanies the comings and goings of a Shakespearian king.

Notwithstanding his weaknesses, George IV[2] read his speech with great propriety in a beautiful voice, but also with a royal nonchalance which brushed aside some of the banalities to which majesty was pledging itself, as well as the words he could not immediately decipher. One could see clearly that the monarch was delighted when his task was ended, so that the exit went rather more vigorously than the entrance.

Since my last letter I have twice been to the theatre, which I can

[1] Prime Minister since 1812.

[2] A Whig during his Regency, he disappointed liberal hopes when he became King (1820) – indeed his extravagance, succession of mistresses, scandalous quarrel with his wife Caroline all diminished the prestige, and the power, of the Crown during his reign.

only visit if I am not invited anywhere because of the late dinner hour here.

I found that Mozart's *Figaro* was advertised in Drury Lane and rejoiced at the prospect of hearing the sweet notes of our country once more – but was not a little surprised at the unheard-of treatment to which the immortal composer's masterwork has been subjected here. You will scarcely believe me – neither the Count, the Countess, nor Figaro sang, but played these roles entirely as actors; their principal songs, with a few changes in the words, were rendered by the other singers; in addition to this the gardener roared through some interpolated English folksongs, which stood out in Mozart's music like a beauty spot on the face of Venus. The whole opera was moreover *arranged* by a Mr Bishop,[1] that is to say, made more pleasing to English ears by insipid alterations. English national music, the clumsy melodies which one can never fail to recognize, seems to me at least exceptionally unattractive – an expression of brutal feeling, in sorrow and joy, composed of roast beef, plum pudding and porter. So you can imagine what effect these graftings on to Mozart's lovely compositions produced.

Much better was the performance at Covent Garden, where Charles Kemble, one of England's foremost actors, played the role of Charles II splendidly. Kemble is a man of the highest breeding, who has always moved in very good society, and so was in a position to play the monarch royally, which here means with all the ease which is peculiar to those who occupy a high position. He knows how to give an amiable slant to the frivolity of Charles II without ever, even in the moments of greatest abandon, losing that inimitable quality of highest born dignity. Moreover, the costume looked as if it had come from the frame of an old painting, down to the smallest details, a practice which was just as closely followed by all his fellow actors for which Kemble, who was also the director, is very much to be praised.

I must say, however, that in the next piece, in which Frederick the Great was the principal character, the same accuracy and knowledge of *foreign* costumes did not prevail, and the king and his suite looked as if they had borrowed their costumes from the harlequinade pantomime. Zieten made his entrance in a high

---

[1] Musical composer who 'adapted' classical operas for the popular taste.

grenadier's cap, and Seydlitz[1] appeared with long locks à la Murat[2] and as many decorations as that royal comedian wore.

December 3rd

Kemble gave me great pleasure again today as Falstaff. It is certain that even the greatest dramatic poet needs the collaboration of the actors in order to make the most of his work. I have never so fully understood the nature of the notorious knight, or realized so intuitively what his outward bearing must have been like, until I saw him through Kemble exactly as if newborn. His costume and maquillage were indeed striking, but in no way such a caricature as in our German theatre; still less does he present a man without position or breeding, a mere *farceur* as, for instance, Devrient played him in Berlin.[3] Although of a common soul, Falstaff is yet, by habit and inclination, a very experienced courtier, and the roughness which he often assumes in the company of the prince is at least as much an intentional act, which he puts on in order to amuse him (for princes very often love the vulgar because of its contrast with the gloomy loftiness of their position) as to express his own mood.

In the first instance you see Falstaff as a comic man, somewhat like the Maréchal de Bassompierre,[4] ridiculously fat, but distinguished and dignified, never lacking in the innate respect which he owes to the place and surroundings in which he finds himself. In Act Two he is already letting himself go much further, taking all sorts of crude, vulgar liberties, but ever with a marked respect which flatteringly puts the prince in the foreground, while he himself assumes only the privileges of the court fool who seems to be able to say anything that comes into his head; only in the last stage do we see

[1] In the Seven Years' War, which began with Frederick II's invasion of Austria and established Prussia as a major European power, his two generals, Hans von Zieten and Friedrich von Seydlitz, distinguished themselves as brilliant cavalry commanders.

[2] Joachim Murat, general under Napoleon, married to Caroline Bonaparte, made King of the Two Sicilies 1808. Court-martialled and shot, October 13th, 1815.

[3] Celebrated German actor, at the Court Theatre in Berlin since 1815.

[4] Maréchal of France in 1622, known for extravagant tastes and excessive gallantry.

Falstaff in complete *négligé*, all pretences fallen. Like a pig in a puddle, he wallows comfortably in mud and yet, even here, remains an original, raising more smiles than horror. This is the great art of the poet: that he can lay a seal of divinity on the most horrid monsters of sin and shame, something which arouses our interest and, almost to our own astonishment, attracts us. This is dramatic truth, the creative power of genius, of which Walter Scott so graciously says, 'I can only compare Shakespeare with the man in the Arabian Nights, who could transform himself into any form he liked and imitate its feelings and ways'.

As I came in late I found your letter, which, as news of you always does, rejoiced me. Do not let yourself be mistaken about either your own melancholy hours or mine. As regards me, you know how it is: you know that a nothing raises the barometer of my spirit, and that a nothing again makes it fall. It is certainly an all too delicate moral constitution that was handed out to me, and not suited to a humdrum fate which calls for tougher nerves.

[*December 4th*

Since the opening of Parliament society has become rather more lively, though London, as a whole, is still empty. The elegant ladies of the first circles have started to give small parties, access to which is far more difficult to most Englishmen than to foreigners of rank, for the despotism of fashion, as I have already told you, rules in this land of freedom with an iron sceptre. But without indulging too early in general observations, I will describe to you my own way of life in London.

I rise late; read, like a half-nationalised foreigner, three or four newspapers at breakfast; look in my pocketbook what visits I have to pay, and either drive to them in my cabriolet or ride. After my visits have been paid, I ride for several hours about the beautiful environs of London, return when it grows dark, work a little, dress for dinner, which is at seven or eight, and spend the evening either at the theatre or at some small party.

At these occasions there is little general conversation; each gentleman usually singles out a lady who particularly interests him, and does not leave her side for the rest of the evening. Everybody of course speaks French, as with us 'tant bien que mal', but this often annoys the ladies so much after a time, that a man who can speak English tolerably has no little advantage.]

December 5th

Oberon, Weber's swansong, occupied this evening for me. Music and singing in the performance left much to be desired, yet the opera was, for London, excellently presented. But I should have begun by telling you that I started the day early when I was presented to the King at a great levée. As proof of the extraordinary voluntary seclusion of the reigning monarch, I can state that the secretary of our legation was presented with me for the first time – although he has been stationed here for two years.

His Majesty has a very good memory and immediately recalled my earlier stay in England, though he mistook the date by a few years. I made good use of the opportunity and complimented him on the beautification of London which had been effected since that time, for which, indeed, the King is almost exclusively to be thanked. After many gracious replies I moved on, and settled myself in a convenient position from which to watch the play in its entirety. It was original enough.

Everyone went in turn past the King (who, on account of illness, was seated), made his bow, was addressed or not, and thereupon either placed himself in the row on the other side, or at once left the chamber. All who had received an appointment knelt down before the King and kissed his hand, at which the American ambassador, next to whom I happened to be standing, made a satyr-like face. The clergymen and lawyers looked very romantic in their black gowns and white powdered wigs – some long, some short – and one of them was the object of almost general, scarcely suppressed laughter. Kneeling down because he was, as the English have it, to be 'knighted', in this posture, with the long fleece about his head, he looked exactly like a lamb led to the slaughter. His Majesty signalled to the royal Field Marshal to give him his sword. However, for the first time perhaps, the doughty warrior could not draw the sword from its scabbard – he pulled, pushed – all in vain. The King waiting with outstretched arm, the Duke bootlessly exerting all his strength, the unhappy martyr kneeling in silent resignation, as if his end were

at hand, and, round about, the glittering court in anxious expectation – it was a group worthy of Gillray's[1] brush. At last, like a
lightning flash, the court sword flew from its scabbard, and though
His Majesty had been impatiently controlling himself through the
long wait, his arm must have gone to sleep, for with the first blow he
struck, not the new knight, but the old wig which for an instant hid
King and subject behind a pillar of powder.

I will now close with a heartfelt wish that the meagre peepshow
of this town, as I unroll it for you, will not bore you too much. You
wanted pictures of daily life – no handbook of statistics, no topogra-
phy, no regular enumeration of so-called 'things worth seeing'; you
are not expecting from me any systematic treatise on England, nor
am I in a position to provide it, so you will have to put up with it if,
sometimes at least, the modest plain fare is seasoned with a grain of
pepper.

Your true Lou

[1] Famous caricaturist, died 1815.

SIXTH LETTER

Beloved friend,

I dined at the house of a lady of distinction, who talked to me throughout dinner about Napoleon, and, with true English exaggeration, was so enamoured of him that she thought the execution of the Duke d'Enghien[1] and the betrayal of Spain laudable acts. Though I do not go quite that far, I am, as you know, an admirer of the man's colossal greatness and delighted my neighbour by describing to her Napoleon's former magnificence, of which I was an eyewitness. What is certain is that he is still too near for impartial judgement; and experience has amply taught us that it was less his despotic principles than his personal aggrandisement which aroused such inveterate aggression. The principles exist still; but, God be praised, the energy with which he put them into practice is utterly wanting, and that is a great gain for human nature.

I went to the theatre with Mrs—, wife of the well-known Minister and Member of Parliament, and accompanied her after the play to the first genuine 'rout' I have attended during this visit to England. It is the custom to take your friends to parties of this sort, and to present them to the mistress of the house, who will never be satisfied until her rooms are full to suffocation, and a fight has broken out among the carriages below and several men and horses hurt or killed, so that the *Morning Post* can, the next day, carry a long article on the extremely fashionable soirée given by 'Lady Vain' or 'Lady Foolish'.

In the course of the evening I made a more interesting acquaintance than I expected on the staircase (I could get no further into the

---

[1] Only son of the Duke of Bourbon, he fought with the *émigrés* against Napoleon but retired to Baden in 1801. Napoleon violated the neutrality of Baden to capture the Duke, and had him executed at Vincennes.

house), in Lady Charlotte Bury, who has some reputation as an authoress.[1] She is the sister of a duke and a celebrated beauty. The next morning I called on her, and found everything in her house brown – furniture, curtains, carpets, her own and her children's dresses. After I had been there some time, the celebrated bookseller C.[2] entered. This man has made a fortune with Walter Scott's novels, though, I am told, he at first turned down *Waverley*, and in the end only paid a small sum for it. I hope the charming Lady Charlotte Bury had better cause to be satisfied with him. I thought it discreet to leave her with her man of business, and made my bow.]

December 10th

The Portuguese affair[3] is now much discussed in all circles, and the Marquis P. even read out to us today, from a box at the French theatre, the recently printed English statement. Politics here are a main preoccupation of society, as they begin to be in Paris and will in time be even in our sleepy Germany, for the whole world is moving in that direction. But the more frivolous pleasures are suffering from it, and the art of conversation, as once it existed in France, may well soon be entirely lost. Here, judging from present impressions, it has never really existed, except perhaps in the time of Charles II. People are too slavishly subject to all established usages, too systematic in their pleasures, too kneaded into the dough of their prejudices, in a word, not lively enough to achieve that unfettered freedom of spirit which is the only possible basis for an attractive society. I must confess that I know no people more wearisomely like each other and more inbred than the upper classes of this country – with only a few exceptions, and those, for the most part, foreigners or those who have lived for a long time on the Continent. Everything here is ruled by a stony, marble-cold subjection to caste and fashion, and this

[1] Youngest child of the Duke of Argyll, she published sixteen novels.

[2] This is either the publisher Archibald Constable or his partner Robert Cadell; it could also possibly be Henry Colburn, a fashionable publisher of ladies' novels.

[3] John VI's death in March had precipitated a constitutional crisis involving his two sons. English public opinion was divided between support of the liberal, Don Pedro, Emperor of Brazil and his younger brother, absolutist Don Miguel.

makes the upper classes boring, and those beneath ridiculous. Courtesy of the heart and cheerful bonhomie are *entirely* absent here, and in their borrowings from other nations, they have adopted neither the ease of the French nor the naturalness of the Italians but, more than anything, German stiffness and awkwardness, concealed beneath arrogance and haughtiness.

All the same, the halo surrounding a firmly rooted aristocracy and a great deal of money has given to the great English world the *par excellence* stamp throughout Europe, which is conceded to them by all nations. Of course, it cannot be denied that the English show great taste in the use of their advantages; but that foreigners personally get little benefit from it is witnessed by the small number of them in England, and by the yet smaller number that makes a long stay here. Every one of them thanks God from the depths of his heart when he has escaped from English society, but still, from vanity, he goes on praising that non-lifegiving, foggy sun, whose rays have at least shone on his *comfort*.

The English are much more loveable and loving in their domestic and intimate relationships, though here too there is a lot of reserve, for instance the custom prevalent in the upper classes for sons, as soon as they are fledged, to leave the paternal home and to live by themselves. They cannot even turn up for a meal with their father and mother without a formal invitation. As a touching example of conjugal affection, I read recently in the newspapers that the Marquis of Hastings, who died recently in Malta, ordered that his right hand should be cut off as soon as he was dead and sent to his wife as a keepsake. A gentleman of my acquaintance, out of pure tenderness and with her consent, cut off his mother's head when she died, so as to be able to kiss her skull for the rest of his life; whilst other Englishmen, I believe, would rather go to Hell than let a dissecting knife come near their body. The laws prescribe that all such directions of the deceased must be carried out with the most scrupulous exactitude, no matter how insane, unless they come into conflict with these same laws. There is a castle in England where, for the past half-century, a well-dressed corpse has stood in the window, gazing motionless over his former possessions. How dearly that man must have loved domestic life!

[Just as I was going to entertain you with more English originalities, my long-awaited head gardener entered my room, bringing your letters. What a pity you could not have put yourself into the large packet (in all your vitality of course, not like Lord Hastings' hand), so that I might share with you every enjoyment fresh as it arises, without this long interval! As it is, you are melancholy because I was a fortnight ago; or your sympathizing answer to a cheerful letter of mine arrives just as I am labouring under a fresh attack of depression. As you say, such old letters are often like a dead body which, after being long forgotten, is fished up out of the sea.

I now take almost daily excursions in the park with Rehder,[1] to make his visit to England as useful as possible. There are in the neighbourhood of London a great number of very interesting seats, all of them situated on very pleasant and animated roads. Amongst these is Kenwood, a villa of Lord Mansfield's; Sion House, belonging to the Duke of Northumberland and laid out by Brown,[2] is also extremely worth seeing on account of its remarkable greenhouses and the multitude of gigantic exotic trees in the open air, which would not bear our climate. Kew, on the opposite bank of the river, unquestionably possesses the most complete collection of exotic plants in Europe. The park has also a great advantage in its beautiful situation on the Thames, but is in general rather neglected. I have said nothing of the enchanting valley of Richmond. Every traveller falls into an ecstasy about it, and with justice; but his descriptions do not always excite a similar feeling in the reader. I therefore avoid them, and remark only that the excellent aristocratic inn [the Star and Garter], from which one overlooks this paradise, enhances the pleasure.]

December 23rd

Thanks for the news from Berlin. I was especially pleased about Alexander von Humboldt's[3] appointment. It must be a joy for every patriot to see a man like him at last settled in his fatherland, which is rightly proud of his reputation in all parts of the world. It must, too,

---

[1] Pückler's head gardener.
[2] 'Capability Brown' was so called because he liked to say, 'This landscape is capable of improvement'.
[3] Traveller, geographer, botanist, mineralogist; given a Prussian pension in 1827.

be a blessed even for local society that salt is going to be added to its mixture, for the lack of it has long made it quite unenjoyable.

My mood is of the same gloomy character – probably because of the eternal fogs, which are sometimes so bad that they have to keep the street lamps on until midday, and even then you can see nothing. In such a state of mind your portrait is my best consolation, and it is to you, my only friend and my friend forever, that I turn at last with wet eyes thanking you, from the bottom of my heart, for all your ways of love and kindness, and I lay my sorrows in your faithful bosom, as I do my joys and all my hopes, whose most brilliant fulfilment would, without you, lose all value. I must leave you now to do my duty, a most repugnant one, and go to a large party where I have decided to do as I do in life and lose myself in the crowd. It is my last sortie into the world for the moment, as I am preparing to set out with Rehder on a park and garden excursion, which will take us at least a month. The present time is the very best for those who wish to study these things, because the leafless trees allow one to see in all directions and so, on a single tour, to survey all that art has done for the landscape, to appreciate the effects achieved, to judge of the whole as if it were a plan on paper, and to recognize the components of every plantation in the order intended for them.

Since our departure is set for tomorrow morning I am sending off this letter, even though it has not grown to the usual corpulence. How mean are yours in comparison! If ever our descendants come across the tattered correspondence of their ancestors in a corner of the old library, they will certainly be equally astonished at my extravagance and your parsimony.

Apropos, do not dissipate yourself too much in Berlin, nor forget to give a thought, if only for the very shortest time, to the most faithful of your friends,

Lou

SEVENTH LETTER

Watford, December 25th, 1826

Dear and faithful one,

This morning we set out at last, unhappily in horrid rainy weather. Ten miles from London we began our operations in the pleasant district of Stanmore, with the inspection of two villas and a great park. At ten o'clock we reached Cashiobury Park, the seat of the Earl of Essex. I had my name sent in to him, and he sent me his son-in-law, Mr M. F., to show me around. I had already met this gentleman in Dresden, and it was pleasant to renew our acquaintance.

The castle is modern Gothic and splendidly furnished. You go first into a hall, with stained-glass windows, which gives on to an inner court, converted into a flower garden. You go from the side of the hall into a long gallery, hung with weapons, past the richly-carved, wooden staircase leading to the upper storeys, and into the library, which serves as the main salon for company. All this is on the ground floor. The library has two little cabinets leading into the garden, both filled with rare objects.

From the library, you go into an equally rich second drawing room, and out of this into the dining room. Alongside both of these is a conservatory in the form of a chapel. All the windows, which stretch down to the floor, command splendid views over the park, through which flows a river. Its walls are all covered with oaken woodwork, with costly mouldings and carvings; the furniture is of rosewood, silk and satin, and the walls are adorned with valuable paintings in antique gold frames. The proportions of the room are those of a hall, and it is all regularly heated by steam to 4° Réamur. The stables, somewhat distant, and the rest of the domestic buildings are to the left of the castle, and connected with it by a crenellated wall, so that the whole stretches for a good thousand feet without interruption.

I paid my respects to the old Earl, who was kept to his room by gout, and received from the kindly old man the most valuable information and, even more important, the entrée for my future journeyings.

[*Woburn, December 26th*

We have made a calculation, dear Lucie, that if you were with us (a wish ever present in the minds of your faithful servants) you could not, with your aversion to foot-exercise, see more than a quarter of a park a day; and that it would take you at least four hundred and twenty years to see all the parks of England, of which there are undoubtedly at least a hundred thousand, for they swarm in every direction. Of course we only visit the great ones, or look *en passant* at any little villa that particularly strikes and pleases us. Before I say any more about what we have seen, however, I must praise the excellence of English inns. A detailed description of this morning's breakfast will give you a good idea of the comfortable living of travellers here.

The following is what I found set out when I left my bedroom – in a little town scarcely as big as one of our villages. In the middle of the table smoked a large tea-urn, prettily surrounded by silver tea-canisters, a slop-basin and a milk jug. There were three small Wedgwood plates, as many knives and forks and two large cups of beautiful porcelain; by them stood an inviting plate of boiled eggs, another of broiled *oreilles de cochon*, a plate of muffins, kept warm by a hot water-plate; another of cold ham, flaky white bread, dry and buttered toast, fresh butter in an elegant glass vessel; salt and pepper, English mustard and *moutarde de maille* and, lastly, a silver tea-caddy with very good green and black tea. (NB I had ordered nothing but tea.)

This most luxurious meal is actually very cheap: it was charged in the bill at only two shillings. However, on the whole travelling here is very expensive, especially the stage-posting which is exactly four times as much as with us.]

Leamington, December 27th

Leamington is a great watering-place of which I have not yet seen much since I arrived here at eleven o'clock last night. A great part of yesterday was spent in looking at the interesting Woburn Abbey. This fine palace, built simply and nobly in the Italian style, is infinitely more soothing than the colossal would-be Gothic nonsense. With its stables, rides, ball-house, conservatories, statues and picture galleries, it constitutes a little town.

For three hundred years, which is rare even for England, this property has been passed down regularly from the possessor to his heir, and, with an income of a million of our money, it is not to be wondered at that there should be a confluence of splendour here.

The actual castle is a regular square, and the *bel étage*, which in this country is always on the ground floor, constitutes an unbroken line of rooms running round the square. These rooms are adorned with valuable pictures and furnished with pieces upholstered in heavy materials; door and window embrasures are of white stucco relieved with gold, or costly carvings, all as simple as they are genuine. In one room there was a remarkable collection of family miniatures, from the first Russell (the family name of the Dukes of Bedford) down to the present Duke, assembled in an unbroken line. In such circumstances, a man can indeed be proud of his family and his nobility.

Since the mail is just leaving, I am enclosing this letter in one for L., so that, through his kindness, you may receive it sooner than you did the last.

Remember the wanderer in your peaceful solitude, and know that, even if fate should hurl him to the Antipodes, his heart will always be with you.

Your Lou

EIGHTH LETTER

Beloved friend,

By heaven – only now am I filled with true and immeasurable enthusiasm! What I have earlier described was smiling Nature combined with everything that art and money could bestow upon it. I left it well pleased, and although I have seen things like it before – indeed possessed them myself – not without admiration. But what I have seen today was more than this; it was an enchanted spot, enveloped in the most charming robe of poetry, surrounded with all the majesty of history, the sight of which still fills me with delightful astonishment. You, you experienced historian and reader of memoirs, know better than I that the Earls of Warwick were once the mightiest vassals in England, and the great Beauchamp,[1] Earl of Warwick, boasted that he had dethroned three kings and set as many upon the vacant throne.

His castle has been standing since the ninth century and has remained in the possession of the family since the reign of Elizabeth. One tower of the castle, said to have been built by Beauchamp himself, has been preserved without any alterations, and the whole stands there colossal and mighty in its intricacies like a vision of the Middle Ages.

Even from a distance you can already glimpse the dark stone mass over the ancient cedars of Lebanon, chestnuts, pines and plane trees, rising perpendicularly out of the rocks on the bank of the Avon more than two hundred feet above the water level. The ragged pier of a bridge, overhung with trees, stands in the middle of the river which, lower down, exactly where the castle buildings begin, forms a foaming waterfall and drives the sails of the castle mill.

---

[1] One of the few times Pückler gets a name wrong – it should be Neville, not Beauchamp.

You lose sight of the castle for a while as you journey towards it, and find yourself in front of a high, crenellated wall built of broad ashlars, which time has covered with moss and creeping plants. The wings of a high wrought-iron gate open slowly to admit you into a deep defile blasted through the rocks. The carriage rolls with a hollow sound over the rocky ground, dark beneath its vault of old and lofty oaks. Suddenly, at a turning in the path, the castle breaks forth from the woods into the open light of Heaven. Between the two giant towers at whose feet you now find yourself, the wide sweep of the entrance dwindles to the size of an unassuming gate. A yet greater surprise awaits you when you pass through the second wrought-iron gate of the castle. Nothing more picturesque and at the same time more impressive can be imagined! Let your fancy conjure up a space about as large again as the interior of the Roman Coliseum, then transport yourself into a wood of romantic luxuriance. You are now looking at the broad courtyard of the castle, surrounded by mossy trees and majestic buildings which, although of every size and shape, yet constitute one noble and consistent *whole*, whose lines, now rising, now falling against the blue sky with the everchanging green of the earth beneath, produce not symmetry so much as a *higher harmony*, elsewhere proper to the works of nature alone.

The first downward glance falls upon a broad carpet of grass, round which a gently curving gravel path leads to all the entrances and exits of this giant building. When you look back, you see both the black towers stretching upwards, of which the elder, called Guy's Tower, rearing its head above the surrounding vegetation in threatening majesty, is as firm as if cast in bronze; the other, built by Beauchamp, is half-hidden by a century-old pine and a magnificent chestnut. Broad-leaved ivy and wild vine run riot, now embracing the tower, now climbing up the walls to its highest point. On your left is the inhabited part of the castle and the chapel, adorned with many high windows of different sizes and shapes, whilst the opposite side of the square, almost entirely without windows, presents only crenellated masses of stone, picturesquely broken by several larch trees of colossal size and bushes as big as trees which, protected in their long shelter, grow wonderfully tall. *Before* you, however, if you raise your eyes to the heights, there awaits the noblest sight of all. On this fourth side, the courtyard forms a low, bushy hollow into which the lines of the buildings sink for a space, and then the terrain rises steeply again in the form of a conical mountain, which the jagged walls of the castle climb. This hill, and the keep which crowns it, are thickly covered to the very top with undergrowth which fills the foot of the tower and walls. High above the stone masses tower the giant, ancient trees, whose smooth stems seem to be swaying in the breeze, whilst, on the highest peak, a bold bridge is seemingly fastened to the trees on both sides like some lofty Heaven's gate. Suddenly, as the clouds drift across the blue sky, the broadest, most glittering stretch of light breaks through from under the towering arch and dark coronet of trees.

Just imagine – suddenly seeing this magic scene and as you see it remembering that here nine centuries of untamed power, of brave victory and annihilating defeat, of bloody deeds and savage greatness, perhaps of soft love and noble magnanimity, have left behind some of their visible traces, or where they have not, their unconscious, romantic memories – then judge with what feelings I put myself in the place of the man to whom this view daily calls back memories of the lives of his forebears, and who is still living in the unchanged castle of the first possessor of the fortress of Warwick, the same half-fabled Guy who lived more than a thousand years ago, and whose battered armour, together with a hundred weapons of famous ancestors, is hanging in the entrance hall. Is there any man so lacking in poetry that he does not see, even today, the glory of these memorials shining around even the most unworthy representative of such a noble line?

It is only a few steps up from the courtyard to the living quarters, first into a passage and from there into the hall, on both sides of which the reception rooms stretch in an unbroken line for 340 feet. Although almost on the same level as the courtyard, these rooms on the other side are more than fifty feet above the Avon. The eight to fourteen-feet thick walls make of each window a cabinet, ten to twelve feet broad, with the most beautiful and manifold views over the wildly foaming river beneath, which then gently winds through the park and flows into the misty distance.

From my first sight of the castle, I have been conducted from surprise to surprise. I believed myself to be transported into past centuries when I walked into the gigantic *baronial hall*, as Walter Scott describes it, its walls panelled with carved cedar wood and filled with all kinds of knightly weapons, enough to supply many battles at once; then I saw before me a marble fireplace in which I could comfortably stand next to the fire with my hat on my head and in which a three-hundred-year-old gridiron, strangely formed in the shape of a basket, blazed like a funeral pyre. At the side, faithful to ancient custom, a stack of unsplit oak logs was heaped up on a base, also of cedar wood, which was placed in the middle of the stone floor and only partly covered by a faded carpet. From time to time the mighty fire was given fresh life, nourishment in the form of a three-foot log, by a brown-suited servant, whose costume, with its gold garters, lanyard and trimmings, made him look sufficiently old-world. Everywhere here the difference between the real old feudal greatness and the mere modern imitations is just as striking as that between the mossy ruins of the weatherbeaten castle on its rocky peak and the ruins erected yesterday in the pleasure garden of a newly rich contractor.

The art treasures are inestimable, and the innumerable paintings, among which there is not a single mediocrity to be found, are almost all by the great masters and have, moreover, a quite special family interest, since there are a great many ancestral portraits painted by Titian, Van Dyck and Rubens. The greatest treasure is one of Raphael's most enchanting pictures, the lovely Joan of Aragon,[1] of whom, strangely enough, there are four pictures, all of the greatest excellence and all declared the true original; three of them, without doubt, must be copies, but are as good as indistinguishable from the model. One is in Paris, another in Rome, a third in Vienna, the fourth here. I know all four of them, and must unconditionally give the palm to the one here. There is charm in this splendid woman which it is impossible to describe. An eye that leads into the depths of the soul, royal dignity twinned with womanly readiness for love, fire in her glance twinned with a sweet sadness; all this with a swelling fullness of the lovely bosom, a transparent softness of the skin, a brilliance and grace of the garments and of all the adornments of her costume and a truth, such as only a divine genius could call into perfect existence. [Among the most interesting portraits in the gallery, both for the subject and the handling of it, is

---

[1] Joanna the Mad, sister to Catherine of Aragon, Queen of Castile and Leon, mother of Emperor Charles V.

Titian's *Machiavelli* – who is precisely as I imagine him. A face of great acuteness and prudence, and of suffering, as if lamenting, after long study, over the worthless side of human nature; that hound-like character which loves where it is spurned, follows where it fears, and is faithful where it is fed. A trace of compassionate scorn plays round the thin lips, while the dark eye appears turned reflectingly inward.

It appears strange, at first sight, that this great and classic writer should so long have been misunderstood in such a gross manner. Either he has been represented as a moral scarecrow (and how miserable is Voltaire's refutation of that notion!); or the most fantastic hypothesis is put forward that his book is a satire. On closer observation, one must arrive at the conviction that it was reserved for modern times – when politics have at last begun to be viewed and understood from a higher and really humane point of view – to form a correct judgement of Machiavelli's *Prince*.

To all arbitrary princes – and under that name I class all those who think themselves invested with power solely '*par la grâce de Dieu*' and for their own advantage, all conquerors and children of fortune – to all such as these, this profound and acute writer shows the true and only way to prosper; the exhaustive system which they must of necessity follow in order to maintain a power sprung from the soil of sin and error. His book is, and must ever be, the true, inimitable gospel of such rulers; and we Prussians, especially, have reason to congratulate ourselves that Napoleon had learned his Machiavelli so ill, or we should otherwise probably be still groaning under his yoke.

By proving, as he incontestably does, that arbitrary power can be maintained only by the utter disregard of all morality, and by seriously inculculating this doctrine on princes, he demonstrates only too plainly that the whole frame of society, in his time, contained within itself a principle of demoralization; that no true happiness, no true civilization was possible to any people till that principle was detected and destroyed. The events of modern times, and their consequences, have at last opened their eyes to this truth and they will not close them again!

Many valuable Etruscan vases and other works of art, besides the pictures and antiques, decorate the various apartments, and with great good taste are arranged so as to appear as harmonious accessories rather than heaped up in a gallery as dead masses, for show.]

I was shown as a phenomenon of the exact and enduring architecture of the castle that, notwithstanding its age, when all the doors of the suite of rooms are closed, you can see through the keyholes along the suite's whole extent of 350 feet a bust standing exactly in the middle of the end room. Remarkable exactitude indeed, which our craftsmen would neither understand nor carry out. Although, as I told you, the walls of the hall are covered with a vast number of weapons, there is also an extremely well-endowed armour room in the castle. Here, among other things, they have preserved Lord Brook's leather jerkin, still splashed with blackened blood, in which the renowned ancestor of the present Earl was killed at the battle of Lichfield.

Here I finally took a lingering farewell of Warwick Castle and laid its memories, like a noble dream of the past, to my heart. In the glimmering moonlight, I felt like a child to whom a fantastic giant's head, from far-off times, is nodding kindly over the tree-tops. With such fancies, dear Lucie, I wish to fall asleep and in the morning go to where Romance again beckons me – the ruins of Kenilworth!

Birmingham, December 29th, evening

A few stages from Leamington, in a district of increasing dreariness and poverty, lies Kenilworth.

The day was gloomy, black clouds rolled across the sky, a wan, yellow sun broke forth but rarely, and the wind whispered in the ivy and whistled through the empty windows. Occasionally a stone loosened from the crumbling walls, clattered down upon the ramparts. No human being was to be seen; all was lonely, shuddering, a gloomy but noble monument to annihilation.

I was seized with wonder at the incessant changes in the lives of men, and it transported me, in the evening, into a shrieking contrast between the lifeless ruins and the prosaic bustle of a crowd, busied only with gain, in the steaming, smoking, swarming, teeming factory town of Birmingham. The last romantic sight I saw was the fires which at the onset of darkness light up the town on every side from the long chimneys of the ironworks. Then I renounced the play of fancy until a more opportune time.

December 30th

Birmingham is one of the most considerable and at the same time one of the ugliest towns in England. She numbers 120,000 inhabitants, of whom certainly two-thirds are factory workers; she also presents the very appearance of a boundless workshop.

I betook myself, immediately after breakfast, to the factory of Mr Thomasson, our consul, which is the second in size and importance. The most considerable of all, where 1,000 workers are daily employed and where an 80-horse-power steam engine turns out countless objects, right down to livery buttons and pins, has been hermetically closed to all foreigners since the visit of the Austrian prince[1] (whose suite must have overheard some important secrets).

I passed several hours here in horrid, dirty, stinking holes which serve as the various workshops, but were yet interesting, and I myself made a button, which Rehder will deliver to you as a sign of my industry.

On the lower storey they have set out to better advantage all the products of the factory, in gold, silver, bronze, plate and lacquer (imitations which surpass the Chinese originals), steel goods of every sort, all in a profusion and elegance which really arouses astonishment. Among other things, we saw here a copy of the gigantic Warwick Vase, of the same size as the original, cast in bronze, and costing £4,000, as well as splendid table services in silver and plate, the latter so well worked that you cannot distinguish it from silver, so that even the great men here are mixing plate with silver, as the Parisian ladies mix false stones and pearls with real ones.

I made a multitude of new and pleasant discoveries concerning luxuries great and small, and did not altogether resist the buying mania, which has so much to feed on here, but I confined myself entirely to trifles which will reach you at the earliest in a well-packed chest.

The ironworks, with their gigantic steam-engines, the needle

[1] Possibly Metternich.

factories, the steel manufactories, where you find everything from the smallest scissors to the largest fireplace and whole staircases, polished as bright as a mirror, heaped up together – to see all this fills up a day very pleasantly, but let me off a more exact description, *ce n'est pas mon métier.*

Chester, January 1st, 1827

Another year gone! Not one of the worst for me, apart from the separation from you. I lit the reading lamp in the carriage, and comfortably read through Lady Morgan's[1] latest novel while we rolled at a gallop across the plain. As soon as the hands of his watch stood at twelve, Rehder congratulated me and gave good wishes to myself and to you for the New Year. Twelve hours later we reached Chester.

Although we made the nineteen German miles from Birmingham to here in thirteen hours, I still find that in England, as in France, the further one gets from the capital the more one notices a gradual decrease in the good things of life. The inns are less good, the post horses worse, the postilions dirtier, the servants less well-dressed, and life, with its varied urgencies, becomes lonelier. Moreover, there is an increase in expense in this unswept state of things, and one is subjected to occasional swindles such as almost never occur nearer to London, because of the strong competition.

[As we had time to spare, we visited the royal castle of Chester, which is now converted into an excellent county gaol. The whole arrangement of it seemed to me most humane and perfect. Imagine a high terrace of rock, on which stands a castle with two wings. The main building is dedicated to the Courts of Justice which are very spacious, and the wings to the debtors. The courtyard is laid out as a little garden, in which they may walk. Under the court are cells in which the criminals are confined; the further end on the right is appropriated to the women. The cells are separate, and radiate from a centre; in front of each is a little piece of garden in which the prisoner is permitted to walk; before trial his dress is grey; after it,

---

[1] Popular and very successful Irish novelist, who showed much kindness to Pückler when he visited Ireland.

red and green. In each division of the building behind the cells is a large common room, with a fire, in which the prisoners work. The cells are clean and airy; the food varies with the degree of crime – the lowest is bread, potatoes and salt. Today being New Year's Day, all the prisoners had roast beef, plum pudding and ale. Most of them, especially the women, became very animated, and made a horrible noise, with hurrahs to the health of the mayor who had given them this feast.

The view from the upper terrace, over the gardens and the prison – with the river winding below, the roofs and towers of the city in picturesque confusion, and in the distance the mountains of Wales – is magnificent, and, taking it all into account, I must admit that our country counsellors of justice are seldom as well lodged as the rogues and thieves here.]

The weather was even less favourable to us in the New Year than in the old. It rained the whole day. I thank Heaven that tomorrow we set out on the return journey, since I am utterly sick of sightseeing and parks. Meanwhile I am sending this letter today to the capital, so as to give you the benefit of a rest, and pray God to take you under His good and faithful protection.

Your ever devoted Lou

NINTH LETTER

Hawkestone Park, January 2nd, 1827

Beloved friend,

Although I felt very tired of parks yesterday, and did not think that I could summon up a really lively interest in any of them, today I am converted, and must give to Hawkestone, above all the others that I have seen, *the* superiority, which comes, not from art nor grandeur nor aristocratic splendour, but from Nature alone, which here she has achieved to such an extraordinary extent that if I were given the power to add something to the beauty of this place (buildings excepted) I could not imagine what.

Here are united all the elements for a favoured spot, as you will be able to gather even from a simple description.

So cast the eyes of your spirit upon a spot of earth of such an extent that, from its highest point, you glance can sweep over fifteen different counties. Three sides of this broad panorama rise and fall in everchanging, many-folded hills and low ranges, like the waves of a troubled sea, and on the horizon are surrounded by the strangely shaped rocks and jagged mountains of Wales, gently sinking at both ends to the fourth side of the prospect, a fertile plain shaded by a thousand lofty trees and bounded in the glimmering distance by the white streak of the sea.

The Welsh mountains are partly covered with snow, and all the fertile land between is so closely interwoven with hedges and trees that it looks like nothing so much as a thick wood, here and there cut into by stretches of water of innumerable different sizes, and little meadows and fields. On one of the gloomiest spots in this wilderness rise the ruins of the 'red castle', a splendid relic from the days of William the Conqueror. Picture to yourself a romantic group of hills rising quite alone out of the plain, almost in the form of a regular cross, around which flow the silver waves of the river Hawke. This naturally enclosed space is now the park of Hawkestone. It is recognized, even in the neighbourhood, as a charming spot, and married couples from the nearby towns of Liverpool and Shrewsbury when their marriage takes place in the lovely season of the year, are in the habit of spending the first weeks of their new, sweet happiness at Hawkestone. Perhaps the reason for this is that Hawkestone Park, quite contrary to English custom, is used more by the public than by its owner, who does not live here at all, and whose house, indeed, cowers like an *hors d'oeuvre*, neglected and insignificant, in a corner of the park. On the other hand they have built a fine inn, where the aforesaid married couples, as well as Nature's friends of all kinds, are entertained with first-rate beds, and strengthened with splendid food and drink.

Here we too pitched our tent and, after a good breakfast, set out on foot – for one cannot drive through the park because of the difficult terrain. The ascending promenade, which in winter is also somewhat dangerous, lasted four hours.

Newport, January 3rd

It has now become winter in earnest, the ground is covered with ice and six inches of snow, and the cold, in rooms inadequately heated by fireplaces, is almost unbearable. Since I spent most of today in the carriage, there is nothing more to report.

Birmingham, January 4th

The whole day was again, as on my earlier visit, devoted to factories and looking at exhibitions of goods. The poor workers sometimes have a bad time of it! They certainly earn enough, but some of their occupations can be fearfully dangerous, if there is the least negligence or oversight.

Everything has its dark side, including this great growth of industry, but that does not mean it should be rejected. Even virtue has its drawbacks when it goes the smallest way beyond the happy mean, and on the other hand even evil, indeed crime itself, has its bright spots.

Stratford, January 6th

Today's journey was not long but its value was great, for the place, the name of which stands at the top of my letter, is the very birthplace of Shakespeare! It is a most gripping experience to see those insignificant objects which, hundreds of years ago, were in daily, intimate touch with such a great and beloved man, and to be on the very spot where his bones have so long been mouldering – and thus, in a few moments, to have traversed the long way from his cradle to his grave. The house in which he was born, and the room itself in which this great event took place, are almost unaltered. The room is just like any petty bourgeois room in our small towns, entirely characteristic of the time when England stood on the same level of culture as the common man among us today. Millions of names, written by kings and beggars, cover the walls of the little room and although I am, as a rule, no friend of this clinging to foreign great men, as vermin cling to marble palaces, yet here I could not resist the urge to add my name, with deep feelings of gratitude and awe, to all the others.

The church on the Avon (the same river that splashes the reverend walls of Warwick Castle) where Shakespeare's bones lie, is a fine relic of the old days, and adorned with many monuments, among which of course that of the immortal poet stands supreme. Like his bust, it was formerly painted in bright colours and gilded, but, through the stupidity of a certain Malone,[1] was whitewashed over about a hundred years ago, as a result of which it must have lost much of its individuality. The bust is, moreover, of no artistic value and quite expressionless and, they say, without any resemblance. I succeeded, only with a lot of trouble and money, in getting from the verger a little picture of the monument in the original colours, which I am enclosing in this letter.

Besides that, I bought in the bookshop several views of the places I have mentioned. On the Town Hall is a large picture of Shakespeare, painted in more recent times, and a still better one of Garrick who, especially in the manner of his bearing, in many ways resembles Iffland.[2]

[1] Eighteenth-century editor and critic of Shakespeare.
[2] German playwright and actor-manager at Mannheim. He wrote sixty-five plays, and helped establish the 'domestic drama' in Germany.

Oxford, January 7th

After we had let our park mania rest for two days, we made up for lost time today by visiting four great parks, of which the last was the famous Blenheim.

The frightful fog grew ever thicker, so we saw Blenheim only, as it were, by twilight. In splendour and size it must undoubtedly be called extraordinary and what I saw, or rather felt, pleased me very much, since it was all enveloped in a magic veil through which the sun, without rays, looked like the moon.

Blenheim is said to have been built largely on the site of the ancient royal park of Woodstock (which you remember from Walter Scott's latest novel[1]), and a great part of the oak wood is still standing from the time of the unhappy Rosamund[2] – still green, and dying only slowly in a hundred-year agony. Here you find oaks and cedars that are real giants in form and size. Around many the ivy has so wound itself that it has killed them, but at the same time in its own leaves has provided a new and lovelier evergreen foliage, that now envelops the weathered trunks like one of Nature's magnificent winding sheets, until they fall to dust.

January 8th

Oxford is a unique town. Nowhere else will you see such a multitude of old and splendid Gothic buildings of between three hundred and a thousand years old gathered in one spot. The detail of many, indeed almost all of the colleges and churches is very beautiful, and it produces the most picturesque effect. It has often puzzled me why various aspects of this architecture have not been adopted for our dwellings, for instance the windows, which, positioned unsymmetrically and sometimes alternated with great turrets, are as beautiful as they are practical; for only custom could make the regular rows of square holes which we call windows bearable to us.

[1] *Woodstock*, published in 1826.
[2] 'The fair Rosamond', mistress of Henry II, reputed to have been offered by Eleanor of Aquitaine the choice between a dagger and a bowl of poison.

January 9th

Today I walked around Oxford for the first time, and cannot express with what deep pleasure I wandered through this Gothic town, from college to college, and brought back for myself the old times. Among other things there is a splendid grove of elms, which was planted in the same year as the buildings you can see from there – 1530. From this queen of all groves, in which not *one* tree is missing, and which leads through the meadows down to the water, you can see on one side a charming landscape, on the other a part of the town with five or six of the most beautiful Gothic towers, which in itself is a splendid view, but today, with the wind driving the black clouds over an overcast sky like a wild army and the loveliest rainbow spanning the Heavens, as if rising from one of the towers and sinking into another, it was almost fabulously enchanting.

London, January 13th

By bright gaslight, which always looks like a festive illumination here, we drove into town, and as I felt the need of a complete change of scene after the long park and garden life, I went down to Covent Garden Theatre in order to see the first Christmas pantomime. This is a much loved theatrical form in England, which is intended primarily for children, so I was quite at home.

[When the curtain first rises, you see nothing on the stage but clouds, a very good effect which they obtain by means of several layers of gauze. The clouds clear to reveal a clear blue sky and a landscape with a small cottage. On the rooftop is a gigantic cock, which stretches its neck and utters a triumphant Cock-a-doodle-doo! Then it bends down and starts pecking at an enormous cat which is sleeping on an angle of the roof. The cat purrs, sits up, washes its face and stretches itself. The actor who plays this animal must have spent many long hours in the study of cats. How the status of the acting profession has risen! Instead of being rivalled by monkeys and poodles, they are now allowed to represent these privileged animals!

The door of the cottage opens, and out comes Mother Shipton, a frightful old witch, accompanied by her son, who is very like herself. She is a very powerful enchantress, and all the farm animals cluster

79

round and fawn upon her. But unfortunately she has awakened this morning in a very bad mood. She curses all the poor beasts and immediately changes them into the characters of the Italian *commedia dell' arte*, Pantaloon, Harlequin, Columbine and the rest. They then spend the rest of the play making a nuisance of themselves to each other.

In the next scene we are transported to a village street, the centre of which is occupied by a tailor's workshop. In the open front of this sit several apprentices stitching industriously. A gigantic pair of shears is fastened above the lintel as a shop sign. Harlequin races in and, with a gigantic spring and a somersault, crashes through a first-floor window. Pantaloon and his friends now rush in in pursuit, gesticulating to each other, and one of them points to the broken window. Pantaloon enters the shop but, as he is rushing up the stairs, Harlequin emerges from the chimney and escapes over the rooftops. Pantaloon then enters the upper room, puts his head out through the broken window and turns this way and that in search of Harlequin; unfortunately at that moment the great blades of the shears close and cut his head off. Not in the least discouraged, Pantaloon withdraws from the window, comes downstairs and begins to look about the street for his head. At this moment a poodle comes on, sees the head and runs off with it, with Pantaloon in hot pursuit. Before Pantaloon gets off the stage, he is met by Harlequin who is now disguised as a doctor. He explains his plight (by gestures), and Harlequin takes from his pocket a jar of ointment with which he rubs the stump of Pantaloon's neck. This causes the head to reappear out of the neck. Pantaloon recognizes Harlequin and sets off after him. His followers cannon into each other and fall on top of one another on their way off the stage.

The last scene is one of the best – the witch's kitchen. In it there is a huge fireplace before which a complete ox, a stag and a pig are turning on a spit. The chef is dressed in a parody of a chef's costume as are his assistants, all of whom are armed with enormous knives and forks. Chef drills them *en peloton* and marches them off carrying their utensils like muskets over their shoulders.

The scene now changes to the path, which winds up a mountainside towards a lofty castle in perfect perspective scale, so that everyone who is climbing up it diminishes in size proportionately. Gradually they all disappear, and finally the colossal pie, which is being carried by the hindmost assistant, goes down like the setting moon.

We now find ourselves in the great hall of the castle, which belongs to a beneficent magician who banishes Mother Shipton and her son to the centre of the earth and restores all the characters to their proper human form. Harlequin is recognized as the rightful prince and marries Columbine.

Clouds now cover the stage, and from the midst of them rises a balloon in which there is a pretty little boy. This ascends to the roof of the theatre and, as it is circling round the chandelier, the whole stage scene disappears through the floor and stars shine through the clouds − a very pretty illusion. The balloon now descends, the earthly scene rises again, and the whole spectacle ends with tight-rope artists and acrobats.]

Now, my good, dear Lucie, *il faut que tout finisse*, even this long tale of travel which certainly gives you a page for every year of my life.

Your Lou

TENTH LETTER

[*London, January 19th, 1827*

Dearest Lucie,

Rehder left London today for Harwich, and will be with you in a fortnight. I know how glad you will be to have a living witness of the sayings and doings of your Lou; someone whom you can question about all the things which, even with the best intentions, cannot always find a place in letters.

I have now settled myself into town life again. Yesterday I dined with Prince Esterhazy,[1] where the – secretary of legation kept us constantly amused. I have often admired the talent of the French, and envied it too, for making the most humorous stories out of the most commonplace incidents, and nobody possesses this talent in a higher degree than Monsieur R.

At the same time, one must acknowledge that however brilliant such agreeable chatter may be at the time, it goes out like a light and leaves nothing to the memory; so that the pedantic German feels a sort of uneasiness after listening to it, and regrets having spent his time so unprofitably. Had it been possible to give to that Germanism which formed our language the lightness, roundness and equivocality – qualities in which the French excel – the conversation of the German would certainly be the more satisfactory of the two, for he would never neglect to connect the useful with the agreeable. As it is, we Germans contribute little to society except the sort of talent the French call 'l'esprit des escaliers' – namely that of thinking of the clever things one might have said in the salon as one is going down stairs.]

---

[1] Member of a powerful Hungarian family and Ambassador to the Court of St James until 1842.

January 22nd

The poor Duke of York has, after a long illness, finally died, and now lies in state in great splendour. I saw him last in October and found him, even then, only a shadow of the sturdy, stately man whom I had so often seen in former days at Lady Lansdowne's and in his own house, where six bottles of claret drunk after dinner made very little change in his countenance. I remember that, on one such evening – it was already after midnight – he conducted several of his guests, among whom were the Austrian Ambassador, Count Meerveldt, Count Beroldingen and myself, into his fine arms room. We attempted to swing several Turkish sabres but none of us was strong enough, and so it happened that the Duke and Count Meerveldt both scratched themselves on a kind of straight Indian sword. The latter then wanted to know whether it cut as well as a Damáscene, and at once tried to cut one of the six candles on the table through the middle. But the experiment succeeded so badly that both candles and candlestick fell to the floor. While we were groping around in the dark and trying to find the door, the Duke's adjutant, Colonel C., began to stammer woefully: 'By God, sir, I remember the sword is poisoned!' You can imagine the feelings of the wounded men when they heard this news. Fortunately it transpired, on closer inspection, that the Colonel's declaration arose from claret and not from poison. [1]

[The Duke's death seems to be much regretted, and the whole country wears deep mourning for him, with crape on their hats and black gloves. People's servants are put into black liveries and everyone writes on black-edged paper. Meanwhile the Christmas pantomimes go on as merrily as ever. It is strange to see Harlequin and Columbine skipping about the stage in all conceivable frivolities and antics, while the coal-black audience claps and shouts with delight.]

---

[1] At the time of the scene of 'the poisoned sword' the Duke's mistress, Mary Anne Clarke, was serving a prison sentence for trafficking in commissions while her lover was commander-in-chief. He was removed from the head of the army when this scandal broke, but later reinstated.

January 28th

I have for several days vegetated too completely to be able to write much to you. However I was very surprised this morning to see Rehder, whom I had thought by this time would almost have reached you, walk into my room. He had been shipwrecked halfway to Hamburg, and, driven back by storms to Harwich, spent a whole night between life and death. He has been so terrified by all this that he will hear no more of the sea as long as he lives. I am therefore sending him by Calais in this time of perilous shipwrecks, and am only writing about it so that you will not be anxious on his account. Unfortunately, he has lost several of the things he was taking for you.

[My house has grown very musical, for Miss A, a newly appointed opera singer, has come to live in it. The thin English walls give me the advantage of hearing her every morning gratis.] I have not been really well for several days; the air of the town does not suit me and is forcing me into a régime such as your chanson describes, since I eat daily not much more:

qu'un bouillon
d'un rognon
de papillon.

Cobham Hall, February 2nd

Lord Darnley, whose wife I got to know in London, has invited me to visit him for several days at his country house, which I accepted the more willingly since Cobham Hall is the place of which Repton[1] says that he worked with the owner on its beautification for nearly forty years. Indeed it does both of them the greatest honour although, from all that I have experienced and seen, it seems to me most probable that the greater part of the credit should go to the excellent taste of the owner – sometimes in opposition to Repton who, in particular, did not show enough respect for old trees. Still, in gratitude to the man to whom landscape gardening is so much indebted, there has been erected in the park a seat dedicated to him which commands a wonderful view. As Repton's son, who was with

[1] Famous landscape gardener.

us, had told Lady Darnley a great deal about Muskau, we found it a very attractive point of contact and diligently walked for some hours around the flower gardens which were more tasteful than splendid, and adorned with several marble statues by Canova.[1]

I did not see the master of the house, who suffers from gout, until I came down to dinner, when I met a great company including Lord Melville[2] who has been inspecting the warships near here on the Thames.

Lord Darnley was lying on a sofa in the middle of the drawing room, covered by a Scottish plaid, and rather embarrassed me with his form of address.

'You do not recognize me,' he said, 'and yet we saw each other often thirty years ago.' Since I was at that time sweeping about in petticoats, I asked for a more exact explanation, but was not best pleased to hear my age so exactly announced before the whole company, for you know that I boast of looking no more than thirty. However, I must admire Lord Darnley's memory, for he remembered so clearly every trifle of his visit to my parents [at Muskau] with the Duke of Portland, that he reminded me of many things from that long forgotten time.

February 3rd

I must describe to you, once and for all, *la vie de château* in England, for this institution is everywhere the same, and I find it unaltered from when I was here before. It offers, without any doubt, the pleasantest side of English life, since there reigns a great freedom and a ban on all the most burdensome ceremonies which with us weary both host and guest.

The attitude of 'please yourself', which of course lies at the root of this life, cannot, if only in the interests of good entertainment, be lightly dispensed with.

To save space, visitors usually get only one large bedroom on the second floor, and the English rarely enter this apartment for any purpose other than to sleep and to perform their twice daily toilette which, even without company and in the most strictly domestic

[1] Famous Venetian sculptor.
[2] First Lord of the Admiralty 1812–27.

circles, is always *de rigueur*, for all meals are taken together, and whoever has anything to write usually does it in the library. There you also arrange rendezvous, general as well as with particular persons, in which you are entirely unconstrained. Often you have the chance to chat for hours at a stretch with the young ladies, who are always literary-minded. Many a marriage, or seduction of the already married, is woven between the *corpus juris* on the one side and Bouffler's works on the other, while the novel of the moment lies between as a means of communication.

Breakfast is at ten or eleven o'clock, at which you can appear in the greatest *negligée*. It is always of the same kind as that already described to you in the inn, only of course more elegant and more complete, and the ladies do the honours very gracefully. If you come down later when breakfast has been removed, there is a valet who takes care of you until one o'clock and even later and ensures that the last straggler does not go empty away. That there lie on the table several newspapers to read as you wish, goes without saying.

The gentlemen now go hunting, or about other business; the host does the same without troubling himself in the least about his guests (a real benefit!) and it is only half an hour before dinner that one finds oneself, elegantly dressed, in the drawing room together with the others.

I have already told you what goes on at table, but there is only one strange custom which I have not mentioned and cannot omit in the interests of completeness, to which, immediately after the departure of the ladies and immediately beside the table, free rein is given: a relic of barbarism which is extremely repugnant to our notions of propriety.

This struck me especially today when an old admiral who, clad in his dress uniform, probably on account of Lord Melville's presence, made use of this facility for a good ten minutes, during which period we felt as if we were listening to the last drops from a roof gutter after a long past thunderstorm.

After midnight, and a light supper consisting of fruit and cold meats at which everyone looks after himself, you retire. For this purpose there stand on a side table several little flat candlesticks, from which everyone takes his own and lights himself up to bed – most of the domestic staff, who formerly had to stay up, have sensibly long since gone to bed. The endless sitting of servants in the antechamber is not the fashion here and, except at prescribed times when their help is expected, you see them very little and look after yourself.

For the night there awaited me in my room a splendid old Chinese four-poster, big enough for a sultan to sleep in with his six wives, but I froze alone like an icicle until I produced my own warmth, for the distant fireplace gave none.

February 5th

Between ourselves let it be said that, however pleasant and unconstrained it may be to stay in another's house, it is always too constrained, too unfamiliar, above all too lacking in independence for me, proud and condescending as I am, to feel entirely *à mon aise*. This I can be only between my own four walls, and after that in the carriage or an inn. This preference may not be the best, but all the same it is mine! So I shall not stay out all the days of my invitation, but leave my great bed tomorrow to another, perhaps less corpulent mortal, and hasten to Brighton, a watering-place which is now very fashionable.

I took leave of Lady Darnley in her own room, a little sanctuary which I found overflowing with charming disorder and superfluity, the walls full of little mirror brackets bearing choice curiosities, and the floor covered with splendid camellias, in baskets, looking as if they were growing there. Permit me, dear Lucie, to take leave of you here among these flowers and grant this letter just as long an answer, so that it may not weigh upon your conscience that I love you (at least in writing) far more than you love me.

The friend of your heart, Lou

ELEVENTH LETTER

Brighton, February 7th, 1827

Best beloved,

I have covered the sixty miles here very fast and in the most comfortable indolence, without even looking up, for one must occasionally travel like a distinguished Englishman.

A better temperature seems to prevail here than in the rest of the Land of Fogs; I was awakened today by the most brilliant sunshine at nine o'clock. Soon after that I went out, first to the Marine Parade, which stretches for a long distance along the sea; then I took a turn through this great, clean and very gay town, which with its broad streets is like the newest quarters of London, and finished with visits to various London acquaintances. After that I went for a ride, since my horses had been sent on before me. In vain did I look about me for a tree. The region is entirely bare, nothing is to be seen but hilly dunes covered with short grass.

Sea and sky provide the only picturesque spectacles – moreover, they greeted me today, just at the right moment, with the most beautiful sunset. The majestic star was enveloped in rose-red mist, so that it cast no rays but rather looked like the intensive glow of a thick mass of gold which, as it touched the water, seemed to melt and flow over a great part of the blue sea. At length the ocean swallowed up the fiery ball, the burning colours faded from red to violet, then gradually to a whitish grey, and in the gloaming the waves roared, driven by the evening wind, and dashed onto the flat shore, as if in triumph over the buried sun.

[February 8th

Public rooms, lists of visitors (*Badelisten*) etc. do not exist here. Brighton has only the name of a bathing place in our sense of the word, and is chiefly resorted to by inhabitants of London for recreation and pure air. People who have no country house, or who find London too expensive, spend the winter, and the fashionable season here. The King used to be very fond of Brighton, and built a strange Oriental palace which, with its cupolas and minarets, looks exactly like the pieces on a chessboard. The interior is splendidly if fantastically furnished. Although it cost enormous sums, its owner, long sick of it, is said to have shown a desire to pull it down, which would indeed not be a subject of great lamentation.

The only large trees I have seen in the neighbourhood are in the gardens of this palace, but the walks by the sea are so agreeable that one does very well without; especially the large Chain Pier, which extends a thousand feet into the sea, and from which steam vessels sail for Dieppe and Boulogne.

Not far from there an Indian has set up Oriental baths where people are cleansed in the Turkish fashion, which is said to be very healthy and invigorating, and is in great favour with the fashionable world. I cannot help thinking, however, that the sudden cold after profuse perspiration is very dangerous.]

February 9th

The sun has again disappeared, and such a cold has set in that I am writing to you in gloves so as to preserve my white hands by which, like Lord Byron, I set great store. I confess that I am not of the opinion that one must be a fop for trying to take care of the few beauties the dear Lord has given one; frost-chapped hands have always been my horror.

[A visit from Count Flahaut,[1] one of the most agreeable and respectable representatives of Napoleon's time, who carried into the Imperial Court *les souvenirs de l'ancien régime*, and into the present one the reputation of spotless integrity and loyalty (a most rare instance!) here interrupted me. He came to invite me to dinner tomorrow. This has detained me – it is too late to ride; I am in no

---

[1] French general and diplomat, he was with Napoleon at Waterloo but escaped exile owing to the influence of Talleyrand, whose natural son he may have been. He settled in England and married Margaret Elphinstone (Baroness Keith).

humour to seek club society; I shall put on a second dressing gown, dream about you and Muskau, read over your letters and patiently freeze in my room.

February 10th

Today I made up for the confinement to my room and wandered about the neighbourhood for many hours. I enjoyed my freedom all the more as I was to attend a great subscription ball in the evening.]

The country here is certainly very individual, for during a four-hour ride I did not see a single full-grown tree. However the many hills, the great town in the distance, the scattering of smaller ones closer to hand, the sea and its ships, as well as the constantly changing light, sufficiently enliven the landscape – and even the contrast with the rest of England, everywhere so rich in trees, was not without its charm. At last the sun went incognito to rest, the weather cleared up entirely and the moon rose, clear and bright over the waters. Now I turned my horse down from the hills to the sea, and rode hard along the strand the five or six miles which separated me from Brighton.

I love nothing more than to ride by moonlight along the empty seashore, solitary but for the splashing and rustling and rush of the waves so near the mysterious sea, so awe-inspiring that even the horse will only remain by the flood if forced to it, and guided by instinct hastens with redoubled speed back to dry land.

[How different from this poetical scene was the prosaic ball! A narrow staircase led into the ballroom, which was ill-lighted and miserably furnished, worsted cords around it to divide the dancers from the spectators. An orchestra for the musicians was hung with ill-washed white draperies, which looked like sheets hung out to dry. The numerous company – all in black, including their gloves – was engaged in a melancholy style of dancing, without the least trace of joyousness, so that the only feeling you have is of compassion for the wasted fatigue the poor people are enduring . . . Now you have a true idea of the Brighton Almack's, for so these very fashionable balls are called.

Almack's balls in London are the resort of people of the highest rank during the season, which lasts from April to June; and five or six of the most intensely fashionable ladies, including Princess Lieven,[1] who are called patronesses, distribute the tickets. It is an immense favour to obtain one, and for people who do not belong to the very highest or most modish world, very difficult. Intrigues are organized months beforehand, the patronesses flattered in the most servile manner to secure an advantage; for anyone who has never been seen at Almack's is regarded as utterly unfashionable – I might almost say disreputable.

When I entered, I saw no one of my acquaintance, and therefore addressed myself to a gentleman near me to show me the Marchioness of—, from whom I had received my ticket through the intervention of Countess F. I was obliged to present myself to her, to make my thanks, and found her a very kind, amiable, domestic woman. She introduced me to her daughters and also to a certain Lady—, who spoke very good German. This is the fashion now, and the young ladies labour hard to accomplish it.

Afterwards I found a gentleman of my acquaintance who introduced me to several very pretty young ladies, among whom Miss W., a niece of Lord C., was particularly distinguished. She was by far the prettiest and most graceful girl in the room, so that I was almost tempted to give up my longstanding resolution to dance no more (for I always danced badly). I might have attempted it here safely enough, for, God knows, nowhere do people jump about so awkwardly, and a man who waltzes in time is a real curiosity.]

February 11th

This morning I went to church in order to be pious, but I had no success. Everything was too dry and unaesthetic; I commend an artistic, even if sensuous, divine service. If only we followed Nature who, in religions as in forms of government (for she rules entirely constitutionally), remains always the best schoolmistress. Does she not infuse in us profound religious feelings through her most splendid, sublime spectacles: through the painting of sunrise and sunset, the music of the raging storm and of the roaring sea, the sculpture of

---

[1] A Prussian by birth, Princess Lieven became a leading London hostess. 'It is not fashionable where I am not,' she declared.

the rocks and mountains? So, dear people, do not be cleverer than the good God, but imitate Him as well as you can.

But in this I would be preaching to deaf ears – apart from yours, dear Lucie, for they have long been hearing, with me, the heavenly music of the spheres which rings forever in the splendid creation of the Eternal to those who do not positively stick cotton wool in their ears to deaden it.

The sermon which I heard, though previously prepared and read from a script, was also entirely wooden and lacking in substance. Preachers in general would achieve a much more beneficial effect if they abandoned the jogtrot of always taking their themes from the Bible, and took them rather from everyday life and human society, and especially if they spoke less of dogma and more of the poetic religion which dwells in every man, and also if they taught morality not only as commandments, but also as the beautiful and the useful, as what is necessary for the happiness of the individual and of society. If from the pulpit the common man were better instructed in thinking rather than in believing, his vices would soon become fewer, he would begin to show a real interest, a need for the church and the preacher in his development, whereas now he visits them for anything but edifying reasons, or without any reflection. Also the laws of the land, as well as the Ten Commandments, should be elucidated from the pulpit, and the reasons for them made easy for the congregation, because many sin in this matter without, as Christ says, knowing what they do.

Above all, in a well-organized society all preachers must be appointed at a fixed salary (this can be provided from the State or from the faithful), and neither for the blessings of true religion, nor for the ceremonies of the conventional should there be cash payments. It is simply dreadful to see a poor peasant putting two *groschen* behind the altar for the Body of Christ which he has received, and at christenings slipping them into the clergyman's hand like a tip. But if all you hear from the pulpit is raging and scolding because the offering is constantly growing smaller, and the condemning of this withdrawal of his receipts as a sign of the decline in religion – then one begins to wonder what so many priests are there for, and what they really think of their vocation.

The afternoon was more soothing. I climbed about the hills above the town, and finally crept on to the floor of a windmill in order to see from there the whole panorama of Brighton. The storm whirled the sails of the mill so violently on their axle that the whole building swayed like a ship. The miller's boy, who had shown me the way up, now brought out a small spyglass from a meal chest but, in spite of its soft bed, it was unfortunately broken. All the same, I greatly enjoyed the beautiful view, which was much enlivened by many hundreds of fishing boats struggling with the wind, and then hastened back with the sinking sun to take up my social duties.

The gathering at the Count Flahaut's was small but interesting, first because of the host himself, then because of a lady famed for her beauty, and finally because of a very famous former leader of Parisian society, D'Orsay,[1] who now lives for a great part of the year in England, apparently not without political ends. He is one of those men now become rather rare, who live in great style without one's knowing quite on what, who know how to assume a certain authority without one's knowing whence, and behind whom one is always looking for something special, in fact secret, without knowing why. This man is at least very amiable, when he wants to be. He is a splendid raconteur, and has forgotten nothing from a varied and turbulent life which can give spice to his conversation. The French make the best such magnanimous adventurers, and their knowledge of human nature is always to be admired, even if they often use it to get the better of others. Their less than warm hearts enable them, if I may so express myself, to live economically with their intellect and retain a firm hold on it forever.

They spoke a lot about Napoleon, whom our host, like everyone who has spent any time with him, remembers only with awe. He related one incident which struck me. The Emperor, he said, was so incredibly exhausted from the gigantic strain of the Hundred Days and the events that followed that, on the retreat from Waterloo (quite contrary to our usual version of the affair), he could only progress very slowly, protected by a battalion of his Guard. Two or three times he fell asleep on his horse and would undoubtedly have fallen from it if Count Flahaut himself had not held him on. Apart from this physical strain he never, the Count assured us, gave the slightest sign of inner agitation.

---

[1] Renowned dandy and artist, D'Orsay attached himself to the Countess of Blessington in 1822 and set up a fashionable coterie with her in London.

An original Scotsman, whom I have heard described as a real madcap who has already killed two or three men in a duel, visited me this morning and brought with him his printed family tree, with the whole history of his race or clan. He complained bitterly that another of his name wished to contest with him the rank of chieftain and took pains to convince me from the work he had brought with him that he was the real one, but thought that a 'trial by combat' between them would soon settle it for the best. Then he opened his coat of arms, a bloody hand on a blue background, and gave the following account of its origins:

Two brothers who were returning from a foray against one of the Scottish islands had agreed between themselves that the one whose flesh and blood (a Scottish expression) first touched dry land should become the lord of it. Even with all the strength of their oars, the ship could make no progress in a turbulent sea, and both brothers flung themselves into the water in order to swim to the island. The elder now saw that his younger brother was outstripping him so he drew his short sword, laid his left hand on one of the jutting rocks, hacked it off with one blow, seized it by the fingers and flung it past his brother on to the shore, shouting as he did so: 'God is my witness that my flesh and blood has touched the land first.' And so he became king of the island, which his descendants have ruled undisturbed for seven generations.

The story of the bloody hand seemed to me not unpoetic, and a striking picture of that rough but mighty time. I did not fail to relate to him a companion story out of the *Nibelungenlied* concerning my (probably just as legendary) ancestors, and we parted over the ghosts of our names the best of friends.

[There are now private balls every evening; in rooms to which a respectable German would not venture to invite twelve people, several hundreds are packed like Negro slaves. It is even worse than in London; and the space allotted to quadrilles allows only the mathematical possibility of making something like a dancing demonstration. A ball without this crowd would be despised, and a visitor of any standing who arrived to find the staircase empty would probably drive away again.

Once you are in, however, I must confess that nowhere do you see more pretty girls, against whom you are squeezed indiscriminately. At one o'clock a cold supper is served; the supper room is usually on the ground floor, and as the table cannot contain more than twenty persons at a time, the company goes down in groups which meet, pushing and elbowing, on the narrow staircase. If you succeed in getting a seat you may rest a little; and many, with little regard for the previous occupants or the ladies, are determined to avail themselves of this privilege. On the other hand, the servants are very active in replacing the dishes and bottles as fast as they are emptied, on the side of the table to which the guests have no access.

In order to see the whole occasion, I stayed until four in the morning in one of the best houses, and found the end of the ball, after three-quarters of the company were gone, the most agreeable; the more so because the daughters of the house were remarkably pretty, amiable girls. There were some real originals, however, at the ball; among others a fat lady of at least 55, dressed in black velvet with white trimmings and a turban with floating ostrich feathers, who waltzed like a bacchante whenever she could find room. Her pretty daughters tried in vain to rival their mama. My curiosity being excited by such a display of Herculean vigour, I discovered that the lady's large fortune had been made by speculations in cattle.]

February 16th

I read yesterday 'that strong passions grow stronger through absence'. Mine for you must then be a very strong one, for tender friendship most certainly is a passion, since I love you more dearly than ever. Besides, the matter can be easily explained. If anyone truly loves another, he sees in absence only their true and lovable qualities; their unpleasant side, little faults which everyone has and which yet, face to face, sometimes wound, is quite forgotten, while love increases, quite naturally, in absence. What do you think?

I am travelling tomorrow express to London in order to give this letter with my own hands to our ambassador, since the last ones were so long in reaching you. Before setting off I took a long walk this morning, not quite alone but with one of the many kinds of young woman whom I have got to know here. In this respect they give unmarried girls in England uncommon freedom, once they are 'out'. This young girl is just seventeen, but has been finished in Paris.

Heaven grant us both better spiritual and bodily health, and grant me above all your tender friendship, which is a necessary part of my wellbeing.

Your faithful Lou

TWELFTH LETTER

Brighton, February 22nd, 1827

Best beloved,

I have just come in from a great Almack's fancy-dress ball, which everyone had to attend either in a fantastic costume or in uniform – not the happiest of combinations. You can be sure that my friend the Highland chieftain turned up in his Scottish ceremonial dress. Indeed this costume is very fine, extremely picturesque and manly, and only the shoes with their big buckles do not please me. The sword is of exactly the same form as our student's rapier and with it he also carries a dagger, pistols and a powder horn, all studded with precious stones; an eagle feather, the sign of a chieftain, adorns the jaunty cap.

I took two ladies to the ball; the first, Mrs C., is a high-spirited, clever and very pretty woman of about thirty-five, who loves the world and is very popular in it – moreover, she cares most tenderly for a sick husband, the truest kind of fidelity. Her figure is pleasant, her manner kind; altogether a very suitable person *pour en faire une amie dans le monde*. The other lady, her bosom friend, is a young, very charming widow, insignificant perhaps but a likeable, kindly little woman, who can be made entirely content if one compares her teeth with pearls and her eyes with violets.

I had nothing to be ashamed of in the person or in the appearance of my ladies, but they, like all present, were cast into the shade by the young Miss F., the beauty of Brighton, indeed one of the most beautiful girls in existence: a little sylphide who must have stolen her wonderful foot and graces from another land. Moreover, she is just sixteen and as wild and lively as quicksilver, as tireless in dancing as in frolic. Today I was fortunate enough to make myself very popular with her with a lucky present. This consisted of a cornet of especially well-made explosive bonbons, distributing which she had already amused herself immeasurably at earlier balls, to the extreme annoyance of the mamas. I had providently laid in a stock at the confectioner's and now handed them to her unexpectedly, and I doubt whether the present of a million to me, the poorest of men, could have given so much pleasure as I gave with this trifle. The little one rejoiced immeasurably, and then uncovered her batteries – which were all the more successful because the enemy considered herself quite safe. At every explosion she laughed herself sick, and whenever I came near her she smiled at me out of her bright eyes, always so beautiful and kind, like a little angel. The poor child! This perfect innocence, this overflow of great happiness and joy, touched me deeply for alas! she will soon, like all the others, be undeceived.

Many of the other girls are indeed very beautiful, but too carefully groomed; some of them were dripping with jewels and other precious objects – but none of them came near the little F. whose grace, in the eyes of ugly, selfish men, would be complete if it were not, unfortunately, united with poverty.

It is my pride that chiefly suffers in this wife-hunting, and this insuperable feeling may prove a great hindrance to me.

February 24th

At these balls there is a custom which is very favourable for the gentleman. When a dance is finished, he takes his partner on his arm and walks about with her until the next dance. By this means many men have time to get over their shyness, and only our large apartments and solitary halls could make it pleasanter.

Here they cannot stretch it out further than down the stairs, into the supper room and up the stairs again, but the crowd itself ensures greater privacy, for no one takes any notice of anyone else. Since they pester me on all sides to dance (a German who does not waltz seems to them incomprehensible) I have given out that I am bound by a vow, and at the same time let it be thought that it is a tender one. This tale the ladies find difficult to reconcile with the conviction that I am here only to seek a wife, something that is fixed hard and fast in their minds. This brings me a certain amount of homage, which spices the daily monotony but, God be praised, there is nothing which could in the least disturb my peace, a very comfortable state of affairs. Things went much worse for a poor Englishman who today flung himself from the pier into the sea for unrequited love, and only yesterday was dancing as if stung by a tarantula.

I have many times lamented the fact that Brighton has no vegetation, but the sunsets over the sea and the cloud pictures which accompany them I have never seen in such varied forms anywhere else. It rained all day today and as it cleared up in the evening there arose on the horizon a dark mountain over the watery mirror, growing gradually ever more solid, and when at last the flaming gold sun broke through the black mass, I seemed once more to be seeing Vesuvius with the lava pouring down its sides.

March 5th

Ah, Schnucke,[1] if only you had 150,000 talers! I would marry you again now. *Cela suffirait pour nous maintenant, et je ne demanderais plus davantage.* Security is the only thing that one cannot do without.

London, March 17th

I am back once more in Albemarle Street and yesterday morning, after my long absence, I paid no fewer than twenty-two visits, attended a club dinner and then a ball at the house of the lady admirer of Napoleon's whom I have already mentioned, and closed the day with a soirée at Mrs Hope's, a fashionable and pretty woman.

Yet another proof that I have enemies who do not rest is an article in a Paris newspaper which says *que j'avais divorcé de la fille du Prince Hardenberg pour épouser la veuve du Roi Christophe.* Although this article has also been published in a newspaper here it has not injured me in any way, but has made me better known, which is an advantage. They are so used to this kind of thing that they only laugh *sans y attacher la moindre conséquence.* That the intention was to cause trouble and that it originated in Berlin is all the more certain because this princess is not here, and is anything but rich; in fact she is living in *misère* in the Netherlands.

---

[1] Endearment, translates roughly 'lambkin'.

March 18th

The Italian Opera has now begun and is, apart from the French theatre, the only spectacle *du bel air*. Everyone must appear in evening dress, even in the *parterre*, which is a splendid sight. The performance itself was bad, orchestra as well as singers, and the ballet no better. The lighting in this theatre is arranged more to be seen than to see, because in front of every box there hangs a chandelier which blinds one in a very unpleasant way and throws the players into darkness. The opera lasts until after one o'clock, which gives the audience enough time to visit it without neglecting other society, since, now that the merry-go-round has begun in earnest, you seldom get home before three or four o'clock; and if anyone really wants to enjoy himself – which in fact the exclusive set do not, but which is amusing to a foreigner – the latter can easily get a dozen invitations for every evening.

Before two o'clock in the afternoon the great world has not come to life. From four to six are the hours for the park, when the ladies, in their elegant equipages and morning dresses, have themselves driven slowly about in their thousands, while the gentlemen ride among them on their fine horses, flitting from flower to flower, and displaying as many graces as the good Lord has bestowed upon them. Almost all Englishmen sit well on horseback, and ride naturally much better than our riding masters, who think they know all there is to know if they can sit a skilfully broken horse through its different paces, looking like pegs on a clothes line.

March 25th

[It would be too tiresome if I were to send you a daily list of the parties I go to: I shall only mention them if anything strikes me as remarkable, and perhaps hereafter try and give you a general *aperçu* of the whole. The technical part of social life – the arrangement for physical comfort and entertainment – is well understood here. The most distinguished specimen of this is the house of the Duke of Devonshire, a king of fashion and elegance.

Very few of the great nobles have in London what we on the Continent would call a palace. Their castles, their luxury and greatness are to be found in the country. The Duke of Devonshire is an exception, and his mansion in town affords, as well as a great deal of taste and richness, a great number of art treasures. The company there is always of the most select although, as is always the case in England, too numerous; but the great number of rooms makes it less tiresome than usual. The concerts at Devonshire House are especially fine, and only the most outstanding talent then in the capital is engaged for them. Moreover, the arrangements for the suppers and 'buffets' are excellent.

Sometimes, after concert and supper, the dancing then begins at two in the morning, and one drives home by daylight. This suits me admirably, for as you know I always did have a taste for Minerva's bird. On such a night-morning I often enjoy a drive in the park, for – thank Heaven! – spring is visibly coming, and the tender green of the young leaves and pink almond blossom peep over the garden walls amid the dark network of swelling branches.]

April 3rd

You are already used to my leading you from palace to hovel, and from the richly ornamented salon to the greater beauties of Nature. Today, come with me to my dentist's, the celebrated Mr Cartwright. This man through his skill, earns a yearly income of £10,000 and behaves in the most grandiose style. First, he himself does not visit anyone apart from the King; everyone else, gentleman or lady, must come to him. But that is not all. You must make an appointment eight to fourteen days in advance, and ask for an audience. Then you receive a card with the following inscription: 'Mr Cartwright will have the pleasure of seeing — at — o'clock on the — th.' When you arrive, you are shown into an elegant room – a pianoforte, etchings, various books and other means of entertainment are laid out to while away the time, a very necessary precaution for you may well wait here one to two hours. When I arrived, I found the room already occupied by the Duchess of Montrose and the Lady Melville, with their daughters, who were called in one after the other. After an hour my turn came round. If you get as far as that you will be entirely content, for Mr Cartwright is the most skilful and knowledgeable man in his calling I know, and entirely free from any charlatanry. Moreover, he has a fixed price and never overcharges. *Mais c'est un grand seigneur de dentiste!*

I looked in on four or five places this evening to find something to interest you and finally found it at Lady —'s, through the good offices of a half-German captain who has just returned from the East. Among other things he told me about Lady Hester Stanhope, a niece of Pitt's, who left England 10 years ago, turned Arab and established herself in Syria.

She is now venerated by the Arabs as a prophetess, and lives with all the consideration and splendour of a native princess, though she allows very few Europeans to visit her.

With a great deal of trouble and through the most complicated intrigues, my friend at last succeeded in visiting her. The first thing she said to him was to demand his word of honour that he would never write anything about her. As soon as he had taken this oath (by which, thank God, I am not bound), she became very gay and talkative, and showed herself to be as unconstrained as she was witty. She made no secret of the fact that she had abandoned the Christian faith, but confided to him that she was awaiting the true son of God whose path she herself was appointed to prepare. Thereupon she showed the captain a magnificent Arab mare, which had a very strangely formed bone growing from her back giving her the appearance of being saddled. 'This horse,' said she, with an expression from which the captain could not guess whether she was deranged or joking, 'this horse God himself has saddled for his son, and woe to the man who dares to throw a leg over it! Under my protection she can safely await her true Master.'[1]

In the course of the conversation she also assured him, *en passant*, that Adam is still alive, that she herself well knows where he abides, but could not clearly explain the location.

Our hostess, Lady Ch., of whose boundless admiration for Napoleon I have already spoken to you, listened to us and assured the captain that Lady Hester had really been taking him in, for she knew her very well, and considered that a clearer, more determined and, at the same time, more devious female mind had never existed. In any case, with such a personality it is good to exchange the West

[1] Lady Stanhope had kept house for her uncle, William Pitt, till his death in 1806, after which she had travelled to the Levant, finally settling at Daer Djoun in 1814. When Pückler himself visited her in 1837, he too was shown the sacred steed on which the New Messiah would ride into Jerusalem. She died in 1839.

for the East. She *rules*, is quite independent, and as free as a bird on the wing; in the midst of civilization she would perhaps never have been able to shed the trammels which are the dark side of civilized life.

April 4th

Sir Alexander Johnston,[1] a great Orientalist, invited me to dinner, and spiced the meal with his witty and learned conversation. Later in the evening I saw a wonderfully beautiful painting, a Venus by Titian, clad only in her own charms and blissfully reposing upon soft pillows; a dream seems to thrill convulsively through her and she shields herself with her little hands, like Venus surprised in the bath.

I have never in my life seen anything lovelier than this heavenly being, so becomingly lighted by the glow from the brightly burning fire, the clear light of which is softened by the half-drawn curtain. Her lovely limbs are as white as snow, not a blemish to be seen on that full, classical body over which stream luxuriant brown locks, affording stolen glimpses of the rosebuds of her virginal bosom. A lovely hand, an adorable foot, which was never disfigured by too narrow a shoe, a mouth made for kissing and a yearning, pearly face which, even if the eyes were closed, would be lit by a wistful, ravishing smile; in all, she appears the most moving type of womanly beauty.

I was lost in contemplation, imagining that, oh Heaven! the dark eyes had opened and were gazing kindly at me – my consciousness left me, and I did not awake until four o'clock in the afternoon. Good morning or good evening, *comme il vous plaira.*

April 6th

You will have not made much out of my last picture. It is a riddle, and until you have solved it let us speak of something else.

---

[1] When Sir Alexander heard that he was mentioned in Sarah Austin's book, he was greatly alarmed and called on her to ask if he was abused in it. 'Certainly not, Sir Alexander, can you imagine it?' she assured him, to which he replied, 'Why, he is rather a Mephistopheles, one can't feel sure.'

Tell me, why is it that it is only what is mirrored in art that awakens pure pleasure, while to reality there is always something wanting? We behold the torture of Laocoon in marble with undisturbed enjoyment, whilst the scene itself would awaken nothing but horror. A fish market in Holland, depicted by a talented artist with deceptive reality, delights, whilst in the real world we should scurry through it with averted eyes and nose. The sufferings and joys of heroes, as depicted by the poets, move us with the same inner pleasure; whilst, in ourselves and others, true sorrow always causes pain, true joy always leaves something to be desired, and even perfect happiness, if it were possible to attain it, would bring with it the hard thought: 'How long will it last?' Schiller rightly says, 'Life is sober, art is gay.' So art alone, which enshrines the creations of the imagination, can offer us true happiness, and let us rejoice a little that in us, too, there lives a lively fancy which can give us pleasures that reality does not possess.

Shall I now lay on for myself such an innocent feast and fly to you over the sea? For we have been parted all too long.

What really provokes me about reality just now is that I have for quite a time been without a letter from you, and I urgently need one to strengthen my nerves. For I am now sitting very sad, with only myself to look at. But do not believe that I have bitter thoughts, for I am just dressing to go to a few Russian balls, as they call them here.

April 8th

What adds considerably to the dullness of English society is the arrogant fashion in which Englishmen (in their own country, be it noted, for abroad they are civil enough) never address a stranger, and if anyone approaches them in this manner they look on it almost as an insult. They sometimes joke about this themselves, though without ever behaving any differently.

They tell this story: a lady saw a man fall into the water and urgently begged the dandy who was with her (a famous swimmer) to go to the aid of the unhappy being. Her friend, with the phlegm which is an indispensable element of the present fashion, seized his lorgnette, gazed earnestly at the drowning man, whose head was just coming up for the last time, and blandly replied: 'Impossible, ma'am; I have never been introduced to the gentleman.'

A ball at Mrs Hope's was extremely splendid, *c'est toujours la même chose*. At the party to which I went before it I was presented to the Duke of Gloucester, which I mention only to remark that the royal princes here observe a more courteous etiquette than is practised in many courts on the Continent, for the prince, who was playing whist, stood up from the table and did not sit down again until after his short conversation with me.

This evening, I met a man of a very different nature, the Persian *chargé d'affaires*, an Oriental of very pleasing manners, whose magnificent garments and black beard were to my mind spoilt only by his pointed Persian sheepskin cap.

He speaks very good English and made some very acute observations about European society. Among other things he said that we are in many respects far more advanced than they, but that on the other hand they held to their beliefs far more firmly, and so everyone was content with his lot, whilst here he could not help noticing a permanent unrest, an unceasing discontent in the masses as well as in individuals. In fact he had to confess that he already felt himself infected by this, and would have a lot of trouble getting back to the old happy way in Persia, where a man who is miserable consoles himself by exclaiming, 'Whose dog am I then, that I should wish to be happy?'

But let me go back, for a moment, to the beginning of the day. The gardens round about are now in full bloom, the weather is fine and so my morning ride led me a good twenty miles from town.

I would gladly have ridden on and on, and at last turned back with a heavy heart, only because I had to. The meadows around me were so lush that only in the distance did they appear green; near to they shimmered blue, yellow, red and lilac. Cows waded belly-deep among these bright flowers, or rested in the shade of colossal domes of foliage, which allowed through not a single ray of sun. It was splendid, and the household of the dear Lord is here more richly adorned than anything manmade luxury can achieve. After an hour, I reached a hill on which the ruins of a noble church stood in the middle of a little garden. From behind a covering cloud the sun cast rays over the entire heaven, like a giant torch, with its head resting exactly over the world's capital, whose unceasing babble, together with its hundred thousand sins, its fogs and smoke, its treasures and misery, was spread unfathomably before me. It could not be helped, I had to go back, back from the spring and its bursting blossoms, back from the green meadows, back to the swamp, to the deadly monotony of dinners and routs.

Now take your leave of me. My next letter will only go on describing what happened to Daniel in the Lions' Den.

Your faithful friend, Lou

THIRTEENTH LETTER

London, April 15th, 1827

Dearest friend,

At last the longed for letter has arrived, even two of them. Why were they so long upon the way? *Quien sabe?* as the South Americans say. The official censor must have grown lazy and let them lie too long before skilfully sealing them up again.

[All goes on here as usual. This evening a splendid party at Lord H.'s closed the Easter festivities. Most fashionable people now make a short stay in the country, and in a fortnight's time the *season proper* begins. I am going back to Brighton for a few days, but shall wait for the Lord Mayor's dinner.

April 16th

This took place today in Guildhall; and now that I have recovered from exhaustion, I am extremely glad I went.

It lasted fully six hours, and six hundred people were present. The tables were set parallel from top to bottom of the hall, except for one which was placed across it, at the top. At this sat the Lord Mayor himself and his most distinguished guests. The view from there was imposing; the vast hall with its lofty columns, the tables extending further than the eye could reach, and the huge mirrors behind them, so that they seemed prolonged into infinity. The brilliant lighting turned night into day; and two bands of music, in a balcony at the end of the hall, played during the toasts, which were all of a national character. The Lord Mayor made twenty-six speeches, long and short. At every toast, a sort of master of ceremonies decorated with a silver chain, who stood behind the Lord Mayor's chair, called out, 'My lords and gentlemen, fill your glasses!' The ladies were frightfully dressed, with figures to match. I was seated next to an American, the niece of a former President of the United States so she told me – but I really forget which.

107

At twelve o'clock the ball began; I was, however, so tired from sitting six mortal hours at dinner, in full uniform, that I drove home as fast as I could and for once went to bed at midnight.

Brighton, April 17th

Immediately after breakfast I drove out with Count D., a very amusing Dane, and spent the evening at Lady —'s, where I met many of the people I had seen here before, including Lady —, whom you may remember in Paris as the object of the Duke of Wellington's affections.]

Apropos of him, do you read the newspapers? In the political world here a great crisis has arisen. The appointment of Canning as premier has given such offence to a number of ministers that, with the exception of three, the remaining seven have resigned! They say that the party will find it difficult to carry on without some of them – for example Lord Melville. The Duke of Wellington also stands to lose heavily by this, as a ministerial journal today expressed it, with the customary exaggeration of the local party spirit, 'He who was everything is now politically dead.' There is, however, something great in so sacrificing all personal considerations to one's principles.

April 20th

I usually spend my evenings now at Lady Keith's[1] or at Mrs Fitzherbert's,[2] and play écarté and whist with the gentlemen or loo with the young ladies. These little circles are much pleasanter than the great parties of the metropolis, for though they understand everything there, they do not understand sociability. Artists are now brought forward entirely as fashionable objects; to respect them, to get pleasure from their conversation, is simply not understood. Here

[1] Great heiress, called 'the fops' despair' in her youth because she refused so many suitors including the Duke of Clarence, the Duke of Devonshire and Lord Cochrane; admired by Lord Byron (who thought of proposing marriage to her in 1814); married Count Flahaut in 1817; confidante of Princess Charlotte and a patroness of Almack's.
[2] A Roman Catholic, Marie Fitzherbert secretly married the Prince of Wales (George IV) in 1785. He left her in 1795 to marry Caroline of Brunswick, but their relationship continued until 1803 and she remained a great society hostess.

the only real education is of a political nature, and all but the party spirit and the fashionable spirit of class simply pass society by. From this there arises a general lack of unity as well as strict social divisions which, given the unsociable nature of the English, are very unfavourable to the foreigner, unless intimate family circles have been opened to him or he can adopt a lively political interest.

The most fortunate and most worthy of attention in this respect are, without a doubt, the prosperous middle classes; their active politics they confine strictly within the limits of their province, and among those of similar views and principles. This unfashionable class alone is truly hospitable. They do not seek the foreigner out but, if one comes in their way, are both kind and interested. They passionately love their native land, but without personal interest and intrigue. Admittedly, this class of people is often ridiculous, but always worthy of respect, and their natural egotism is confined within more modest bounds than that of their superiors.

You can now say with perfect truth of England what you could once say about France: *les deux bouts du fruit sont gâtés*; the aristocracy and the people. The first must, of course, be looked up to for their splendid position – but without great moderation, and without great concessions brought about by good sense and time, this position may not last for more than perhaps another half-century. I said this once to Prince Esterhazy, and he laughed at me, *mais nous verrons!*

I am sending you a few excerpts from the newspapers to give you an idea of the freedom of the local press.

1. Every ship in England should display its gala flags, for Lord Melville was an incubus that weighed down the Service. Salaried officers may now be able to get promotion; under Lord Melville they could have hoped for none.

2. We hear from a reliable source that the Great Captain (the Duke of Wellington) is taking an extraordinary amount of trouble to get back into the Cabinet, but in vain. This spoilt darling of fortune cannot have imagined that his departure could embarrass the Government for a moment. We believe, moreover, that he is not the only ex-minister who is now bitterly regretting his foolishness and arrogance.

3. The ministerial septemvirate who wished to rise to a higher

station should be very grateful to Mr Hume's new Act, for under the old law, servants who tried to extort a higher wage from their masters were, quite rightly, sent to the treadmill.

4. We are assured that a prominent septembrist (the Duke of Wellington) has offered to return to the Service but only on condition that they make him principal Minister, Lord High Constable, and Archbishop of Canterbury.

Our ministers would indeed be surprised if our blotting-paper journals were to make as free with them.

Tomorrow I shall betake myself back to town for, just as the Romans once called Rome 'the city', the English call London 'town'.

London, April 22nd

[I arrived just in time to attend a dinner party at the new Prime Minister's, to which I had received an invitation in Brighton.

This distinguished man is as remarkable for the grace and charm with which he does the honours of his house, as for the eloquence with which he holds sway over his audience. *Bel esprit* and statesman both, he wants nothing but better health; he seemed to me to be very unwell and suffering. Mrs Canning is also a very intelligent woman. I have been assured that she runs the newspaper department – that is, she reads them, informs her husband of all the important matters they contain, and has even occasionally written articles herself.]

April 25th

After a long interval, I visited the theatre today. I struck lucky for Liston was playing in a little farce, set in Paris in the time of Louis XV. A rich English merchant who was suffering from the spleen travels to Paris in search of distraction. Scarcely is he settled in his inn than they announce to him a visit from the Commissioner of Police, who forthwith enters, correctly dressed in the costume of the time, and reveals to the astonished traveller that he is on the trail of a gang of violent robbers, who, suspecting him to be very rich, intend to break into the inn that very night and to rob and murder him. Everything now depends on the way he comports himself, the

Commissioner goes on. If he shows the least sign of fear, if he appears less cheerful or does anything unusual which betrays anxiety, he may hasten the robbers' undertaking and no one will be able to help him. Indeed, his life would be in the greatest danger, for it is not certain that the people of the house are not in the plot. He must, therefore, go to bed as usual at ten o'clock, and wait and see what happens.

Mr Jackson, more dead than alive when he hears this news, wishes to leave the house immediately, but the Commissioner earnestly dissuades him. 'Calm yourself,' he says, 'everything will be all right, if only you will put a good face on it.'

You can imagine what ridiculous scenes arise from the old merchant's attempts to conceal his terror under cheerfulness. His servant, a real Englishman – always thirsty – has in the meantime found some wine which he greedily swallows down, but it turns out to be tartar emetic, and in a few minutes he is seized with acute dizziness which thoroughly convinces his master that instead of stabbing or shooting him, the gang intend to poison him. At this moment, the hostess appears with a cup of chocolate. Beside himself, Liston seizes her by the throat and forces her to drink it herself which, although much astonished by the strange manners of the English, she is quite ready to do. Liston's dumb play and the way in which he suddenly remembers his promise is excruciatingly funny as is his attempt to make a joke of it all.

At last, ten o'clock arrives and after a great deal of comic by-play, Mr Jackson lies down in his bed with a dagger and pistol in the band of his trousers and draws the curtains closely together. Unfortunately the daughter of the house has a lover, and before the foreigner hired the room, she had arranged a rendezvous with him there. In order to avoid detection, she now comes tiptoeing in, carefully extinguishes the light, and goes to the window, where her lover is already climbing in. As the latter springs into the middle of the room and begins to speak, they hear strange sounds of woe from the bed, and *one* pistol falls from the bed with a clatter, closely followed by the *other*. The curtains open, Liston makes a weak thrust with the dagger which falls from his trembling hand, whereupon he bursts from the bed, falls at the knees of the astonished girl and brokenly pleads for his life, whilst the lover stealthily slips behind the bed. Then the door opens, and the Commissioner of

Police enters with torches to inform the trembling Jackson that the gang has been arrested. And he continues with a smile, looking at the group before him, 'I congratulate you on having employed your time so well.'

[*April 26th*

I visited a strange place today! A church called Areopagus, in which a clergyman, the Rev. Robert Taylor, preaches *against* Christianity and permits anyone to oppose him publicly. He has retained one aspect of the Anglo-Christian church – that of making you pay a shilling for your seat. Mr Taylor has some learning and is no bad speaker, but as passionate a fanatic for the destruction of Christianity as others are for its support.[1] The place was thronged with all kinds of people – in a nation which is at such a low point of religious education, it is easy to understand that a negative apostle of this sort may attract a great gathering. In Germany, where people are more advanced in the rational path of gradual reform, an undertaking of this kind would fill some with pious horror, and attract nobody – even if the police did not prevent its taking place.

The first Almack's ball took place this evening; it so little answered my expectations that I was perfectly astonished. A large bare room, with a bad floor and ropes around it, like the horses' enclosure in an Arab camp; two or three other equally bare rooms where the most wretched refreshments were served; and a company into which, despite the immense difficulty in getting tickets, a great many nobodies had forced their way, and in which poor deportment and tasteless dress prevailed; in a word, a gathering fit for an inn – the music and lighting were the only good things. And yet Almack's is the pinnacle of the English fashionable world. The oddest thing is that one ticket, for which so many English men and women strive, actually costs only ten shillings.

This exaggerated simplicity was, in fact, originally intended to counteract the show of rich parvenus with something entirely free of ostentation. They had hoped to make the balls inaccessible, but

[1] Rev. Taylor was twice imprisoned for blasphemy and narrowly escaped an action for breach of promise in 1833 by fleeing to France with an elderly woman of property whom he subsequently married.

money and inferior company (in the aristocratic sense of the word) have managed to break in. The only characteristic which has been retained is the lowly place, which is not unlike the location of a shooting ball in our large towns, and forms a most ludicrous contrast with the general splendour and luxury of England.]

May 1st

From four o'clock in the afternoon until ten o'clock at night, I sat in the House of Commons; crowded, in frightful heat, most uncomfortable, but with such excited attention, so absorbed in what I saw, that the six hours passed like an instant. There is something great about this gathering of the country's representatives. The simplicity in appearance, the dignity and experience, this gigantic power in the outside world and unassuming family relationship on the inside. Today's debate was, moreover, exceedingly interesting.

The former ministry has, as you know, for the most part resigned, including some of the most important men in England and (since the deaths of Napoleon and Blücher[1]) the greatest marshal in Europe. Canning, the champion of the Liberal party, has overthrown this ministry and in spite of all their efforts has become the chief of the new one, the selection of which, as is usual in England in such cases, will be left entirely to him. But the whole might of the exasperated ultra-aristocracy and their supporters now presses heavily upon him – in fact one of his most important friends, a Commoner like him, is among the resigning ministers and has allied himself with the enemy party. This man, Mr Peel, today opened the battle in a long, clever, somewhat repetitive speech.

It would take me far beyond the bounds of a correspondence such as ours if I were to enter in detail into the political questions now under consideration. My object is only to lay before you the tactics with which, on the one side, the most gifted members of the new Opposition opened the attack, followed by several minor associates who planted a stroke here and there; while on the other the old Opposition, the Whigs, who are now supporting the Liberal

---

[1] Blücher came to London in 1814 for the celebrations after Napoleon's abdication and was fêted as a hero. He returned the compliment by saying that London would be a fine city to sack.

ministry with all their strength, took the opposite course. They very efficiently opened with small fire and only later, as heavy artillery, called on one of their champions, Brougham.[1] In a splendid speech which flowed on like a clear stream, he sought to disarm his opponents, now pricking them with sarcasm, now taking a higher flight, and convinced his entire audience.

It was only now that Canning himself, the hero of the day, made his entrance. If the former speaker resembled a clever, elegant and 'witty' boxer, Canning presented the complete picture of a gladiator of antiquity. Everything about him was noble, admirable, simple and then suddenly his eloquence broke forth like lightning, great and breathtaking. A kind of weariness and weakness that, whether the result of the illness from which he has so recently recovered or of his crushing workload, seemed somewhat to decrease his energy, possibly won him yet more in the form of sympathy.

His speech was in every respect the most genuine, the most spontaneous, the most gripping, the culmination of this day! Never shall I forget the impression it made on me, together with that already famous one he gave a few weeks ago on the Portuguese Affair. On both occasions I felt deeply that the highest power man can wield over his fellow man, the most blinding splendour with which he can surround himself and before which even that of the happy warrior pales like the light of phosphorus in the sunlight, resides in the divine gift of oratory. Only to the great masters in this field is it given to move the heart and mind of a whole nation in that kind of magnetic somnambulism which cannot but command blind obedience; and the magic wand of the magnetiser holds equal sway over rage and gentleness, over peace and war, over tears and laughter.

The next day the House of Lords was opened in circumstances as remarkable as those of yesterday in the House of Commons, but no one there showed talent equal to Brougham and, above all, Canning.

[The late ministers were accused of having resigned as a result of a conspiracy, and of having thus been guilty of the great offence of

---

[1] Historian, scientist, man of letters and politician, Brougham was Lord Chancellor in the 1830 administration which passed the Reform Bill (1832). Samuel Rogers said of him: 'There goes Solon, Lycurgus, Demosthenes, Sir Isaac Newton, Lord Chesterfield and a great many more, all in one post-chaise.'

trying to diminish the constitutional prerogative of the King to change his ministers of his own free will. They were therefore called upon to justify themselves fully – here I saw the great Wellington in a terrible strait. He is no orator and was compelled to enter into his own defence like an accused person. There was something touching to me in seeing the hero of this century so subdued by a situation. He stammered, interrupted and confused himself; he occasionally said strong things – probably stronger than he meant, for he was not in control of his speech. The following words particularly pleased me: 'I am a soldier and no orator. I am utterly deficient in the talents requisite to play a part in this great assembly. I must be more than mad if I ever entertained the insane thought (of which I am accused) of becoming Prime Minister.'[1]

All the Lords who had resigned made their apology in turn, as well as they could. Old Lord Eldon[2] tried the effect of tears, which he has always at hand on great occasions; but I did not see them produce any corresponding emotion in the audience. He was answered by the new peer and minister Lord Goderich, formerly Mr Robinson, for himself and the Premier who, being a Commoner, cannot appear in the Lords, though he governs England and is become too illustrious, as Mr Canning, to exchange that name for a title. Lord Grey[3] far excelled the rest in dignity of manner, a thing which is lacking in most English orators. The want of decorum, remarkable in the Lower House – which is like a dirty coffeehouse, where most of the members sprawl on the benches with their hats on and talk of all sorts of trifles while their colleagues are speaking – seldom appears here.

My overall impression of this day was that it was both elevating and depressing; the former when I fancied myself an Englishman, the latter when I remembered that I was German. In contemplating this twofold senate of the people of England one begins to understand why the English nation is, as yet, the first on the face of the earth – in spite of all the defects and blemishes common to human nature which are blended in its composition.]

---

[1] By the following year the Duke was, in fact, Prime Minister.
[2] Former Lord Chancellor.
[3] Whig statesman, later Prime Minister in the 1830 administration which passed the Reform Bill.

May 3rd

My morning visits today were useful, since they procured for me three tickets for the next Almack's, and I even prevailed on one of the terrifying, dreaded patronesses to give me a ticket for an obscure little miss of my acquaintance – a great favour. Still, I had to intrigue and plead for a long time before I obtained it. The young lady and her companions were almost ready to kiss my hand and behaved as if they had each and every one won the big lottery. *Je crois qu'après cela, il y a peu de choses qu'elle me refuserait.*

Apart from Almack's, English ladies are best reached through politics. Lately one has heard nothing, at table, at the opera, even at the ball, but Canning and Wellington from every lovely mouth; indeed Lord Ellenborough complained that his wife plagued him with politics even at night. She had terrified him by crying out suddenly, in her sleep: 'Will the Prime Minister stand or fall?'

If I improve myself here in nothing else, at least I shall succeed in politics and the driving of cabriolets. This last one learns to perfection: you wind, at a spanking pace, between carriages and coaches where formerly you were held up for minutes. Above all, after a long residence in a capital like this you really see everything on a less petty scale: you see things more broadly and more *en bloc*.

May 10th

At a dinner and soiree this evening at Prince Polignac's there were several interesting persons present: among them the Governor of Odessa, one of the most agreeable Russians I have met, and Sir Thomas Lawrence,[1] the celebrated painter. I was told that he regularly loses at billiards (of which he mistakenly fancies himself a master) the enormous sums he gains by his art. He is a man of interesting appearance, with something 'mediæval' in his features which reminds one strongly of the pictures of the Venetian school.

Prince Polignac's niece told me that her uncle's hair, which is perfectly white (while the rest of his appearance is youthful and agreeable), had turned grey when he was 25 years of age, from the anxiety and horror of a revolutionary dungeon. He may well find the

---

[1] The most famous portrait painter of the day.

present change acceptable – but alas! the Restoration cannot restore the colour of his hair.[1] This story interested me for I must tell you, my dear Lucie, that my hair has also patriotically begun to assume our national colours, white and black.

A foreigner who wishes to experience the whole range of social life can hardly last out a London season. More than forty invitations are now lying on my table – five or six a day. All these party-givers must be called upon in the morning, and to be courteous one must go in person. *C'est la mer à boire* – and yet on my way to parties I often pass ten or more houses I don't know, where the same numbers of carriages are standing before the door.

A ball at which I was present recently was particularly brilliant, and was attended by some of the royal princes. When this is the case, the fashion now is to satisfy the vanity of the host by mentioning on the card: 'To meet his Royal Highness', etc. – a laughable phrase. The whole garden was covered over, and divided into large rooms which were hung with draperies of rose-coloured muslin, enormous ornamental mirrors and numerous chandeliers, and perfumed with every kind of flower. The Duchess of Clarence[2] honoured the party with her presence, and all pressed forward to see her – for she is one of the few princesses whose personality inspires more respect than her rank, and whose infinite goodness of heart has gained her a popularity in England of which we Germans should be proud; the more so as she will probably be Queen.

May 15th

Riding this morning with several ladies, we raised the question of which road one should take to enjoy the lovely spring at its best. Then we saw a balloon in the highest heaven, and the question was answered. For more than ten miles, the indefatigable ladies followed their airy guide as if they were at a steeple chase; at last it entirely disappeared from our sight.

Midday was devoted to a great diplomatic luncheon at which

[1] Extreme reactionary and royalist, Polignac conspired against Napoleon and was imprisoned for two years. Ambassador to the Court of St James 1823–9.

[2] Daughter of the Duke of Saxe-Coburg-Meiningen and later (1830–7), Queen Adelaide, wife of William IV.

several of the new ministers were present; the evening to a ball in a German house, solid and tasteful, its appointments equal to those of the best English houses and, because of the attractive originality of the host, surpassing most of them. I am speaking of Prince Esterhazy.

But my journal is soon going to be as boring as the travelogue of Bernouilly, which also treats of invitations, luncheons and evening entertainments. You must realize how things go. Pretend this diary is a garment on which very different patches, rich and poor, are sewn. The enduring, long-lasting material represents my unchanging love for you and the wish to live my future life with you. But the other patches, which are only copies of the experiences themselves, take on their colours – now glowing, now pale – and it would not be surprising if they became quite faded in this gloomy town, which never provides such lovely pictures as does glorious Nature.

May 20th

The truth is that the whole question of marriage is personally intolerable and as soon as I consider anyone seriously she immediately seems almost frightful to me. That is why I would so much like to preserve my freedom of choice until the last moment. Meanwhile, it is no laughing matter and so I am of a mind to proceed in earnest without delay in one direction or another, if you are convinced that it cannot go on any longer, something you alone can decide. I have four choices. First Miss G[ibbins], a doctor's daughter, pretty and accomplished, with £50,000; second, a merchant's daughter, [Miss Windham] very pretty, kind and stupid, with £40,000; third, a well-bred, ugly girl with £100,000; fourth, a gentle, pretty, clever and well-bred one, with only £25,000. Number one is the worst, on account of her father and mother who will not be parted from her.[1] The others would accompany me alone. By the

[1] At first Puckler could not understand why Miss Gibbins antagonized him so much; she was, after all, pretty, accomplished, rich *and* willing – but then he met her parents and the mystery was solved. The mother was vulgar, the father a boring pedant and, worst of all, they firmly intended to set up home with their daughter and her husband. Nevertheless, in a dark hour late in 1828, he even got as far as drafting a proposal to her – but he never sent it.

way, if no influential enemy intervenes, I do not think that I need fear a refusal from any of them.

May 27th

I had the honour to dine with the Duke of Clarence where the Princess Augusta, the Duchess of Kent and her daughter,[1] and the Duchess of Gloucester were also present. The Duke was a very kindly host, who most graciously remembered the different times and places in which we had previously met. He is a typical Englishman, in the best sense of the word, and also has the English love of domesticity.

Among the other guests I must mention Admiral Sir George Cockburn, who took Napoleon to St Helena. After dinner he told me a lot about the Emperor's uncommon talent for winning anything to which he put his mind. He also admired the frankness with which Napoleon spoke of himself, as if of some other historical person; among other things he candidly declared that the Russians had so completed outwitted him in Moscow that, up to the very last day, he had hoped for peace. '*C'était sans doute une grande faute,*' he added indifferently.

In the evening Pasta[2] sang splendidly at the Countess St Antonio's and two or three balls concluded the day.

May 31st

I dined with Lord Darnley, where I met the Archbishop of York, a majestic old man, who began life as a private tutor, and has reached this elevated station by the patronage of his pupils. Nothing is uglier, and at the same time more comical, than the demi-toilette of an English archbishop. A short schoolmaster's wig, badly powdered, a black French coat and a little black silk lady's apron worn in front over their trousers, of the kind that our miners wear behind. Our host laughed loudly when I asked him, puzzled, '*si ce tablier faisait allusion au voeu de chasteté?*' I did not at that moment

---

[1] Princess Feodora of Leiningen, Queen Victoria's half-sister and her elder by 12 years; they were tenderly attached to each other.
[2] Italian opera singer.

remember that English archbishops, otherwise so very Catholic, have reserved to themselves the right to marry. Yet it is true that their wives are treated just like mistreses, since they may not bear the names of their husbands.

We were very well entertained with venison from the park and splendid fruit from Cobham; and after dinner we were taken to a concert, which was very different from what is customary here. It was organised by several cultivated noblemen, admirers of the music of Handel, Mozart and the old Italian masters, whose compositions were the only ones performed.

It is a long time since I have experienced such pleasure. What are all these modern trills and tremolos compared with the nobility of this old church music? I felt as if I were actually transported back to the years of my childhood, a sensation that strengthens the soul for many days and gives her a more soaring flight. The singing was throughout excellent, often supernaturally beautiful in its simplicity, for it is incredible what power God has given to the human voice when it is rightly used and rings simply and surely from a lovely mouth. During Handel's Chorus I could really feel the horror of the night which stretched over Egypt, and hear the tumult of Pharaoh's army and the roaring of the sea which engulfed them beneath its waves.

I could not bring myself, after such holy sounds, to listen to the fiddles of the ball, so I took myself home at twelve o'clock, abandoning Almack's and another ball of the fashionable world. I want to take the reverberation of that music of the spheres into my dreams and to set out with you upon its wings on a shining night journey.

Your Lou

FOURTEENTH LETTER

London, June 5th, 1827

As an example of everything a dandy requires, I am passing on to you the statement of my fashionable washerwoman, who is employed by some of the most outstanding *élégants*, and who alone knows how to give cravats the right stiffness and to arrange them in the correct folds. As a rule, this kind of *élégant* requires every week: twenty-four shirts, nine summer trousers, thirty neck-bands, unless he wears black ones, a dozen waistcoats and stockings *à discretion*. From here I can see the horror of your housewifely soul. But since a dandy cannot conveniently get away with fewer than three or four toilettes a day, all this is quite natural.

One, he appears at breakfast in his breakfast toilette, a Chinese dressing gown and Indian slippers. Two, the morning toilette for riding, a frock coat, boots and spurs. Three, toilette for dinner, a tail coat and shoes. Four, toilette for the ball and pumps, a word that means shoes as light as paper, which are freshly varnished every day.

June 13th

At six o'clock the park was so full that it resembled a rout on horseback, but far more charming, for instead of clammy heat there was fresh coolness, and instead of tiring one's own legs, one made the horse do the work.

Tomorrow I am going with Captain Ross[1] to Ascot to give a little variety to my monotonous life. They think that these races will be particularly brilliant because the King will be attending them and some of his horses will be running.

[1] Soldier, sportsman and renowned marksman; he had joined the light dragoons in 1819.

After a rapid journey of 25 English miles, we reached the wide, barren heath of Ascot, where the races are held. The course looks like an amusement park. Countless rows of tents for horses and men, lines of carriages along the course for the most part adorned with lovely ladies, stands as high as houses, and the King's box in the centre – all of this enlivened by 20,000 to 50,000 people, many of whom have been here for six days. These are the main features of the picture. One part is occupied by a sort of fair where, among other stalls and tents and in accordance with an old privilege, are to be found many sorts of gambling, elsewhere strictly forbidden.

The ladies in the carriages are every day provided with champagne and splendid breakfasts, which they share with great hospitality. I found many old friends and made some new acquaintances, among others a most attractive woman, Lady Garvagh, who invited me and Ross to dinner at her cottage. As the races finished for the day at six o'clock, we drove to Titness Park through wonderfully beautiful country so thickly planted with trees that, in spite of the cultivated meadows, it had the appearance of a wood. We arrived before the family and found the house wide open, without either servants or a single other human being in it. It was like the enchanted dwelling of a fairy, and a more charming abode could not be imagined. If only you could have seen it! Upon a hill, half-hidden by grand old trees, stood a house, added on to by its many forebears at different periods and then concealed in shrubberies which at no point allow the eye to take in the whole at one time. A terrace of rose bushes, streaming with flowers, led directly into the hall, and passing through several other rooms and along a corridor we reached the dining room, where a table was already richly furnished – though still no one was to be seen. The garden lay before us, a true paradise lit by the rich rays of the sunset. Along the whole side of the house alternated verandahs, flanked by plants of every kind, which served as a backdrop to the most brilliant flower garden covering the whole of the hillside. At its edge was a deep narrow valley and, beyond, the terrain sloped up again to a meadow which rose to the crest of a range of hills studded with ancient beeches. In the distance we could see over the treetops the round tower of Windsor Castle, with the gigantic royal standard fluttering above it and reaching into the blue sky. It was the only reminder in this solitude that Nature and some beneficent fairy did not reign alone here, but that mankind with its joys, its needs and its splendours was also near at hand. It stood like a beacon of ambition, looking down upon the peaceful cottage, beckoning to a higher and more responsible enjoyment – which he who attains will only pay for with heartache – while peace and contentment remain behind in the valley of holy silence.

I was interrupted in my poetic ecstasy by my lovely hostess, who took great delight in my description of her enchanted castle, and now hurried off to see that rooms were prepared for us so that we could change our clothes, which the heat and the dust had rendered very necessary. We heartily enjoyed an excellent dinner, with iced champagne and splendid fruit, and remained at table until midnight. A few more hours were occupied with coffee and tea and music but, to tell the truth, we would willingly have left the last named, I mean the music, to the family. My endurance was taxed to the utmost by the gigantic strain of holding back my laughter, when the old mother of the lady of the house sat herself down at the piano and gave of her best in an aria of Rousseau's composition, whose refrain '*Je t'aimerai toujours*' I shall remember until my life's end. She treated the 'ai' of *aimerai* to a trill which at first resembled a lament, then imitated the cooing of a turtle dove, and finally became the cry of a courting capercaillie. The song seemed as if it would never end and young Ross, who is as subject to fits of laughter as I am, was already wound up like a fiddle bow with the tortured squeezings of his body, and making the most extraordinary faces behind his great moustache; as for me, I was calling so hard on my moral strength for help that I found myself thinking without interruption of you, dear Lucie, and the pattern of composure you present on such occasions.

These people had been so extraordinarily kind and friendly that I would literally rather have wept blood than laughed at them; but what can one do when overcome by an irresistible inclination? At the approach of the danger spot I actually prayed to God that He would guide the good old lady just this time to sing '*Je t'aimerai toujours*' without ornamentation. But in vain; scarcely was the threatening 'ai' struck than there followed implacably that pitiless trill. By the seventh verse I could hold out no longer – for the first time Rousseau's work seemed to me immortal. I parried the old lady's stroke, as the students say; before she could strike that threatening note again I seized her hand, shook it heartily, thanked her for her kindness, assured her that I was conscious of our indiscretion in having troubled her for so long, pressed the hand of her lovely daughter in the same way (*car c'est l'usage ici*), as well as those of the other members of the family, and found myself in a '*clin d'oeil*' with Ross in the carriage which had already been waiting fully harnessed for an hour in the driveway. You can imagine with what relief we loosened our laughter muscles. And all the way to Windsor we rejoiced over the memory of those inimitable trills.

Richmond, June 15th

This morning we looked at Windsor Castle, which is now being completed, and is already the largest and most splendid of the royal residences occupied by any European prince. Time was too short to inspect the interior, which I had to postpone for another occasion. I visited only the Duchess of C., who lives in the largest tower and enjoys a heavenly view from her high balcony. Among her staff was a beautiful Greek boy in his national dress, scarlet, blue and gold, his legs and feet bare. At the massacre of Scio he was hidden in a baker's oven and thus saved. He is now become a complete Englishman, but has retained in his air something uncommonly noble and foreign. At one o'clock we betook ourselves again to the race course, and I received my breakfast this time from another beauty. When the race meeting was over we drove to Richmond, where Ross's regiment is garrisoned, and passed a very happy and noisy evening there, with the officers' corps. The general English prosperity allows a much more luxurious life than military men enjoy with us. These gentlemen deny themselves nothing and their mess is, in every way, much better supplied than many a prince's table in Germany.

In the morning the regiment of Hussars, as well as a regiment of Ulans, will muster for a general inspection, which I shall wait to see before returning again to London.

The regiment discharged its business very well, with less affectation and also less precision than our wonderful, three-year trained riders, but with more true military confidence and long-accustomed self-reliance; also all their movements were quicker because of the splendid horses, with which those of the Continent are simply not to be compared. Moreover, the English cavalry has quite uncommonly improved since the last war because of the care bestowed upon it by the Duke of Wellington. The men had their horses as well under control as the best of ours. In my opinion, the unceremoniousness of the occasion was a remarkable sight: there were at least fifty to sixty officers in civil clothes, among them several generals – some in top boots and morning coat, others in frock coat and brightly coloured neckcloths – taking part in the revue. Apart from the regiment which was being inspected, the inspecting general was the only one, with his two adjutants, to appear in uniform. Indeed, even a few supernumerary officers of that regiment, not presently on active service, rode about with him in civil clothes and shoes – a sight that would have so astonished a Russian general as to cost him his reason. In a word, you see here more of the real and, with us, more of the form. Here, in fact, clothes do not make the man, and this simplicity is sometimes very impressive.

Ross told me that this regiment was originally formed from the Guild of London Tailors at the time of the threatened French invasion, and in the beginning consisted only of tailors. They have now transformed themselves into very efficient martial hussars, and fought with great distinction at Belle-Alliance.

Today I found all my beauties as disagreeable as ever! *C'est une fière médicine que je suis obligé d'avaler tôt ou tard.* In theory it is all going easily, but in reality it awakens a dreadful nausea.

Since the season is now (thank God) nearing its end, I am thinking of embarking shortly on a journey to the North of England and

Scotland, for which I have in fact several invitations; however I would rather keep myself free so as to journey through the country as it pleases me, if time and circumstance permit.

[Children's balls are now the order of the day, and I went to one of the prettiest this evening at Lady Jersey's. These highborn northern children had every possible advantage of dress, and many were not without grace, but it really afflicted me to observe how early they had ceased to be children; the poor things were, for the most part, as unnatural, as unjoyous and as much occupied with themselves as we larger figures around them. Italian peasant children would have been a hundred times more graceful and engaging. It was only at supper that the animal instinct was openly and reservedly displayed, breaking through all forms and all disguises and reinstating Nature in her rightful place. The most pure, lovely natural feeling was, however, the tenderness of the mothers, which betrayed itself without affectation in their eyes, made many ugly women tolerable and gave to the beautiful a higher beauty.

A second ball at Lady R's presented the hundredth repetition of the usual stupid throng; poor Prince Borghese,[1] for whose corpulence these crowds are little adapted, fainted and, leaning on the bannister, gasped for air like a dying carp. Pleasure and happiness are certainly pursued in very odd ways in this world.]

July 10th

It is now oppressively hot, something that I would hardly have thought possible in this Land of Fogs! The lawns in Hyde Park are the colour of sand, the trees faded and dried out, and the squares in the city look not much better.

With the heat, London too is becoming more empty every day, and the season is as good as over. Today I found myself for the first time without any invitations, and immediately used this freedom for various excursions. Among other things, I inspected the prisons of King's Bench and Newgate.

The first, which is principally devoted to debtors, presents an entirely isolated world in miniature, not unlike a small town, except

---

[1] Married to Napoleon's sister, Pauline.

that it is surrounded by thirty-foot high walls; neither cook-shops nor lending libraries, coffee-houses, tradesmen's stalls of all kinds – nor even a market place are wanting. On the last there was a very noisy ball-game taking place when I arrived. Anyone who has money lives within these confines as well and pleasantly as possible until he is set free. There is no lack even of good company, of ladies and gentlemen, in the little community of a thousand people; only the man who has nothing fares badly here. For such men, however, every spot on earth is a prison! Lord Cochrane spent some time in King's Bench for allowing a false rumour to be circulated,[1] the rich and well-respected Sir Francis Burdett also sat here for a considerable time because of a lampoon he had written.[2] The prisoner who conducted me around had already been an inhabitant of this place for twelve years and declared, with the best of humour, that he had no hope of ever getting out. An old and very distinguished Frenchwoman said much the same; she did not wish to inform her relatives of her situation, was living very contentedly, and did not know what would happen to her in France.

Things look worse at Newgate, the prison for criminals. But here too there is much mildness in their treatment, and also an exemplary cleanliness. They give every prisoner half a can of thick barley soup and a pound of good bread every day at midday, and on alternate days half a pound of meat or meat soup. They are also allowed to buy yet more food and half a bottle of wine per day. There are normally seven or eight prisoners to a cell. For those who wish to work there is a workshop, but many smoke and play from morn to evening in the courtyards which belong to each group of cells. At nine o'clock in the morning all must go to prayers. Everyone gets a mattress and two covers for sleeping, also coals for cooking and, in the winter, for heating. Those condemned to death are in smaller, less comfortable cells, with two or three to each. By day, these too have their own courtyard for recreation, and for eating they have a separate room. I saw six boys all under sentence of death, the eldest

[1] Lord Cochrane was arrested in 1814 for spreading a rumour of Napoleon's overthrow from which he was said to have made £10,000. He was sentenced to a fine of £1,000 and a year's imprisonment, but later granted a 'free pardon'.

[2] Leading radical, MP for Westminster (1807–37). Arrested in 1820, he was imprisoned and fined £1,000 for his letter on the 'Peterloo Massacres'.

of whom was hardly fourteen, smoking and playing very cheerfully. The sentence was not yet confirmed so they were still mixing with the other prisoners. It was believed that they would be reprieved and only sent for life to Botany Bay.

Four older men in the same situation, but with the difference that, because their crime was more serious, they could hope for no reprieve and must expect their lives to end in a few weeks, seemed to accept their fate even more humorously than the former. Three of them were playing whist with the dummy amid much jest and laughter while the fourth sat upon the windowsill industriously studying a grammar in order to learn French! *C'était bien un philosophe sans le savoir.*

July 12th

Last night I went for the first time to Vauxhall, a public garden in the style of Tivoli in Paris, but far more splendid and grandiose. The illuminations, thousands of lamps in brilliant colours, are absolutely splendid. Especially beautiful were colossal bunches of flowers hanging from the trees, made of red, blue, violet and yellow lamps, and the leaves and stems of green. There were chandeliers of a gay Turkish type in all shades, and a temple for the musicians with the royal coat of arms and crest above it. Several triumphal arches were made not of wood, as is usually the case, but of cast iron, of transparent patterns, just as strong and far more elegant.

Beyond stretched the gardens with all their variety and different exhibitions. At eight o'clock there is the opera. This is followed by other sideshows which continue until ten o'clock, when they perform the Battle of Waterloo. An open part of the garden surrounded by ancient chestnut trees with undergrowth at their feet serves as a stage. Between four of these trees, whose foliage is so thick that it will hardly admit the light of heaven, a 'tribune' had been erected with benches for twelve hundred or so people which was at least 40 feet high. In a frightful press, which involved some painful pushing and shoving, we got to our seats. It was a marvellous warm night. The moon shone brightly and showed between two gigantic trees a great red curtain, painted with the combined arms of Great Britain.

After a moment's silence, a cannon shot thundered through the wood and at the same time the fine military music of the 2nd Regiment of Guards rang out in the distance. The curtain swung open, and we glimpsed the breastworks of Houguemont (not a stage decoration but structures of wood hung with painted linen, true imitations of buildings). Out of the wood advanced the French Guards with the bearded *Sapeurs* at their head. They formed themselves into ranks and Napoleon, on his white horse and in his grey overcoat, accompanied by several marshals, rode past them *en revue*. From a thousand throats echoed '*Vive l'Empéreur!*' The emperor touched his hat and went off at a gallop, while the troops bivouacked in closely packed groups, and marched off. Soon afterwards Wellington appeared with his general staff, all very good copies of the originals. He harangued his troops and slowly rode off. The great original himself was in the audience and laughed loudly at his representation.

Now the fight begins with skirmishes; then whole columns rush at each other and attack with the bayonet, while the French cuirassiers charge the Scottish squares. Since there were about a thousand men and two hundred horses in the action, and no lack of gunpowder, at moments it was just like a real engagement. The thick smoke of a real fire enveloped the combatants who, for a time, could be seen only by the lightning flash of the artillery, whilst the foreground was occupied by the dead and dying. As the smoke cleared away Houguemont was seen in flames, surrounded by the English as victors and the French as prisoners, and in the distance was Napoleon on horseback, with his carriage and four horses behind him, fleeing across the stage. Wellington the victor was greeted under the roar of the cannon with shouts of 'Hurrah, hurrah, hurrah!'

The most ludicrous feature of the performance was Napoleon, who had to be hunted across the stage several times, and made to serve for the delight of the plebs. Such is the lot of the greatest man on earth! The world conqueror before whom the earth once trembled – for whom the blood of many millions was willingly shed, and on whose nod kings waited – is now a child's plaything, a legend of his time, vanished like a dream.

Although after midnight, there was still time enough to betake myself from that stage, so strangely lit with its mixture of garish illumination and moonlight, to a brilliant ball at Lady Lansdowne's, where I found a great many diamonds, lovely women, costly refreshments, greedy suppers and colossal boredom. It was therefore only five o'clock in the morning when I got to bed.

July 13th

The Haymarket Theatre now engages very good actors, and is the rendezvous of all those gay ladies who find themselves out of work at the end of the season. Last evening I was sitting in my box with all my attention on the play, when suddenly the most charming foot, enveloped in a pretty shoe and pearl coloured stockings, was stuck up on the seat beside me. I turned round and a pair of magnificent, laughing brown eyes looked at me out of a shepherdess' face, half-hidden by a great Italian straw hat, while an entirely simple, spotless white dress, caught together beneath the breast with a red ribbon, displayed the charms of this little person who could not have numbered more than sixteen summers.

All the dandies and many young people of the great world – which dandies now are not – are in the habit of getting their mistresses here: they lease a house for them, set them up in it and spend their idle hours there. Just like the *petites maisons* in France. They enter upon quite a regular domestic footing with them, and are just as systematic in this relationship as in any other. It is true that this type of woman is seldom faithful forever, but they are often far better educated in manners and in mind than their like in other lands . . .

The little one behind me seemed to have the idea of starting a regular relation, which she showed in a kind of well-mannered coquetry towards me and an extremely guarded demeanour towards others who wished to come near her. Soon a kind of understanding developed between us without a word having been spoken. Moreover she was not lacking in the status symbol of a mother beside her, as chaperone.

It is not too great a leap if I conduct you now to Bedlam, actually to Betlem, which I visited this morning. Nowhere are the madmen lodged better: by which I mean the madmen who are locked up. There is a pleasure ground before the door of the mansion, and nothing could be cleaner or more efficiently arranged than its interior. As I went into the first women's gallery, conducted by a very pretty young wardress, one of the mad girls gazed at me attentively, and then suddenly ran up to me, saying: 'You are a foreigner – I know you – why aren't you wearing your uniform when you come to visit me?' She went on: 'It suits you much better. Oh, how handsome Charles looked in his!'

'The poor soul,' said the wardress, who was aware that I was a foreigner. 'She was seduced by a foreign prince and now thinks that every foreigner she sees is like him. Sometimes she weeps all day long, and will not let anyone come near her. After that she is again quite sensible for weeks at a time. Once she was very beautiful, but sorrow has taken every charm from her.'

I was particularly struck by a rich, very well-educated young man, who had one fixed idea: that he was a Stuart, and therefore had a legitimate right to the throne. I talked with him for half an hour without being able to get him on to this subject. He did not show in his bearing or exterior the slightest trace of insanity. At last I succeeded in making him a little more excited, when I chanced to speak of Sir Walter Scott's novels, and then when I said privately to him: 'I know that you yourself are a Stuart,' he seemed to be terrified; he laid a finger to his mouth and said: 'Yes I am a Stuart, but I can only hope for justice from Heaven.' 'I am going to Wales,' I rejoined (he is from Wales and his father is a rich landowner). 'Would you like to give me your father's address, so that I may convey your greetings to him?' 'With great pleasure,' he replied. 'Give me your pocketbook, I will write the address in it.' I gave it to him and he wrote his real name in it, and as he smilingly handed it back to me he said in my ear: 'That is the name my father goes under there. Goodbye' – and with a pleasant wave of his hand he left me.

July 14th

I have already visited the architect, Mr Nash, several times, and have him to thank for much information about my art [landscape gardening]. They say that he has accumulated a fortune of £500,000. He owns a splendid country house, and no artist is more gracefully lodged in town.

As I was driving from his house to dinner, I saw in the Thames a boat full of stark naked men, like savages, from which a man dived now and then – an indecency in the middle of London which astonished me all the more since I had read only yesterday in the newspaper that an officer, under whose windows a man was bathing naked with his son, and refused to go away when called on to do so, had, without more ado, shot him right through the body. In court he declared that the bathers were shamelessly exposing themselves before the eyes of his wife, something which he could not put up with, and if it were to happen again he would behave in the same way. Characteristically he was discharged by the jury.

At home I found your letter, with all kinds of loving reproaches, among them that of too much neglecting personal news for outside things. Even if this were sometimes the case, do not think because of it that my heart is ever less full of you. Flowers, too, smell more strongly at some times than at others; indeed, sometimes there is not a flower on the rosebush at all even though, in season, they burst forth and bloom again – but the nature of the plant remains the same.

People are disagreeable to you, you say. Ah God, how disagreeable they are to me! If you have lived so long in the greatest intimacy of the exchange of every feeling, the honesty of every thought with another, intercourse with the banal, unconcerned world becomes no more than void and savourless.

This hypothesis that souls, congenial here, fuse in another world into one being is very charming, but I would not like to be united to you in this fashion, because a being must love himself absolutely, just as two choose freely to love each other. Only that is worthwhile! So we do indeed wish to meet each other again but also to become one only through mutual love and faithfulness, as we are now and, for the present, may remain in this world as long as we can.

Good Schnucke, confess: if you yourself were the editor of the morning paper, you could not have a more diligent reporter than I – whether it goes well or ill with me, whether I am glad or sad, I always do my duty. At this moment it is not going too well with me. I am unwell and have lost a lot of money at whist. By the way, it is remarkable here in England how soon you come to look on a pound as being worth the same as a taler.[1] Although I well know the

---

[1] There were about twelve talers to a pound.

difference, and often experience it in an unpleasant fashion, yet still do I mindlessly look on the pound here exactly as I do the taler at home, for which I often laugh at myself. I wish that Fate would, for once, change our talers into pounds. But if we think about the things that have been bestowed on us, if we wish to beautify the Nature created by God, as I do, we have done well if we make others happier and more content, I through giving work to others and you, more directly, by benevolent acts to the needy. Shrewdness was never our strong point, and if you have more of it than I, that is simply because you are a woman and must always hold yourself on the defensive. Shrewdness is much more an art of defence than one of aggression.

July 19th

A friendly sunbeam lured me into the open which, in fact, I soon exchanged for the subterranean. That is, I inspected the famous tunnel, the wonderful 1,200-foot long connecting way under the Thames. You must have read in the papers that, a few weeks ago, the water of the river broke in and entirely flooded the tower at its entrance, which is 150 feet high and 50 feet broad, as well as the completed double path, 540 feet in length. Whether good news or bad, a caricature is always ready a few days after the event. So, in the one representing the tunnel catastrophe, a fat man, croaching like a toad, is trying to save himself and shouting 'Fire!' from a wide open mouth. With the aid of diving-bells they filled in the hole in the bed of the river with bags full of clay. In order to continue the tunnel, they have strengthened the riverbed with a 15-foot mixture so that, they say, no such danger need ever be feared again. A steam machine of the strongest kind has been set up at the top of the tower, and has almost entirely pumped out the invading water so that you can now see the whole project. It is a gigantic work which could only be carried out here, where people do not know what to do with their money.

July 22nd

During the last weeks I have had to suffer much. First, because of a succession of pitiable social events, gossip etc., I have almost parted company with fashionable high society. To tell you about them would be unbearingly boring, and they can only be recounted verbally. Secondly, I have lost the whole of my gambling winnings. Thirdly, I have fallen sick and, fourthly, I have received a sort of refusal. *Il y a de quoi décourager quatre personnes*, and I, poor, sensitive Lou, must bear this all alone.

August 8th

Canning is dead! A man in the fullness of his intellectual powers who, only a few weeks ago, had arrived at last at the goal of his active life – as ruler of England – and who was, for that reason, undoubtedly the most influential man in Europe; endowed with a fiery spirit and with a soul which was capable of embracing the wellbeing of mankind. One blow has destroyed this proud tower, so many years in the building, and the brave man must die like a criminal, suddenly, with the most fearful sufferings – a sacrifice to pitiless Nature, which with iron foot strides on and on, crushing what lies in her way, whether it is the young sapling, the swelling blossom, the kingly tree or the dying plant. What will the consequences of this death be? It will be years before they are known; and perhaps it will hasten on a solution which seems to threaten us on many sides, and to which only an enlightened and magnanimous statesman like Canning would be capable of giving unity and a favourable direction. Perhaps the party, which is now rejoicing so barbarously and unfeelingly over his premature death, will face its first serious danger through his death, for Lord Chesterfield said long ago, with a prophetic eye: '*Je prévois que dans cent ans d'ici les métiers de gentilhomme et de moine ne seront plus de la moitié aussi lucratifs qu'ils sont aujourd'hui*'.

But why should I worry about politics? If I could only maintain an appropriate equilibrium in myself, I would be content. That of Europe will establish itself. Cleverness and stupidity arrive at the same end – Necessity.

Canning's death is naturally the talk of the town, and the details of his sufferings are shocking. The pious, to whom because of his free-thinking opinions he was most repugnant, are trying to spread it abroad that, during his last sufferings, he was out of his mind; one of his friends, on the other hand, who spent a long time beside his deathbed, could not say enough of the stoical courage and gentleness with which he bore his cruel fate until the last moment of consciousness, filled only with his plans for the wellbeing of England and of mankind, and anxiously longing to bring them to fruition.

August 15th

[The anxiety with which the rich English shut up their property from the prying eyes of the stranger is sometimes truly amusing, but may occasionally be painful. I was riding one day in the neighbourhood of London, and attracted by the sight of a fine house and grounds, asked the porter at the lodge whether he would allow me to look at the garden. He was very unsure, but finally opened the gate, taking charge of my horse in the meantime. I must have walked for about a quarter of an hour, and was just looking at the neatly kept pleasure-ground, when a rather fat person appeared in his shirt at a window of the house; he seemed to have been running about in great distress and at last threw open the window with great vehemence and cried out to me in half-suppressed rage, '*Qui êtes-vous, monsieur? Que cherchez-vous ici?*' I thought it too ridiculous to shout back the answer from such a distance and soon found it unnecessary, for several servants, alarmed by the ringing of a bell, ran towards me from all directions. I let the proprietor know by one of them that I was a foreigner who had been attracted by a fondness for gardening; that I had not climbed over the wall as he seemed to believe but had entered through the usual entrance, where my horse was waiting; that I was heartily sorry for having caused him such a shock in his illness, and only wished that it might have no serious consequences; and at the same time assured him of my best respects and that I would immediately leave the garden.

I soon reached my horse and rode off laughing – for this was the amusing side of the affair. About a fortnight later I happened to pass near the same house, and approached the lodge again and rang the bell. Another man appeared and I mischievously inquired after the health of his master, and whether I would be allowed to see the garden. 'God forbid!' was the answer. 'On no account!' I then heard from the servant, to my sincere grief, that the poor fellow, his predecessor, had been dismissed with his wife and children though he had been in the service of the family for many years, merely for having let a stranger enter without permission. And this severe gentleman is one of the patent-liberals of England. What would an illiberal one have done?]

The walks and rides in the vicinity are once more very inviting, since the autumn has set in early. The burnt grass decks itself again in bright green, and the trees keep their leaves longer and fresher than with us, although they begin to colour earlier. The winter comes very late, often not at all, to swathe itself in its white winding-sheet. At the same time there is no ceasing in the mowing of the lawns and the cleaning of the squares and gardens. Indeed, in the country, where autumn and winter are *the* season, this is just the time when such things are most carefully tended.

London, however, is deserted by the fashionables, and with such affectation that many who are obliged to remain seek to hide themselves in lodgings. The streets in the west end are as empty as in a ghost town. Only the girls of the town are to be seen, pursuing every passer-by in the most indecorous manner and with the most explicit gestures.

The day ended very pleasantly for me with the arrival of my friend L., for whom I now leave you and this letter, so frightfully long and, alas, so poor in matter. I close with the assurance, so old but for you always with the charm of novelty, that, far or near, you are always in my heart and so remain.

Your faithful Lou

FIFTEENTH LETTER

———————————·~·~·~·~———————————

Dear faithful one,

Curiosity led me again today to the works on the tunnel. I went down to the bed of the river in the diving-bell and, for half an hour, watched the stopping of the breach with sacks of clay. Apart from a pretty severe pain in the ears, I found that the deeper we went, the cosier we were in the metal box. On top it has thick glass windows, furnished with two vents to let fresh air in and stale air out. There is no floor, only a narrow board on which to put your feet, and two fixed benches at the sides. Several miners' lanterns give the necessary light. The workers had magnificent wading boots which keep out the water for twenty-four hours, and it gave me great pleasure to write the name of the manufacturer in my pocketbook on the bed of the river, down among the fishes, '*auf des Stromes tiefunterstem Grunde*'.

[*August 21st*

As I was driving home today I was given in change a quantity of small coins by the turnpikes, and amused myself by letting a penny fall quietly out of the carriage every time I saw a poor, ragged person. Not one of them noticed it – and Fortune behaves in the same way with us! She drives through the world continually in her chariot, and throws out her gifts blindfold. How seldom do any of us see them, and stoop to pick them up. We are generally looking in another direction at the lucky moment.

   On my return home I found a real gift of fate, and a very precious one – a long letter from you.

Salthill, August 25th

I have at last left town with L., who will accompany me for some days, after which I shall continue my travels alone. The first resting place is a delightful inn, like a gentleman's villa, in the neighbourhood of Windsor. The incessant rain has painted everything emerald green, and the freshness of country has the most benign influence on my mind and spirits. I can talk of you too, my dear Lucie, to L., whose company is very agreeable to me.]

August 26th

Early this morning we drove to Stoke Park, the seat of the grandson of the famous Quaker, William Penn; in the mansion they still keep a part of the tree under which he signed the treaty with the Indians [on the site of Philadelphia] from which Pennsylvania derives its name. We saw, in a fine park, a great variety of fallow deer – black, white, striped, spotted, black with white blazes and brown with white feet.

After we had looked at another park, we drove to Windsor to look at the new castle *en détail*. Unfortunately the King and his suite arrived at almost the same moment, in five phaetons drawn by ponies, so we had to wait for over an hour before he drove out again and we were permitted to enter.

In the meantime we visited Eton College, an ancient educational institution founded by Henry VI. Its exterior is an extensive and beautiful Gothic building with a church attached to it, its interior of a simplicity hardly to be surpassed by our village schools. Whitewashed walls, wooden benches with the names of the boys who have studied here scratched upon them (among them famous men such as Fox, Canning and others), are all that you see in the rooms in which the elite of England is brought up. According to King Henry's provisions, the scholarship boys receive nothing every day but mutton – what could the founder have been thinking of!

When we got back from Eton, the King had already left, and Mr Wyatville his architect, who is supervising the additions to the castle, had the great kindness to give us exact information about everything. This building is a gigantic undertaking, unique in England, and it has been carried out not only with a lot of money and technical skill but also with a great deal of taste – indeed genius. The size and splendour of the castle, which is not yet half-finished and has already cost three million of our money, is, indeed, worthy of the King of England. Its historic interest, its great age and astonishing size and extent combine to render it unique in the world.

The splendour of the interior corresponds with that of the exterior. In the gigantic Gothic windows, for instance, every single pane cost £12 and, in the interior, satin, silk and gilding dazzle the eye. A high terrace on the side of the King's rooms consists of hot-houses within, and on the outside of a high wall of undressed stone, in keeping with the sober character of the whole, which surrounds the most charming flower garden and pleasure-grounds. The four great entrance gates to the castle courtyard are so cleverly placed that each of them offers a most interesting stretch of landscape, enclosed as in a frame.

August 28th

[L. left me yesterday – sooner than he had intended. I am extremely sorry for it, for so agreeable and friendly a companion doubles every pleasure. Afterwards I drove with an acquaintance of the Guards to St Leonard's Hill, which belongs to Field-Marshal Lord Harcourt, to whom Esterhazy had given me a letter.

The weather, which had been overcast and from time to time rainy, was splendid: scarcely a cloud in the sky. On no more beautiful day could I have seen a more beautiful place than St Leonard's Hill. Giant trees, a fresh wood full of variety, enchanting views, and a delightful house with the loveliest of flower gardens – form a whole which has not its equal in England. The owners are a very agreeable old couple, unfortunately without children to whom to leave this paradise. The old lord seemed much pleased with my enthusiasm for the beauties of the place, and invited me to spend the following day with him, which I accepted with pleasure. I was engaged to dine with my friend Captain B. at the Guards' mess at Windsor, where I passed the evening.]

Early next morning I was summoned by Lord Harcourt, who is the Ranger of Windsor Park and wished to show it to me before the King appeared. As soon as he rides out, the private sections are hermetically sealed against everyone except the King's immediate circle. I was somewhat late; the good old gentleman fumed a little and I immediately had to get into the landau, drawn by four splendid horses, and in it we sped hastily through the lofty beech woods.

In his immense park of 15,000 acres, the King has had several carriage ways made for his private use, leading to the most interesting points. We drove along one of them and, after half an hour, reached the royal stables where the much-discussed giraffe is to be found. Unfortunately we learned here that the King had just had his carriages ordered, and they were standing already harnessed in the courtyard. There were seven of these, of various kinds, but all with very low wheels, built very lightly like children's carts and drawn by little ponies – that of the King with four, which he drives himself, the others with two, mostly of different colours. Lord Harcourt saw these equipages with terror; he was afraid that the King might meet us and be *mal à son aise* at the sight of unexpected strangers, for the monarch is strange like that. He finds the sight of any stranger in his domain very unpleasant, and so the park, apart from the main road which crosses it, is perfect solitude. The King's favourite spots are closely hedged in and are daily planted with more vegetation to make everything even more private and hidden. In many places, where men are doing work and might cast a furtive glance at the sanctuary within, three storeys of hedges have been planted one behind the other.

We therefore made great haste so as to at least see the giraffe, which was led out to us by the two Turks who had brought it from Africa. A strange animal indeed! You know her shape, but nothing can convey the beauty of her eyes. Think of a mixture of the eyes of the most beautiful Arab horse and of the most ravishing southern maid, with long, raven-black eyelashes and the most profound expression of kindness mingled with volcanic fire. [Her appetite is good, for she daily drinks the milk of three cows who were lying near her. She uses her long, bright blue tongue like a trunk, and with it she took my umbrella from me and, liking it so much, was loathe to give it up. Her walk was somewhat ungainly as she had sprained her leg on board ship – however the Africans assured us that when in perfect health she was very swift-footed.

140

When one is much pleased, one generally pleases, and accordingly I was pressed into spending a few days in this little paradise. However, as you well know, my restlessness is equal to my indolence, and just as I find it difficult to move from a place once I have fixed myself (witness my long and unprofitable stay in London), so I find it equally difficult to bring myself to remain when the immediate interest is exhausted. I therefore gratefully declined the invitation and returned to Salthill.]

September 1st

I have allowed myself to be over-persuaded by the beautiful Lady Garvagh, a near relation of Canning's, to devote a few days to real country life.

We drove to the races at Egham, I in the phaeton with the charming Lady Garvagh who, unhappily, was married only two years ago, and that to an old, ugly husband merely because of his title! She is as beautiful as she is gentle and amiable, and for me dangerous. Had I found her unmarried, my decision would quickly have been made.

I had a strange conversation with her today, during which I said that I could marry her sister out of love for her. Indeed this sister[1] is a lovable creature, not beautiful but not ugly, and so naive, so innocent and natural that we would never find her like in one so young.

Windsor, September 3rd

I have set the business with the sister so far *en train* that I have enlisted Lady Garvagh as a confidante and have, at the same time, made her acquaintance and found there to be a possibility of marriage with this good-hearted child, who is also worth at least £30,000. We had breakfast together, and lunch, and took a three-hour walk, and then I had at last to leave them! I plucked forget-me-nots, which have the same name in English, and handed these to the ladies, saying that there could be no better expression of my thanks

[1] Harriet Bonham.

than taking leave of them with these flowers. They all accompanied me to the carriage, the beautiful Rosabelle (Lady Garvagh) among them . . . commanding like a mistress among slaves. My little one pressed a forget-me-not into my hand and was very sweet, but Rosabelle drew my eyes like a magnet. She has that soft, thoughtful expression which engages me more than any other womanly charm.

September 5th

I had thought that I could never fall in love again, but I see that it is high time for me to part from Rosabelle, for her presence disturbs me far more than I had anticipated. To love, to seduce this woman would be a delightful sin – to marry the sister virtuously is to me, by comparison, a bitter draught, and yet it all exists in my imagination, but that rules us and not we it. If I could only send you her picture, you would be in admiration of her beauty and the indescribable expression of softness, repose and kindness in that countenance. A slight trace of melancholy which is brightened by a heavenly smile, the mouth like a fresh cherry and the most beautiful teeth, half-hidden behind the lips, showing themselves as if by stealth; when this lovely mouth opens and whispers the softest sounds, its sweet music pierces irresistibly to the heart – that is an approximate portrait. She is still not two years married, and for half a year before that struggled with herself to marry her entirely good but entirely charmless present husband – if she had only held out for two more years! She may perhaps be thinking that too – *mais n'importe, il faut l'oublier.*

September 5th, evening

Tomorrow I am going back to London for a few days. I had luncheon in the barracks, where I am quite at home and always have a good time. It is true that Rosabelle rises from every glass, and gazes earnestly and sadly at me, but I do not change for all that for forget her I must, at least for now, when everything that looks like love is quite *hors de saison.* Dear Schnucke, only my love for you remains unchanged, and is the gold background on which my life is painted.

Your Lou

SIXTEENTH LETTER

London, September 7th, 1827

Dear friend,

I am, as you know, not good at remembering dates and so forth, but I know that tomorrow the day comes round again on which I had to leave my poor Schnucke alone in Bautzen! Since then a year has rolled over the world, and we insects are creeping along the old track – but we love each other as much as ever and that is all that matters.

There is, in fact, nothing now to keep me in London – but Lady Garvagh is here and alone and so attractive! It would be wrong to avoid such a friend, especially as I do not think I am in love with her. But is there not something sweet in the simple friendship of a beautiful woman? I have observed that many men spoil relationships because, in their intimate dealings with women, they always feel obliged to play the lover, and so set the woman at once on the defensive and prevent the gradual growth of trust and unconstrainedness that is the soil in which all the seeds one would wish to sow come to their fairest bloom. So I content myself completely with a tender friendship, especially when what I can read in the glances of soft, languishing blue eyes is spoken by a mouth of rose and pearl and a satin hand, of the most exquisite symmetry, confirms it with its warm pressure. To this portrait you have now but to add the innocent expression of a dove; long, dark-brown ringlets, a slender form of medium height and the most beautiful English complexion, and there you have Lady Garvagh, just as she lives and loves.

September 9th

You know that my Rosabelle is Canning's cousin. She is here, and I am in touch with her because of her sister. *Je tiens les deux fils*, and write very beautiful and passionate letters to her, but cannot,

143

unfortunately, take copies of them because I have such an enormous amount to do with my other business.

If I can get £50,000 with the little Harriet, who will be like soft wax in my hands, I shall take her; but I am very much afraid that she has only £30,000 and thus I would find it hard to take the plunge after all – when there is a thunderstorm threatening, the man is a fool who refuses to take shelter except in a palace, especially if he does not know if he has time to reach one! What do you think?

September 12th

I ate in the club as usual, and spent a long time with Lady Garvagh, who had arranged an innocent little rendezvous with me in the square where she lives, since she cannot receive visitors in her house while her husband is absent. She seems to me to be not unwilling, but our relationship is a singular one for I am always dealing, at one and the same time, with my love for her and marriage with her sister. With £30,000 everything would be all right, but I have now decided that, come what may, I will not do it for under £50,000, which is the least sum with which a radical cure of Muskau's affairs can be effected. Besides, I am in fact very unwilling to marry at all, whoever it might be – even Lady Garvagh, I think – so why should I crucify myself without at least completely wiping out my money troubles?

Lady Garvagh assures me that the little one is in love with me, though I can hardly believe it. My rank, I think, charms her more than my person. I am, in fact, what the English call 'outworn', frayed with worries and cares and disappointments. Even my little passion for Rosabelle, hardly begun, has already wasted away. I desire things as children do playthings – as soon as I know that I can grasp them, they lose all value. In fact, I no longer expect anything really good: I see myself as being inevitably and unalterably destined for mediocrity, which is what befits my personality. Indeed, it may be a consequence of it. But do not think that I am melancholy; far from it. On the contrary I am, in my own way, in very good spirits but I am no longer as I once was. Bold youth and fresh courage are gone!

September 14th

Today I learned – if I am truthful, with more pleasure than annoyance – that life is made up of disappointed expectations. It is at the same time a proof of how difficult it is to get hold of reliable information. How everything, in England as elsewhere, is exaggerated! After I had brought the matter of the little Harriet right out into the open, with great expenditure of trouble and cunning, I found that – although everyone is of the opinion that Lady Garvagh received £40,000 on her marriage, and that their old Papa is one of the directors of the East India Company and passes for extremely rich – the little one will bring with her no more than £10,000 and Lady Garvagh got only £8,000. *Ainsi il ne faut plus y penser* and, anyway, she was not the right one! I thank Heaven now that Lady Garvagh was not free, for I would have found it harder to renounce her.

Doncaster, September 17th

I was on the point of dating this from London, so quickly have I flown, in twenty hours, over the 120 miles between here and there!

The Doncaster races are the most frequented in England, and its racecourse surpasses all others in the country in taste, efficiency and a good view of the events. From the towering, extremely elegant stands, you can watch the entire race from beginning to end. The horses run round the course – the same spot serving as starting point and winning post. The crowd of ordinary people, of beautiful and fashionable society, is quite extraordinary.

The St Leger, which was run today, must have cost many a man a sleepless night, for enormous sums were lost. A little mare, who was so slightly regarded that the odds against her were fourteen to one, led the field of twenty-six all the way round and came in first. An acquaintance of mine won £9,000; another must have lost almost his entire fortune – and that was because of the cheating of the owner of one of the favourites, who had betted heavily on it in public, but even more heavily against it in secret, and then purposely had it lose.

With their bustle and thousands of equipages, the races left me with a very striking picture of English wealth. Afterwards, I drove on towards the north, a goal as yet unknown to me, and at one

145

o'clock in the morning, arrived in York, the second capital of England.

I have been wandering all day about this town. I began with York Minster, which bears some resemblance to the cathedral in Milan in its size and the richness of its ornaments.

A quarter of an hour from the Minster there stands, on a hill adjacent to the town, the romantic ruin of the abbey of St Mary, richly overgrown with trees and covered in ivy. They have the far from praiseworthy intention of erecting a public building quite close by on the same hill, and are even now busied with digging up the ground for this purpose. In doing this they have stumbled on the most beautiful fragments of the old abbey, works of art as well preserved as if they had been finished yesterday. I saw several capitals still in the earth and, in a nearby house, magnificent bas-reliefs which had been brought there in the course of the work. We then crossed the river (the Ouse) in a punt, and continued our walk along the top of the old town wall, a picturesque but almost impassable route. The surrounding district is very fresh and green and varied by many Gothic towers and churches, which in turn offer splendid views. After a quarter of an hour's walk, we reached the so-called Mickle Gate, which still retains much of its original form although they have just removed the old barbican from it. The brightly hued, gilded coats of arms of York and England shine above in knightly fashion in the sun.

I then betook myself to the poor prisoners in the county gaol. From the outside their dwelling looks quite like a palace, but it looks very different on the inside, and I heartily pitied the poor devils who have to sit in clean but icy, damp cells through the whole winter until the month of March, merely on suspicion, with the pleasant possibility of then being hanged. Nor can they expect any compensation if they are discharged.

In all the cells which I visited I found the order and cleanliness quite praiseworthy. However, the most remarkable feature of this prison was the prisoners' wardrobe, which was arranged with real elegance. A prison warder, with a good cargo of wine on board, stuttered out the following description: 'Here you see the wig of the famous Granby, which disguised him so well that he evaded capture for ten years. He was hanged here in 1786. Here is the fence stake with which George Nayler was struck down two years ago on the road to Doncaster. The delinquent was hanged here last spring. These great iron splints were the only things that could restrain Kirkpatrick; seven times he escaped from the most secure prisons, but these splints – which I fastened on to him myself – they were a bit too much for him.' They were great iron blocks from which even a horse would have found it difficult to free himself. 'He only wore them for two months, for on the first of May he was sent to Heaven. It was a lovely day. Here is the machine with which Cork stamped forged guineas. He was a very respectable gentleman. Hanged in 1810.' The wardrobe was right beside his quarters, and it seemed a much loved collection which owed its existence soley to his enthusiasm. How different are men's hobbies!

Scarborough, September 22nd

If English people so often die of chills and consumption, it is because of their habits rather than the climate. Walks on the wet grass are the favourite, and in every public room there are always several windows open so that one can hardly endure the draught. Even when they are closed the wind whistles through them, for they seldom fit properly and are never double. The climate too, however good for plants, is terrifying for human beings.

A chance which I have lighted on here of sending this letter to London, to the embassy, allows me to share with you the report of my journey. So I am closing for now, though with the condition, like Scheherezade, of beginning again in the morning. So, *sans adieu.*

Your Lou

SEVENTEENTH LETTER

Whitby, September 25th, 1827

Beloved friend,

After a somewhat tiring trip yesterday I slept rather long, and so left Scarborough only at two o'clock. The road as far as Whitby is rather difficult because of the many hills, and the appearance of the region is strange. As far as the eye can see, there is not a bush, a house, a wall, nor a fence. Nothing but endless, undulating hills, thickly covered with heather, which is the most beautiful violet and rose-red near at hand, but in the distance simply spreads the same dusty red-brown colour over the entire countryside. It does, however, provide a rich harvest for the grouse shooters. The only touch of variety is a mass of white dots, slowly moving here and there – and what are these but thousands of 'hill sheep'; very timid, mostly with black heads, and against their wool poodles and Pomeranians would look dingy.

As we were coming down from the bald mountains, about an hour before Whitby, the character of the country changed and, by the time we reached the town, had become very romantic. At the same time, English cleanliness and daintiness were gradually disappearing. Whitby was just like an old German town: just as dirty, with narrow lanes and no footpaths but also with heartier, more friendly inhabitants. Apparently travellers of distinction seldom come to this poor spot, or else they took me for someone else, for they flocked around me as if I were some rare animal. Every time I went out I had an escort of at least a hundred men, who crowded about me very good-humouredly, but very intrusively, in order to contemplate me from head to foot.

A comical anecdote occurred to me at this point, one which I had recently heard from the Duke of Leeds. This gentleman is very gracious towards his tenants, one of whom came up as the Duke was out for a walk and asked permission to make a request. This was

148

kindly received, and he came out with it: his twelve-year-old son had been tormenting him, day and night, to see the Duke and, since they were at that moment not far from his cottage, His Grace might have the great courtesy to allow himself to be looked at by the boy. The Duke smilingly gave his consent and went to the cottage, where the delighted father brought out his son. Hardly had the boy hurtled out than he stood amazed before the elderly and unimpressive-looking Duke, of whose power and greatness he had heard so much. He looked at him for a long time, touched him, and suddenly asked: 'Can 'ee swim?'

'No, no, my good boy.'

'Can 'ee fly?'

'No, I can't do that either.'

'Well, faith, I'd rather have my father's drake, for he can do both.'

Guisborough, evening

I wrote a letter to Lord Mulgrave, the owner of a large alum mine, a fine castle and park on the sea coast, and asked him to allow me to see these things. He sent me a very polite answer and a mounted groom to accompany me everywhere. This made the little town even more tiresome. The magistrate complimented me an hour later by sending over two of his colleagues, who are also the secretaries of its museum, which they took it upon themselves to show me. Because of the many fossils found in the vicinity, the museum is quite remarkable, so I accepted. Half the town was again assembled and followed us, with a rearguard of very noisy youths.

In the museum there was a large crowd of dignitaries on hand and a blossoming of inquisitive ladies, from whose attractive glances I had to keep averting my eyes to turn them upon a crocodile, an old walrus tooth or a fossilized fish. The two secretaries had divided the exhibits between them. One did the honours with the fish and the amphibians, the other with the birds and mammals. Both, however, were so eager for me not to be deprived of anything that each kept interrupting the other; just as one was beginning his oration, the other would regale me with something from his own realm. This was at first funny but soon became tiresome, for while A was clutching my left arm and saying: 'This is the famous little crocodile that was found in the stomach of a boa constrictor, and . . .' B was seizing me by the right arm, turning me round and making me look at a mantle of Papageno feathers and the tattooed head of a New Zealander whose skin had, literally, been pulled over his ears and tanned like leather.

The most interesting exhibit was a canoe, presented by Parry, with the whole fishing apparatus of the Eskimos. It was made entirely of fish bones and seal skin, and so light that it is difficult to understand how they could trust themselves to it on the sea. Although fairly long, it was scarcely *one* foot broad; it was entirely covered over, like a box, except for a single round hole in the middle in which the Eskimo sits and holds himself in equilibrium with a double oar, like a balancing pole.

Leeds, October 1st

The impressions of the evening were quite different from those of the day, but no less fine. As twilight was falling I reached the great manufacturing town of Leeds. A transparent cloud of smoke lay over the broad space which it occupies on the slopes and valleys of several hills. Hundreds of red fires flashed from it, lofty chimneys belched forth black smoke, and between them the great five-storey factory buildings stood out, every window illuminated by two lights behind which the busy workers went to and fro until deep into the night. But even in this maze of industrial lights the romantic was not wanting; high above the houses towered two old Gothic churches, upon whose steeples the moon with majestic calm poured golden light, which seemed to soften the strident fires of busy mankind.

Leeds has almost ten thousand inhabitants but no representatives in Parliament, because it is a new town; at the same time, as is well known, a miserable decaying village with hardly two wretched houses has two, sometimes more Parliamentary seats, which the owner naturally fills with his creatures. A crime and injustice as this misuse may be, English statesmen have not yet ventured to do away with it, perhaps because they are afraid that any change in so complicated a system might be a dangerous operation, only to be undertaken in case of dire necessity.[1]

---

[1] The Great Reform Bill was in fact only five years away.

Sheffield, evening

I reached Sheffield in good time where, because of the smoke, the sun casts no rays and looks just like the moon. I inspected the admirable products in the knife and scissors industry, such as a knife with 180 blades and scissors which can cut invisibly. In spite of the superstition I have bought you enough scissors and pins to last you a lifetime, as well as other recently invented trifles which I hope will give you pleasure.

Nottingham, October 14th

I travelled through the night and saw – only by moonlight and from afar – Newstead Abbey, Lord Byron's now very neglected birthplace and family seat. Apart from the Gothic church, of which almost every town in England can offer a more or less fine example, there is nothing much to see in Nottingham, except for the remarkable manufacturing process of pettinet (a material with a net pattern woven into it), in which the machines do everything quite by themselves; only a single man stands by to take charge if there should be any kind of a hold-up. It looks extremely strange when the iron monsters begin to operate with all their spikes and hooks, and as the finest pettinet, stretched in its frame, slowly emerges from the top, you see beneath the raw thread slowly unwinding from the spindle, without a single human hand touching it throughout.

During the night I reached St Albans, and saw the famous abbey by moon and lantern light. The verger was soon awakened and had to take me round. First I admired the exterior of the building erected eight hundred years ago by Saxons, its Roman tiles entirely undamaged, and then I went into the impressive interior. The nave of the church is, in fact, one of the largest in existence, for it is over 600 feet long. It has been adorned with much splendid work in stone and carving and, although one could see little clearly in the feeble light, the whole effect – the melodramatic and uncertain illumination, our two black figures in its midst and the tolling of the midnight bell from the tower – was most romantic. How solidly they built in those times is best proved by the splendid wooden roof, more than a thousand years old, which is still as beautiful and well-preserved as if it had been built only last year. The bright windows and gilded tomb of St Alban were, unhappily, for the most part destroyed in Cromwell's time.

I reached London in time to get at least half a night's sleep, and my first task in the morning was to finish this letter to you. I hope that in a few hours it will be on its way.

So let the time until then not seem long to you, and receive this letter with the same love and consideration as its many predecessors.

Your faithful Lou

EIGHTEENTH LETTER

London, November 4th, 1827

My dear Schnucke,

[As a Knight of St Louis, I attended a great dinner at the house of Prince Polignac in honour of either the saint's day or the name day of the King of France, I know not which. I then went to *The Continuation* of *Don Juan* at Drury Lane.]

Of course the first act was played in Hell, where Don Juan has already seduced the Furies and even the Devil's grandmother, and for this is unceremoniously thrown out by His Satanic Majesty. When he arrives at the picturesque banks of the flaming Styx, Charon is just ferrying souls from London across the river. Don Juan distracts the old man as he is climbing out of the boat by asking him to change a banknote – for paper money has already reached Hell – and uses this opportunity to hurl the three women from the bank back to earth. Arriving in London, he encounters the usual adventures: duels, seductions etc. The horseman statue at Charing Cross invites him to tea, but his creditors carry him off to King's Bench, from which he is rescued by marriage to a rich wife who wears the trousers – a punishment for all his sins which even Hell could not provide. Madame Vestris as Don Juan is a most charming and seductive youth, who certainly showed no lack of experience.

The piece amused me, but even more entertaining was a new novel which I found on a table in my lodging. Set in the year 2200, admittedly not in itself an original idea, England has again become Catholic and an absolute monarchy, and universal education has made such strides that learning has now become common among the lower classes. Every workman labours quite rationally according to mathematical and chemical formulae; lackeys and kitchen maids, who have names like Abelard and Heloise, talk like a literary magazine, whilst the upper classes, in order to distinguish themselves from the plebs, employ the coarsest words and expressions and carefully conceal all knowledge of reading and writing. This idea is witty, and perhaps prophetic. Moreover the lifestyle of this class is as simple as possible, only coarse food and very little of it appears on their tables while rich food is only encountered in the servants' hall.

That balloons are usual means of transport and steam rules the world goes almost without saying. However, a German professor discovers a way of bringing the dead back to life, and the mummy of King Cheops which has recently been discovered in an as yet unopened pyramid is the first person on whom this experiment is tried. How the living mummy comes to England and how shockingly he behaves there, you can read for yourself when the novel is translated into German. You know, I often feel like a mummy here myself, bound hand and foot, and longingly awaiting my resurrection.

November 20th

Hélas! il faut vous affliger un peu. That is, old Schnucke, I am speaking only of a negative evil, for nothing has come of the jeweller's business[1] and for the most unreasonable reason in the world; but then misfortunes always come in pairs.

There is a rock standing in my way here which it will be difficult to push aside. You may perhaps remember that I wrote and told you, I think, that shortly after my arrival, when I was telling Lady Lansdowne of our divorce and the reasons for it and so on, she said: 'My dear Prince, you will not find a wife here – according to our laws divorce is only possible on grounds of infidelity.[2] No other grounds are recognized, and an English girl in such a second marriage would regard herself only as a sort of mistress.' I looked on this at the time as a half-joke, and took little notice of it because it seemed to me entirely too absurd. But just think, in this instance she spoke only the truth.

The girl's father longs for nothing more ardently than our

[1] Harriet Hamlet was the only daughter of a wealthy jeweller; she was probably the best prospect that came Pückler's way during his entire stay in England, and he applied himself seriously to the task of winning her – even engaging a matrimonial agent to procure an introduction to Mr Hamlet.

[2] On the part of the *wife*.

marriage; he is entirely on my side in the matter, and the girl has confessed to him that I am very pleasing to her, that she thought she could not see me any more without danger to her heart, but that she felt she could not, under such circumstances, become my second wife. The father came to me in consternation to impart this gloomy explanation to me. I worked on him for hours, and at last succeeded in persuading him fully of the foolishness of these scruples. He promised to do his best, but unfortunately came back today without hope. He had tried every means, but in vain. His daughter had burst into tears and begged him, for God's sake not to force her against her will, that her objections were insuperable. [1]

I am now making a last attempt with a letter to her, since I cannot get an interview – but it is only *pour faire mon devoir*, since success is scarcely more to be thought of. The father took leave of me with tears in his eyes, as did I from his £200,000, *car pour la demoiselle, elle prouve par sa bêtise d'être une telle* incurable Englishwoman *et bégueule, que je n'en sens pas le plus petit regret.*

If it calms you, dear Schnucke, to learn that this sequence of events cost me absolutely no sorrow nor care, but affected me for only a single day after the father brought me the first news, I can truthfully assure you of this. On the contrary, it seems to me all the more ridiculous when I think that not only does it have to be said of my poor Schnucke that she allowed herself to be divorced, but also that she must have been unfaithful to me in order, in English eyes, to set me entirely free. [2] At such a price the Mogul's daughter would be too dearly bought, even if I were understanding (unfaithful)[3] in my own sense and not in that of the world! But you must confess that my experiences here are bizarre. This matter had gone so far that any other would have thought it already settled. Now I am so doubtful of ever succeeding that I allow myself hardly a single instant of disappointment, and am very careful not to give you more than a moderately lively hope. Truly I have, if I understand myself aright, only one regret in all this, and that is not to be able to give you more

[1] Harriet Hamlet had already refused two lords because she intended to marry for love.

[2] In fact, one of the major stumbling blocks to Pückler's plans (apart from English squeamishness about divorce) was general sympathy for Lucie, the 'deserted' ex-wife.

[3] Translator's parenthesis.

pleasure, just as Alexander only wanted to conquer the Persians in order to be able to write about it to Athens. Indeed, I believe that if I no longer had you, I would not take another single step towards improving my lot.

November 20th

Since there is now time to visit the theatre, and the best actors are playing, I am devoting many of my evenings to this aesthetic pastime. Last night I saw, with renewed pleasure, Kemble's accomplished performance as Falstaff, of which I have already written to you. I must however mention that his costume of white and red was of the most careful elegance, if a little shabby, and, combined with his handsome, curly white head and beard, gave him a happy mixture of the distinguished and the comic which in my opinion very much heightened the effect and, as it were, refined it.

All the costumes were masterly, but it was indeed an unpardonable destruction of all illusion that, immediately after the departure of Henry IV with his splendid court and many knights glittering in steel and gold, two servants in theatrical livery, with shoes and red stockings, came on stage to take away the throne. It is just as difficult to get used to seeing nothing of Lord Percy but his back during the quarter-hour he is haranguing the King. It is striking that even the most famous actors here fall into this bad habit, whilst with us they run to the opposite fault; for instance the *primo amoroso*, whilst making the most ardent declaration to his fair one, turns his back on her so as to ogle the audience. German actors generally make of Percy, in his behaviour towards his wife as well as the King, a kind of raging calf who has been bitten by a mad dog. These people simply do not know when to play down the poet and when to play him up. Young understands this thoroughly, and knows very well how to combine youthful, stormy outbursts with the nobility of the hero and the dignity of a prince.

November 23rd

It is strange that a man will consider as a miracle what is far removed from him in space or time, but take no notice at all of the daily miracles around him. Yet we must truly be living in the time of the Thousand and One Nights, since today I saw a being who seemed to outstrip all the imagined pictures of that epoch.

Listen to all the things that the monster can do.

First, its food is very cheap for it eats nothing but wood and coal and needs none at all as soon as it stops working. It never gets tired and never sleeps. It never gets sick and only refuses to work when it becomes unusable through old age. It is equally industrious in all climates, and undertakes indefatigably every kind of work. It is here a water-pump, there a miner, here a seaman, there a cotton-spinner, a weaver, a smith or a miller; indeed, it carries out each and every trade and, despite its diminutive size, pulls without any strain ninety ship's tons of merchandise, or draws behind it an entire regiment of soldiers, packed into carriages, with a speed that surpasses that of the fleetest stagecoach. Moreover, it marks its own speed on a dial, and also regulates the degree of heat it requires for its well-being, oils its innermost bowels if they require it in a wonderful manner, and removes at will all unwanted stale air. Although it cannot help itself, if anything goes wrong it immediately warns its proprietors by a loud ringing of the bell. Finally, it is so docile that a four-year-old child could put this giant to work at any moment with just the pressure of his little finger.

If only one could obtain the services of such a spirit without Solomon's ring – and was there ever any witch burnt at the stake for sorcery who could perform such deeds?

Now – a new miracle – if you were to magnetize five hundred gold pieces with the firm intention of changing them into a machine like that, after a little ceremony you would see it at your service. The spirit goes up in steam, but does not disappear thereafter. It remains, with the consent of God and man, your lawful slave. These are the miracles of our time which must surely outweigh those of old heathendom and even of Christendom.

November 28th

A great actor, a true master of his art, surely stands very high! How much he must know and be able to do! And how much genius must he combine with physical grace and skill, how much creative ability with the greatest and most patient routine!

Today, for the first time since my stay in England, I saw *Macbeth*, perhaps the noblest and most complete of Shakespeare's tragedies. Macready, just recently returned from America, played the principal part outstandingly. He seemed to me especially true and gripping in these moments – first in the night scene, after the murder of Duncan, when he comes out with the bloody daggers and tells his wife of the deed he has done. He delivered the whole speech softly (as the nature of the affair demands), like a whisper in the dark, and yet so clearly and with such frightful expression, that it brought all the horror of the night and of the crime into the very soul of the audience. Just as good was the difficult scene with Banquo's ghost. The beautiful passage:

> 'What man dares, I dare!
> Approach then, like the rugged Russian bear,
> the Hyrcan tiger . . .
> And if thou hadst the strength of twenty men
> Yet will I stead thee.
> And my firm nerves will never quake with fear
> Or be alive again.
> And dare me to the desert with thy sword,
> And I shall stead thee.
> Ne'er shake thy bloody locks at me.
> There is no apprehension in those eyes
> That thou dost glare withall.
> Hence, horrible shadow, unreal mockery hence!
> Avaunt and quit my sight, let the earth hide thee.'

and so on. He began very properly, and instead of exaggerating with all the excitement of despairing rage, lowered his voice little by little, overwhelmed with horror, until the last words were only a murmur. Then suddenly he burst out shrieking (in frightful fear of death) and, flinging his cloak over his face, sank half-lifeless back upon his seat. By this means he achieved a supreme effect; shudderingly, as a fellow human being, you felt that even our greatest courage cannot face the horror of another world – and you saw no trace of the purely theatrical hero, who troubles himself very little about Nature and only plays to the gallery for effect, seeking his highest triumph in a climax of shrieking and raging. Macready was also magnificent in the last act, when conscience and fear are alike exhausted and sheer apathy has taken the place of both; when the Last Judgement breaks over the sinner in three blows, following in rapid succession: the death of the queen, the fulfilment of the lying prophecies of the witches and, finally, Macduff's shattering declaration that he was of no woman born.

What formerly tortured Macbeth's mind and permitted him to brood over his position, struggle against the wounds of his conscience, can now only momentarily pierce him through, like a lightning flash. He is weary of himself and of life and fighting, as he himself says 'with bitter scorn', and like a bear at the stake at last he falls – a great sinner but yet a king and a hero.

Lady Macbeth was played by only a second-rate actress for unhappily, since the retirement of Mrs Siddons and Miss O'Neill, there are no more of the first rank; nevertheless she pleased me even in her weak performance more than many a would-be great artist of our Fatherland, whose affected manner is not up to any Shakespearian character.

Not only do I share the well-known opinion of Tieck[1] about this role, but I would like to go still further. The least of men can understand how love for a woman sees everything solely as it regards or affects the beloved object, and therefore, for a while at least, knows virtue and vice only in relation to her. Lady Macbeth, portrayed as a raging Fury who uses her husband only as an instrument of her own ambition, is lacking in all inner truth, and what is more, in all interest. Such a woman would not be capable of her depth of misery, which shows itself so horribly in the sleepwalking scene, whilst in the presence of her husband, in order to give him courage, she always seems the stronger, never displaying fear and remorse, but jeering at them in him and trying to deafen herself to their voice in her own heart.

She cannot, nevertheless, be called a soft, womanly character, but the womanly love she shows for her husband is all the same the main motive for her conduct.

She sacrifices to him not only everything which stands between Macbeth and his secret desires, but also herself, her peace of mind, indeed all womanly feeling for others, and calls on the infernal powers for help and strength. It seems to me that only in this way

---

[1] German Romantic poet, novelist, dramatist and dramatic critic.

can the character be dramatically and psychologically consistent with the latter part of the play. Any other interpretation is a mere caricature, of which Shakespeare's creative genius would have been incapable, for he always painted possible people and never unnatural spectres and imagined devils. So both went down together to destruction – while separately neither would have gone so far – Macbeth apparently with the greater selfishness, so that his torment and his end are equally frightful.

It is a great advantage in presenting this play if the role of Macbeth, rather than that of Lady Macbeth, falls to the player of greater talent. I was thoroughly convinced of this today. If Lady Macbeth becomes the main role because of her superior acting talent, you see the whole tragedy from a wrong point of view. It becomes something entirely different and loses much of its interest, if you see only a cannibalistic Amazon and, under her slipper, a hero who lets himself be used entirely as a tool.

No, in him lies the original seed of sin; from the beginning his wife simply supports him. He is in no way a fundamentally noble man who, led astray by the witches, becomes a monster; but, as in *Romeo and Juliet* the passion of love, in a soul too receptive of its power, leads from the innocent childishness of its first budding through all the stages of delight to despair and death, so in *Macbeth* the subject of the painting is selfish ambition; how it develops, fostered by the evil powers in Macbeth himself, from only apparent innocence and the fame of the fêted hero to the blood lust of the tiger and the end of a hunted beast. But the man in whose soul the poison is working is endowed with so many other lofty qualities that we can follow the struggle and development with sympathy for the hero. What a boundless pleasure it must be to see such a work of genius performed by great actors, with no weak players in any of the roles. This, though, could only be carried out by spirits, as in Hoffmann's ghostly production of *Don Juan*.[1]

[I must just mention one ridiculous thing that occurred here. After the murder of the King, when there is a knocking at the door, Lady Macbeth says to her husband:

---

[1] E. T. A. Hoffmann (of *The Tales of Hoffmann*), author of many macabre tales.

'. . . Hark, more knocking!
Get on your nightgown, lest occasion call us,
And show us to be watchers.'

Now 'nightgown' does indeed mean dressing gown, but yet I could scarcely believe my eyes when Macready entered in a fashionable flowered, chintz gown (perhaps the one he usually wears), loosely thrown over his armour, which glittered with every movement of his body; and in this curious costume drew his sword to kill the chamberlains who were sleeping near the King.

I did not notice that this struck anybody else – indeed the interest was generally so slight, the noise and mischief so incessant that it is difficult to understand how such distinguished artists can perform at all with so brutal, indifferent and ignorant an audience as they almost always have before them. As I told you English theatre is not fashionable, and is hardly ever visited by what is called 'good company'. The only advantage of this state of things is that actors are not spoiled by that indulgence which is so ruinous of them in Germany.]

After *Macbeth, Der Freischütz* was produced the same evening. Weber, like Mozart, had to resign himself to cuts and substitutions by Mr Bishop. It is a real misery, and not only the music but the very story loses its character. It is not Agatha's lover but the king of the free shooters who comes into the wolf's cave, and sings Caspar's favourite song. The devil, in long red robes, dances a regular shawl dance before he comes to rest with Caspar in his hell, which is very gracefully symbolised by means of fiery waterfalls, red from the wings, and heaps of skeletons. Here every comparison with Germany comes out entirely in our favour, just as we lost in tragedy. Still, I wish it were the other way round.

December 2nd

You must doubtless be wondering why I am still lingering in London at this thankless time of the year – but Lady R., to whom I have turned in this lonely life, is still here. Besides, the theatre has begun to interest me, and the peace of this silent life suits me well after the earlier turmoil. It is indeed so quiet that, like the famed prisoner in the Bastille, I have lately begun a liaison with a mouse, a charming little beast and undoubtedly a bewitched Lady who, if I am working, slips shyly forth to look at me with her little eyes like twinkling stars. She is becoming tamer all the time and is charmed with cake crumbs, which I place every day six inches further from her residence in the right-hand corner of the room. At this moment she is devouring one of them with much grace and is tumbling about the room quite unconstrainedly. But what do I hear? An incessant sound of shrieking in the street! My wee mouse dashes in a flash back to her corner.

'What is it?' I ask. 'What is this frightful noise?'

'War has been declared!' calls an 'extra' from the street.

'With whom?'

'I don't know.'

This is one of the branches of industry among poor devils in London. If they cannot think of anything else, they cry out some great novelty and sell an old newspaper to any curious person for half a shilling. People hastily seize it, understand it wrongly, look at the date and laugh at having been led astray.

[As is always the case when I live alone, I have so completely turned day into night that I seldom breakfast before four in the afternoon, dine at ten or eleven after the play, and walk or ride in the night. It is generally not only finer but also brighter at night – the days are so foggy that even if there are lamps and candles you can't see them a yard away. As I galloped home last night through the wide, quiet streets, white and coal-black clouds coursed swiftly across the moon's face and afforded a singularly wild and enchanting spectacle. The air was serene and mild, for the recent cold has been succeeded by almost spring weather.

I have received your long letter, and give you my heartiest thanks for it. Do not be displeased that I so seldom answer in detail, for which neglect you reproach me. Remember that one gives no answer to the rose for its precious fragrance other than to inhale it with delight. To dissect it would not enhance our pleasure. Nevertheless, I regret that I have neither the materials nor the disposition to send you such roses in return. The wall is as bare before me as a white sheet.

Woolmers, December 11th

Sir Gore Ouseley,[1] formerly English ambassador to Persia, has invited me to his country house and I drove there this morning. I arrived late, in darkness and rain, and was obliged to dress immediately to go to a ball at Hatfield, a weekly event given by Lady Salisbury during her stay in the country. Sir Gore took his whole party which included Lord Strangford, the well-known ambassador to Constantinople.

The next morning I delighted myself with a review of the various Persian curiosities which decorate the rooms. I was particularly struck by a splendid manuscript with miniatures, which excelled all the mediaeval European illuminations and was often more correct in drawing. The subject of the book is the history of Tamberlane's family and is said to be worth two thousand pounds in Persia. It was a present from the Shah. Doors inlaid with precious metals; sofas and carpets of curious velvet, embroidered with gold and silver; above all a golden splendidly enamelled plate show that if the Persians are behind us in many things, they surpass us in others.

The weather has cleared a little, and enticed me to a solitary walk. Noble trees, a little river and a grove, under whose thick shade a remarkably copious spring gushes forth as if from the centre of the earth, are the chief beauties of the park. When I returned, it was two o'clock, the hour of luncheon. Afterwards, Sir Gore showed me his Arab horses, and some of them were quickly saddled for a ride. The groom had to jump off and on his horse every minute to open the gates which interrupted our way. This is often the case in English parks, and still more in the fields, which makes riding, except on the high roads, somewhat troublesome. In the afternoon we had music, and the daughter of the house and Mrs F distinguished themselves as admirable pianists. The audience was, however, perfectly unrestrained; they came and went, talked or listened just as they felt inclined.

When the ladies retired to dress, Sir Gore and Lord Strangford told us many anecdotes about the East – a theme of which I never

---

[1] Diplomat and orientalist, ambassador extraordinary to Persia in 1812; an authority on and collector of Persian art.

tire.[1] Both these gentlemen are great partisans of the Turks, and Lord Strangford spoke of the Sultan as a very enlightened man. He was probably, he said, the first ambassador from any Christian power who had had several private conferences with the Grand Signior. At these, a singular etiquette was observed: the Sultan would receive him in the garden of the seraglio in the dress of an officer of his bodyguard, and in that character address Lord Strangford with the greatest deference in the third person; Lord Strangford would not let it appear that he recognized him.

After dinner, at which we had some oriental dishes and I drank genuine Shiraz for the first time (not a very pleasant wine, by the way, for it tastes of goat-skins), we had music again and *petits jeux*. As these were not very successful, the whole party went to bed at a reasonable hour.

December 12th

I have bought one of my host's horses, a coal-black Arab as wild as a roe, and to give him a longer trial rode over to Lady Cowper,[2] who lives in the neighbourhood. The park and house of Panshanger are well worth seeing, especially the picture gallery, which contains two of Raphael's early Madonnas and a singularly fine portrait of Marshal Turenne[3] on horseback by Rembrandt. Lady Cowper received us in her boudoir, which led out into a beautiful garden, even now gay with flowers and bordered by greenhouses and a dairy in the form of a temple.

Panshanger is celebrated for the largest oak in England. It is nineteen feet and a half in circumference six feet from the ground, and very straight and lofty. We have larger oaks than this in Germany.

---

[1] Pückler was later to travel extensively in Turkey and the Near East.

[2] Sister of Lord Melbourne and later wife of Lord Palmerston, Lady Cowper was an outstanding hostess and, according to Pückler, one of the 'gentlest' patronesses of Almack's.

[3] One of Louis XIV's most brilliant generals.

December 13th

In my host's house is an unusual picture gallery – a Persian one, which contains some very curious things, including some large dressed dolls which give a faithful idea of the fair sex in Persia, with long hair painted red or blue, arched and painted eyebrows, large, languishing eyes of fire, pretty gauze pantaloons and gold rings round their ankles.

Lady Ouseley told us many amusing details of the harem, which I will reserve till we meet again that I may not exhaust all my resources. Many things in Persia seem to be very agreeable, many quite the reverse: among them the scorpions and insects, which we are free from in our temperate climates. Let us all therefore be contented with them: a wish I cordially make for you and me.

Your Lou]

NINETEENTH LETTER

London, December 16th, 1827

Dear Schnucke,

[After writing a few verses in the Woolmers album, in which Arabian steeds, Tamberlaine's magnificence and the fair beauties of Teheran met in agreeable confusion, I took leave of my kind hosts and returned to London. The same evening my friend L. took me to a strange exhibition.

In a suburb a good German mile from my lodging, we entered a sort of barn, dirty with only a rough roof for a ceiling. In the middle of it was a boarded space twelve feet square, surrounded by a strong wooden rail; round this was a gallery filled with the most vulgar, perilous-looking faces of both sexes. A ladder led to a higher gallery, which was let out at three shillings a seat to the patrician part of the audience. There was a strange contrast between the 'fashionables' and the populace among whom they were scattered, many of them offering and taking bets of between twenty and fifty pounds. The subject of these was a fine terrier, the illustrious Billy, who, we were promised, would kill a hundred rats in ten minutes.

The arena was empty and there was an anxious pause; in the lower gallery huge pots of beer circulated from mouth to mouth and tobacco smoke rose in dense clouds. At length a strong man appeared bearing what looked like a sack of potatoes, which in fact contained a hundred live rats. These he set free all at once by untying the knot, scattering them about the place and then retreated rapidly into a corner. At a given signal Billy rushed in, and set about his murderous task with incredible fury. As soon as a rat lay dead, Billy's faithful squire would pick it up and put him in the sack; some of them might only have been senseless, or even old practitioners pretending to be dead at first bite. Be that as it may, Billy won in nine and a quarter minutes according to all the watches. This was the first act. In the second, the heroic Billy, who was

166

greeted with continual shouts by an enraptured audience, fought with a badger. Each combatant had a second, who held him by the tail. Only one bite or grip was allowed before they were separated, and immediately let loose again. Billy had the best of it and the poor badger's ears were streaming with blood. At last the victorious terrier retired exhausted.

The entertainments ended with bear-baiting, in which the bear wounded several dogs with seemingly little damage to himself. It was evident throughout that the managers were too careful of their animals to expose them in earnest; as I have said, I suspected some hidden talents for play-acting from the beginning – even from the rats.]

December 31st

Don Miguel of Portugal[1] has arrived here, and I was presented to him this morning. Only the corps diplomatique and a few friends were present. The young Prince is not bad looking and even resembles Napoleon, but was somewhat constrained in his manner. He wore seven stars and seven broad ribbons over his frock coat. The colour of his face is like the olive of his native land, and the expression of his countenance was more melancholy than cheerful.

January 1st, 1828

My best wishes for today and a fond kiss for the beginning of the year. Perhaps this is the good year for which we have been waiting in vain for so long. Its opening was for me at least very cheerful. We spent yesterday with Sir Lewis Moeller,[2] who had invited five or six pretty ladies and girls, and at about midnight drank a toast to the New Year. L and I, on this occasion, followed the German fashion of kissing the ladies which they, after dutiful struggles, allowed right willingly and gladly.

Don Miguel's presence is enlivening London. A soirée was held

---

[1] King of Portugal (1828–34), Don Miguel had been deeply involved in the constitutional crisis which followed the death of his father, John VI, in 1826; he was then to usurp the throne from his niece Maria. Later, he was himself driven from the throne by the Legitimists under the leadership of Don Pedro, his brother.

[2] Privy Councillor of Legation to the Hanoverian government in London.

at the Duke of Clarence's this evening, and tomorrow there will be a grand ball at Lady Keith's. The Prince seems to be generally pleasing and, now that he is more at home, there is something quite formal and distinguished in his air, although it looks as if there is more than one ulterior motive behind his great affability. Etiquette is so strict among the Portuguese that our good Marquess P. must fall upon his knees every morning when he first sees the Prince.

January 6th

[We float in a sea of fêtes. Yesterday the beautiful Marchioness gave hers; today was the Princess Lieven's which lasted until six o'clock. People are busy from morning to night amusing the Prince. It must be agreeable to be this sort of privileged person, whom the highest and the lowest, the wisest and the silliest, are all doing their utmost to please.]

In the midst of this whirl I received a letter from you by means of L., and rejoice at the hundred thousandth assurance of your love contained in it, an assurance which I would not tire of hearing for the millionth time, and after the millionth would cry: *L'appétit vient en mangeant!* Just as little tired, it seems, are the people here with these celebrations. Whilst the horizon becomes ever more overcast with dark clouds, our diplomats dine and dance in the face of the threatening tempest with much laughter and jest.

My mood through all this is well and strong. My manly soul (for I have a womanly soul of my own, apart from yours, which belongs to me) is now *du jour*; and thus I feel more reliant, freer, and less sensitive to exterior influences. This is very suitable for my stay here, for the English are as cold as their flint pebbles, sharp and with cutting edges; but it is the property of steel to strike lively sparks from them which produce light by a beneficent antagonism.

As a rule I am too little excited by them to be either willing or able to act as a steel on the individuals around me. However I can always confront their pride with a still greater one, and have mollified many in this way and alienated others. Both are just what I want, however, since the craniologist very truly said that I have been endowed with an essentially creative spirit, and that people like me can only love those who congenially fit in with them, or those who, in a subordinate position, provide them with a useful instrument on which they can play their own melodies. With all others they are opposed or distant.

January 14th

I drove this morning into the city with the Earl of B. and a son of the famous Madame Tallien[1] in order to see the India House, where many remarkable objects are kept. Among them is Tippoo Sahib's dreambook in which he daily wrote his dreams and their meaning and which, like Wallenstein, he had principally to thank for his downfall.[2] His armour, part of his golden throne and a strange barrel organ are all kept together here. This last is to be found in the stomach of a very well executed metal tiger, of natural colour and life-size. Under the tiger lies a red-uniformed Englishman, whom he is tearing to pieces; by turning the handle of the barrel organ, you can hear the shrieks and whimpers of a man struggling in his death throes, hideously alternating with the roars and grunts of the tiger. The instrument is entirely characteristic of this frightful enemy of the English, who adopted the stripes of a tiger as his coat of arms and who was wont to say of himself that he would rather be a tiger on the prowl for a day than a peacefully grazing sheep for a hundred years.

January 20th

Munster[3] asked me recently, in good-humoured jest, whether I was going to Brighton on the prowl. Not a bad way of putting it. Heaven only provides a quarry that is worth the trouble, and if it is not to be a royal stag, then we must be content with a leveret in order to sate our hunger. So do not reproach me, Schnucke of my heart, if, after vainly striving to obtain a haunch of venison, I sustain my life with

---

[1] Wife of a member of the French National Convention.

[2] Sultan of Mysore, Tippoo Sahib defeated the British in the Second Mysore War when Warren Hastings was governor. He was finally defeated at Malvalli by General George Harris and shot during the siege of Seringapatam. According to Schiller, General Wallenstein's belief in prophetic dreams probably contributed to his ruin: he was assassinated.

[3] Hanoverian statesman much in favour at the Court of St James.

potatoes or even pine cones. The Roman who killed himself because he could no longer eat peacock's tongues was a great fool, and I shall certainly never imitate him. At least I hope not.

Brighton, January 25th

I am now once more active but there is, in fact, nothing to be done here without money or time. Do not worry about the future on this account. If I cannot secure a *fortune*, because I do not have the means of holding out and perhaps also because the circumstances are not favourable, I can at least marry the young Scottish lady (of whom I wrote to you once that I had gone riding with her in London, and who pleases me very much, being gentle, kind and independent, with 100,000 talers) or if in the meantime someone else has got her, there is always the little Harriet with her 70,000 talers. This money would save us, at least for the moment, and as for the future, we are all reaching for the impossible until we die. In the meantime I am making *de mon côté* a few attempts to get money, so as to be able to wait for something better; but if all this fails I shall, as I said, do what is necessary in order at least to make a happy end to the torment. You approve of this, don't you?

It cuts me to the heart, my poor darling, that you have to live in Berlin in such straightened circumstances, but the dear Lord will some day give us better times. Only keep yourself healthy and, when possible, cheerful, even if not in high spirits.

January 25th

Fashion is a great tyrant, and though I realize this I let myself be ruled by her as others are. Several days ago she led me here again, to the amiable Mrs J., the clever Lady L., the charming F., and so forth. Already I am tired of balls and dinners and am flirting with the sea, the only poetic thing in this otherwise prosaic world. I was at its edge just as night was departing, returning from a rout at the furthest end of the town, and stood for a good half-hour under the foam and thunder of the incoming tide. The stars were still sparkling and everlasting peace ruled above while wild roaring and tumbling raged here below – Heaven and earth in their truest likeness! How splendid, how beneficent, how fearsome, how troubling is this world – the world which never begins and never ends – in whose endless circuit the very fancy veils itself and sinks shuddering to the ground. Ah, my dear Schnucke, only love can show the way out of this labyrinth. Does not Goethe say: 'Only the soul that loves is happy'?

February 6th

I have caught a chill and developed a high, nervous fever which has already kept me fourteen days in bed, and has made me extraordinarily exhausted. It was not entirely without danger either, but it is now over. So do not worry.

February 8th

The doctor thinks that I am very patient – dear God, I have indeed learnt patience and, to speak the truth, adversity is a good school for the spirit. Adversity at the deepest level actually arises only from one's own failings, and so carries its own cure. If you accept that, from the beginning, you should always act sensibly and kindly, you will hardly experience any sorrows. But pleasures need to be so refined that you set but little store by earthly things. No more dinners, at which we willingly risk spoiling our stomachs; no more fame, which we chase after with such satisfied vanity; no more sweet, forbidden chariots of love, no more splendour with which to surpass others! It would ultimately – God forgive the thought – be no more than a Philistine's life, a standstill, even if it looked like fulfilment.

Real life, on the other hand, is movement and contrast. It would be the most terrible state of affairs if we all became entirely sensible here below. Still, in my case I do not believe there is any danger of that. You see, my illness has not greatly changed me, and I would not have written about it to you at all if this letter had gone off earlier, or if I had not been entirely recovered. However, you can read it with entire peace of mind and be convinced that, until my last breath, I shall enjoy everything that the dear Lord has bestowed upon us. Farthings or gold pieces, houses of cards or palaces, soap bubbles or rank and due consideration – whatever time and circumstance may bring – and at last death and whatever follows that. Beautiful are the sober virtues, but let us have spice with them. So I am really enjoying my present abstinence; it makes me feel quite ethereally higher than the animals, and nobler than usual.

February 10th

A letter from you always gives me great pleasure, as you know, but how much more in my present situation! Judge then with what joy today's was received.

February 12th

My illness has prevented my going to Scotland, for which I had everything ready and had received many invitations. Now W's expected arrival and the beginning of the season will keep me in London. For the first time today the doctor allowed me to drive out, and I directed my way towards the not too far distant park of Stranmore to give myself entirely over to the pleasures of a romantic walk. However entrance to the gardens was forbidden me, although I showed my card to the caretaker. We are certainly more liberal, but this aristocratic selectivity also has its advantages, for it makes the thing itself, and the satisfaction when at last you do get in, much more valuable.

February 15th

The short outing was really too soon, since it did not suit me at all well. Moreover, the weather has become frightful. A snow storm whipped the sea under my windows so that it foamed with rage and roared; its waves even broke over the high breakwater of the street and came right up to the houses. In the midst of this thunder yesterday I began to write my memoirs, and have already completed eight pages which I enclose with this letter.

February 20th

I have got up and, behold, everything has become strange – wherever I go my acquaintance has almost all left; on the Promenade, as well as indoors, I see nothing but new faces on every side. It was only when I ventured forth into this bare landscape that I found things to be the same as of old, with the sole exception of the green meadows which have been fertilised with – oyster shells!

The single meaning of these many words is always the same – my heartfelt love.

Your Lou

TWENTIETH LETTER

Best and dearest,

I must tell you about an acquaintance I made in Brighton which has a certain interest. You have no doubt heard that a forbear of the Thelluson family made a will according to which his fortune should remain untouched for a hundred and fifty years, so as to pile interest upon interest, and that, when the money was released, only the youngest Thelluson then alive should come into possession of it. This term will run out in twenty years' time, and I saw here Mr Thelluson, a man of forty who possesses very little, and his son, a pretty boy of eight, who is destined to receive twelve million pounds sterling in his twenty-eighth year – ninety-four million talers in our money. An Act of Parliament has forbidden such wills in the future but no one has been able to break this one, although they want to, for so huge a fortune would give an unnatural degree of power to any private citizen. However I could not but heartily congratulate the boy on his high hopes. It is a great thing to have so much money, for it cannot be denied that money is representative of most things in this world. And what marvellous objects might be attained by such a fortune, wisely spent!

My first visit in the capital was to Countess M. who, in spite of her forty years, has added another child to her dozen during my absence. I ate there and admired a beautiful present of plate from the King, the workmanship of which is finer here than anywhere else, so that the cost of the labour is often ten times that of the metal. At table the Earl gave a pleasant example of the legal practices in this country.

'A man whom I know,' he said, 'had a snuffbox stolen from him in the street. He seized the perpetrator and, as he was the stronger, was able to hold him down, though not without some rough handling; he then handed him over to the police – when they arrived. The evidence was indisputable on the testimony of a number of witnesses and, if tried at the Assizes, the delinquent would have been either hanged or transported to Botany Bay. His wife, however, sought out the gentleman and embraced his knees, pleading for mercy. The thief himself, who was not without education, wrote the most touching of letters, and no one will be surprised at the outcome – that is, he found a sympathetic hearing, the plaintiff did not appear on the appointed day, and therefore, in accordance with English law, the guilty man was released.

'This misplaced sympathy, however, proved unlucky for the gentleman. Fourteen days after the aforetold, he was accused by the selfsame man who had stolen his snuffbox of bodily harm and assault on the public street, and this was attested by witnesses. The accused responded that it was true that he had seized the man, but he had done so only because he had caught him stealing his snuffbox. Since the delinquent had been entirely cleared of this, however, and no one can be tried twice for the same offence, no notice was taken of his objection. In short, the victim had to pay one hundred pounds sterling in damages and costs to the thief and the court.'

March 8th

I ate at Esterhazy's at midday, and in the evening went to the play and then to a boring ball. It is unbelievable how few opportunities there are of seeing the person one wishes to see. I am making no progress, and everything is conspiring to make my goal here almost unattainable.

Bülow has given me the real story on this and has explained a great deal – which leaves me little hope – but I still must try to the last. The story of your ill-treatment has got about and they have found out the truth which, according to the stupid ideas here in England, is very damaging for me, especially my desire to live with two women at once, which here they regard as a kind of bigamy. According to Bülow, they are saying in the first circles that my wife would really be only a kind of mistress, and indeed I speak to everyone who will listen with the greatest tenderness and friendship of my first wife, who is living on my property and so on and, as in a

Turkish seraglio, would remain the sultana. Bülow says that it is astonishing how they know every personal trifle, for instance he learnt at an English gathering that you have gone to Muskau from Berlin in order to get everything ready for me. You see, Schnucke of my heart, what a fearful weapon the devil has got hold of here. However, there is nothing to be done. I must return to my last attempt, and after that we will have to draw up a new strategy for ourselves.

I replied to Bülow, who I must confess has been friendly towards me, that the conclusions of the English were silly, that I have never denied the tenderest friendship for you, and that even if I could get Venus with ten millions, you would remain the only person in the world who lives for me, and no one else would or could ever love me so again. I also said that it did not follow that I wanted to live with two wives at once, that our relationship was like that of mother and son, and that the happiness of a young woman whom I married would be just as near to your heart as to mine; that your presence in Muskau was only the result of my insistent request so that, during my absence, matters should be kept in order.

I must speak in this fashion as I am sure you will agree, for, in the short time that I can remain here, why should I completely bar the way to a last attempt? If I should marry the girl I have in mind we can do with her what we will, and I know for certain that I would not remain married to anyone for a month unless she loved and honoured my Schnucke, but one must bow to prejudice as long as it is to be feared. Our position is a sad one, but only because we lack money – and unfortunately I have heard from Bülow that people are only too well-informed about this too, and that is the worst of all.

[*March 9th*

The season is already asserting its prerogative. The streets swarm with elegant equipages; fresh treasures fill the shops; all the houses are full and all the prices have doubled and trebled. Mr Peel gave a brilliant soirée this evening for the Duchess of Clarence. His house is decorated with many fine pictures, among them Rubens' famous *Chapeau de paille*. Mr Peel paid fifteen thousand reichthalers for this picture – a half-length.]

March 11th

A hideous misfortune! The operation of dyeing my hair has fared so badly, the devil knows why, that this evening I had to begin all over again. Great and small misfortunes alternate with each other in such a pleasing way that I cannot become bored. But the reign of the devil cannot last forever, and if care has turned my hair white before its time, art must make it black once more, and so care will turn to joy. Let us not despair, perhaps everything will change in April. Ah, Schnucke, how I long for you.

March 13th

[I must take you again to the theatre, and in the company of the celebrated Lord Lauderdale,[1] an old acquaintance of mine who, after a varied and busy career, now preserves himself by daily washing with vinegar – whereas he formerly pickled others in a pungent, sour sauce both in writing and by word of mouth. We talked of old times, and as we reached the door of Drury Lane, he recited some wild but beautiful verses of Moore's:

'Oh what were Love made for, if 'tis not the same
Through joy and through torment, through glory and shame?
I know not, I ask not, if guilt's in that heart;
But I know that I love thee – whatever thou art.'

No bad motto for Desdemona, who awaited us, though truly the Moor's was a fearful response to such devoted love.

It is a constantly contested point in Germany whether Shakespeare should be given a literal translation, a free one or a still freer paraphrase. I prefer the second – even though a play of wit or words may occasionally be lost by this means. But to alter in any degree the course of the play, to omit scenes, to give to Shakespeare

---

[1] Politician whom Byron described as 'a shrill, Scotch and acute' speaker. A friend and adviser of Lady Lansdowne, at the time of the breaking off of her engagement to Pückler, Lauderdale wrote to assure him that, 'he will ever mention his conduct in the recent unfortunate transaction with the utmost respect', and expressed the wish that 'he may occasionally hear from the Count with whom he will be happy to have a correspondence'.

words and ideas perfectly foreign to him, can only deform and mutilate him, even if done by the greatest poet. People say Shakespeare is better read than seen, and that he cannot be performed in a literal translation without taking us back to the infancy of scenic art; since, according to them, theatrical representations in Shakespeare's time were no more than stories in dialogue with some attempt at costume.

I will not go into the question of the accuracy of this assertion, but this much I know: the performances of *Romeo and Juliet*, *Hamlet* and *Othello* on the English stage – in which even things generally supposed shocking to taste and probability, including the obligato king's trumpeteers, are not omitted – leave a feeling of such full and untroubled satisfaction that reading or hearing read (even by Tieck, the best reader I know of) have never remotely given me. Indeed, I confess that it is only since I have seen them here that I have been sensible to Shakespeare's real greatness. It is true that, to produce this, a degree of concert on the part of all the actors is necessary, and an excellence in those who support them. This is wholly lacking in Germany, for Macbeths in Berlin and Macbeths in London are a very different sort of people. The first actors here, like Kean, Young, Kemble etc., are men of great cultivation, who have seen the best society and devoted their lives to the earnest study of their great national poet. They seldom act any other character than his, and don't mix a tragic hero with one of Iffland's *Geheinräthe* (privy councillors), nor appear today in *Othello*, and tomorrow in *Wollmarkt*.]

Many Germans do not like to hear that other nations outstrip us in any way at all, and I too grieve over such things, but all the same I must express my conviction that, just as we have no dramatic poet of Shakespeare's calibre, so we have no actors who are capable of portraying his characters in their entire significance. It was not always so, as they say, and I myself have retained impressions from my earliest youth of Fleck[1] and Unzelmann which I have never seen bettered on our stage.

To do justice to foreign actors we must first in some degree think ourselves into their national character and become accustomed to certain unfamiliar mannerisms and turns of speech (no matter how

[1] Especially famous for his portrayal of the title-hero in Schiller's *Wallenstein*.

well we understand them) – to this I am sure every sensible man would agree. At first these things are distracting, and I have only seen one artist who was, if I may so express myself, entirely cosmopolitan – the inimitable, perhaps never equalled, certainly never surpassed Miss O'Neill.[1] In her it was only the human spirit and soul that spoke; nationality, time and external appearance vanished from the mind in an all-enveloping enchantment.

But back to the present. We saw *Othello* in which the combination of the three greatest dramatic artists of England provided me with one of the most enjoyable of evenings, and occasioned this rather long digression. It also caused me to miss the aforementioned heroine most painfully. Had she been there, I would have seen the highest of all theatrical performances.

Kean, Young and Kemble, as I said, constitute the triumvirate of the English stage. The first undoubtedly possesses the greatest genius, the second is splendid and consistent in his acting, the third, although not so excellent in high tragedy, is yet always dignified and intelligent. In this performance of *Othello* these three are playing together for the first time. It was indeed a rare enjoyment. After Shylock, Othello is Kean's greatest role. It is admirable with what deep knowledge of human nature he depicts not only the passion of jealousy, first slumbering, gradually awakening and then finally overflowing in rage, but also the southern nature of the Moor, imitating the peculiar individuality of this class of men with wonderful accuracy. There shines through all the noble being of the Moor something animal, which makes one shudder and, at the same time, places his immense suffering before our eyes. The simplicity of his acting at the beginning, the absence of all boasting about the great deeds of the past and his deep love for his chosen woman won the hearts of the spectators, as they had won Desdemona's – the ugly Moor is forgotten in the complete, heroic man until, amid the tortures of lacerating jealousy, that horrifying hidden nature slowly emerges before our very eyes, and at last we can hardly believe that we are looking at a man, but rather at a raging tiger.

I was strengthened anew in my conviction that the great poet needs a great actor in order to be fully understood and appreciated. In Berlin, for instance, the strangling scene appeared not only

---

[1] Eliza O'Neill had retired in 1819 on her marriage to Sir William Becher.

ridiculous but actually indecent. Here the blood literally froze in one's veins, and even the rough English audience was silent for a long time, as if struck by lightning. Indeed I confess that the tragedy of Othello's long martyrdom, so satanically meted out to him by Iago a drop at a time, was at times so painful to me that, with the fear of what I knew was coming growing in me, I involuntarily turned away my face as if from a shocking spectacle. Young's portrayal of Iago is an absolute masterpiece, and it is through his playing that this character has become entirely clear to me. It is perhaps – I should say, Iago is perhaps contrary to Shakespeare's usual method, being not a character firmly founded in Nature but rather a glittering fancy, an invention of the poet's even though carried out with admirable consistency. He is the devil incarnate, a being fed on gall and bitterness who is capable neither of pleasure nor joy, who sees evil as his element, and finds his only comfort in the contemplation and revelation of his own atrocities. His bond with humanity is a tenuous one that he must treat the Moor thus because 'he between my sheets has done my office'. Even this seems only a pretext, which he sets before himself with his last breath of moral feeling, as an excuse, while real joy at misfortune and suffering is ever his principal motive. Yet this monster is never entirely repulsive. His intellectual superiority, his courage, his consistency and finally his steadfastness in misfortune never allow this most thorough-going of villains to sink into common meanness.

Iago always remains a hero compared with a Kotzebueian[1] model of virtue. It is in this spirit that Young plays the character throughout: his outlook is dark and sullen but noble; no smile crosses his lips, and his jests never lose anything through their dryness. He wields his power with calm and superiority, yet also with well-marked nuance. With his wife he is rough, with Roderigo authoritative and moody, with Cassio considerate and masterful and friendly, with the Moor respectful and sincere, but always serious and dignified. Kemble plays Cassio splendidly and, as Shakespeare depicts him, 'a man, made to make women false': young, cheerful, light-hearted, with a noble person, a good-hearted character and

---

[1] August von Kotzebue was a prolific and popular playwright; one of his domestic dramas, *Lovers' Vows*, is the play so strenuously rehearsed in Jane Austen's *Mansfield Park*.

fine manners. Desdemona was, unfortunately, only very mediocrely portrayed. However the contrast between her soft, patient womanliness and the Moor's glowing passion was not entirely lost. Kean played Othello in the dress of a Moorish king out of the Bible, in sandals and a long silk robe, which is extremely conventional. But you soon forgot the costume in his magnificent playing.

Your faithful Lou

TWENTY-FIRST LETTER

[London, March 27th, 1828

Beloved friend,

I have just come back from the Levée, which was very crowded.
The King was seated, on account of his gout, but looked very well.
The Duke of Wellington gave thanks for his elevation to the
premiership by falling on both knees, whereas it is usual only to
kneel on one. Perhaps his gratitude is double on account of his
double status as Prime Minister and former Commander-in-Chief –
as the caricatures represent him: the left half of his body dressed as a
courtier, the right as a field marshal, but both sides of his face
laughing.

As soon as I had changed my clothes I rode in the most delightful
spring weather in the still empty Regent's Park, where hundreds of
almond trees are in blossom; I visited the menagerie which has been
lately established there and saw a tiger-cat, a creature which seemed
to me the perfect model of beauty and elegance among quadrupeds.

I afterwards went to a great dinner at the Marquis of
Thomond's, an Irish peer, where I met one of the most conspicuous
Tories, the Duke of Northumberland. I must confess that he does
not look much like a genius, and the whole party was so stiffly
English that I was very glad to be seated next to Princess Polignac,
whose lively good-natured prattle seemed to me, today, as agreeable
as if it had been the most intellectual conversation in the world. I
concluded the evening with a ball at the Marquis of Beresford's
in honour of the Marchioness of Louly, sister of Don Miguel.
She seemed, however, not a little bored and, as she speaks only
Portuguese, could scarcely converse with anybody but the host.]

April 1st

Schnucke! It's all over, I am married. I have an income of £200,000
and two children!

Are you taken in? Alas, I can only give you good news on the First of April.

[—*Park, April 9th*

I came here yesterday, and am with a large party at the house of a very fashionable lady. The house is tastefully and richly adorned, but too stately and pretentious for me. Besides, there is a certain Luttrell[1] here, an apparent wit whose every word the good-natured company holds itself bound to admire; people affect a great liking for him for fear of his evil tongue. I abhore such intellectual bullies; especially when, as in this case, they unite all the gall and acrimony of satire without any of its grace. They appear in human society like poisonous insects, whom in our weakness we assist in feeding on the blood of others so that they do not suck our own.

Country life here is in some respects too social for my tastes. If, for instance, you want to read, you go to the library where you are seldom alone; if you have letters to write, you sit at a great common writing table, and they are then put in a box with holes and taken to the post by a servant. To do all this in your own room is not usual, and therefore surprises and annoys people. Despite freedom from all our useless ceremonies and complimenting there is still a considerable degree of restraint, which the continual necessity of speaking in a foreign language makes more oppressive.]

April 12th

At midday I was again invited to the country house of the Duchess of St Albans where a pleasant surprise awaited me. When I came in late, they put me between the hostess and a tall, friendly-looking man, already stricken in years, who spoke in a broad, somewhat disagreeable Scottish dialect and would probably not have seemed to me very striking had I not been told, after a few minutes, that I was sitting beside the Great Unknown. It was not long before a number of sharp, dry witticisms dropped from his lips, as well as

---

[1] The natural son of the Earl of Carhampton, Henry Luttrell was a wit and a fashionable diner-out, and his verses won praise from Byron and Thomas Moore.

several unassuming anecdotes, which without being particularly brilliant were always striking. His eyes sparkled when he became animated in such a bright and friendly way, and expressed so much sincere kindness and naturalness, that anyone would have been attracted to him.

Towards the end of the meal he and Sir Francis Burdett exchanged ghost stories, half shivery, half humorous, which emboldened me to tell your famous key story. It was a great success, and it would be funny if you recognized it in the next novel of the fertile Scot. A little concert closed the evening, in which the really pretty daughter of the great bard, a sturdy-looking Highland beauty, took part, and Miss Stephens[1] sang nothing but Scottish ballads. It was not till late that I reached London, my *aide-mémoire* enriched with an extremely lifelike sketch of Sir W. Scott which I owe to the kindness of my hostess. Since none of the engravings I have seen resemble him, I shall enclose an exact copy in this letter.

April 18th

My body went this evening to a ball at Lady Burroughs' but my soul was with you and in Muskau.

A thousand thanks for the splendid boots. I wore them like a rich pasha with a hundred wives, and not like a poor Christian dog who is uselessly tiring himself out trying to find even one suited to his mind and his needs.

April 21st

Ah, Schnucke of my heart, what a sad letter I received from you of the 19th when I woke up! You have been sick and, moreover, what a sad birthday for you. It is the greatest part of my torment to have nothing, you poor soul, with which to cheer you.

April 23rd, 3 o'clock at night

Coming home from dinner and Almack's, I found the case with your picture had arrived at last. It made me so sad that I almost wept.

---

[1] Operatic singer who married the Earl of Essex in 1838.

Explain this feeling for yourself. As I look at it, I do not find in it the likeness of what I love. It is like, but like you when you are conversing with someone you are meeting for the first time who does not interest you; but of your good-humoured, lovable manner when you look at your Lou there is not a trace.

April 24th

Good morning, Schnucke – *mais décidément votre portrait a deux expressions*. Looked at from above it is cold and, as you say, reserved. However, from below it has your expression when you are with me in the company of others, and to look at it gives me great pleasure – although, as I have already said, there is nothing to be seen of your expression when you are alone with me. Ah, Schnucke, Schnucke, where have our breakfasts in the green room gone, and our dinners under the lime trees? Above all, where is my original Schnucke? And what is a picture compared with her? It is strange, but on the whole this picture gives much more pain and sadness than joy. My good dear soul, I sometimes long so dreadfully for you that it makes my heart race, and the thought of losing you is the only thing in the world that I really dread. I followed your advice, yet my sadness was doubled by the thought that all the misery you were suffering with me was bearing you down to an early grave. So remain firm, my Schnucke, and full of love for your poorest Lou.

April 27th

The trouble with these last few days has been their monotony; only a dinner at the Spanish ambassador's reviving in me a pleasant memory, where a Spanish girl full of fire and beauty danced boleros after dinner and awakened in me a taste for this entirely different music. If I may judge from the *fandango*, Spanish society must be very different from ours.

Yesterday I was invited 'to meet the Dukes of Sussex and Clarence', but as it turned out, met instead Mademoiselle Henrietta Sontag[1] whom I had not yet seen, and at whose feet here lie the great

---

[1] Catalini said of this bewitching singer: *'Elle est unique dans son genre, mais son genre est petit'*.

and small. She is indeed a most lovable, charming creature and everyone finds her seductive. You couldn't find a more innocent and yet more effective coquetry – so childish, so lovely – *et cependant le diable n'y perd rien.*

She very quickly found my weak side, and entertained me without the least apparent *arrière-pensée*, but only with those things which were suitable and pleasant for me to hear. Moreover, my native tones fell from her pretty mouth like pearls and diamonds into the stream of conversation, and she seemed to use the most beautiful blue eyes in the world like a spring sun lightly veiled in a transparent cloud. 'Tomorrow Kean is playing Richard III,' said she casually, at length. 'The Duke of Devonshire has lent me his box, would you care to accompany me?' I need not say that such an invitation took precedence over all others.

April 28th

Never have I seen or heard less of a performance than I did today, and yet I must confess that none has seemed shorter to me. And I must also confess that in spite of the presence of a duenna and a visit from Mr Kemble in the intermission, there was hardly a pause in our conversation to which so many reminiscences of home gave constant new interest.

Moreover, the pleasant excitement lingered with me during the subsequent ball at the fashionable Lady Tankerville's, for I felt much less *ennuyé* by that fashionable fête than usual. Excuse me if I write only these few words today, but Helios is coming up and I am going to bed.

[*May 2nd*

Yesterday the wedding of the Duchess of St Albans[1] was celebrated with a very pleasant rural fête at her country house. In the middle of the bowling green there was a maypole decorated with garlands and ribbons, and gaily dressed peasants in old-style English costume

---

[1] The Duchess of St Albans' first husband, the banker Thomas Coutts, had died in 1822.

danced around it. The company wandered about the house and garden as they liked; many shot with bows and arrows; others danced in tents or played all sorts of games till, at five o'clock, a few blasts on a trumpet announced a splendid breakfast, at which all the delicacies that luxury could furnish were served in the greatest profusion.

Garlands of fresh flowers hung from all the bushes, producing an indescribably rich effect. The day, too, was singularly fine so that I was able, for the first time, to see London quite clear of fog and only slightly obscured by smoke.

As night drew on, the effect of the garlands was enhanced by many coloured lamps, tastefully distributed among the trees and thick shrubs. It was past midnight when breakfast ended. There was a concert and a ball at which the lovely German waltzer outshone her rivals – and with the most innocent air, as if she did not see one of her conquests. Perhaps there never was a woman who had so perfected the art of appearing childlike; certainly this captivating sort of coquetry is women's greatest charm, though not their greatest merit.

May 8th

For a week past two or three concerts have resounded in my ears every evening, or, as they more properly say here, every night. They are all of a sudden become the rage, from the highest and most exclusive down to the herd of 'nobodies'. Mesdames Pasta, Sontag etc. sing over and over again the same airs and duets, which people never seem to tire of hearing. They often sing very negligently – doubtless tired themselves of the monotony of it all – but that makes no difference whatever. The ears that hear them are seldom very musical, and those in the middle of the crowd often cannot hear if the bass or prima donna is singing – but must fall into ecstasies like the rest, notwithstanding. For the performers this pastime is profitable enough. Sontag, for instance, receives at every party where she is heard at all forty, sometimes a hundred pounds, and occasionally she attends two or three in an evening. Pasta, whose singing is to my taste sweeter, grander and more tragic, rivals her. The concerts at Prince Leopold's are generally the most agreeable and the insufferable squash is somewhat avoided in his large rooms. This prince is less popular than he deserves; the English cannot forgive him for being a foreigner.]

May 10th

Kind Schnucke, I am suffering. For eight days I have not eaten as much as I would have eaten in one at Muskau. It is the result of many kinds of emotion. Ah, Schnucke, I think that if it were not for you I would not be here much longer. Money would not help; I felt that here very keenly once when I was close to getting it, and again when I contemplated the lives of those who have more than I could ever hope for. Love is all I need, the mother love of my Schnucke, as if I were your only beloved child. Do not leave me, Schnucke, otherwise I shall quickly sink to the bottom and the waves will break over me forever!

May 11th

It has gone so far – they know here in London that your picture is standing on my desk and Bülow recently said to me: 'Prince, this sentimentality is doing you more harm than you think.' At which I laughed and answered: 'Dear Bülow, Judas only betrayed his Lord for pieces of silver.' All this absolutely disgusts me and if we could only attain some strong and secure position, no matter how humble, I would willingly, from my heart and forever, give up the dreams of riches which perhaps are not to be realized without a devil of a marriage to some good, unpretentious child, to whom I owe nothing but who would owe everything to us and would love and honour us.

I have had another disappointing experience today, I must confess, which almost convinced me that in the prevailing circumstances there is no hope for a rich match. I have now only three prospects: one who is rich and well-bred, but at the same time extremely ugly and seems malicious and capricious. Moreover, it is very unlikely that I shall get her. The second is of common family, ugly, thirty years old I think, good-natured and has £30,000. The last is pretty, kind, stupid, very well-bred and so would be entirely desirable, but has only £10,000. A rich relation might, however, double this sum if she wished. Still, this is uncertain and would cost my life's freedom.

Would it not be better to remain as I am and let Fate decide?

May 12th

Your letter of the 2nd arrived today, and is indeed almost comfortless, but still confirms me in my intention under no circumstances to sacrifice me and my better self by entering into an engagement that is repellent to me. That you, my Schnucke, are so utterly devoted to me where my happiness and well-being are concerned, that I can rely on you with unshakeable certainty – that keeps me firm. So do not lose heart. Things will yet work out. I have never felt more than now that the joys money can give have something dead in them. There are only three things that are worth anything: love, friendship and war. This may sound strange but it is true; love makes everything easy and even has bliss in sorrow. Friendship softens and calms, but war brings all powers to their highest potential.

If you cannot help yourself in any other way, then sell the silver. It would be much better to send the two horses over here since, even after the cost of transporting them has been included, I shall certainly be able to get twice as much for them here as you in Muskau or Berlin. I shall think about what is best. Dear, dear Schnucke, forgive me that things are going so badly for you and keep your spirits up as much as you can.

June 6th

Spent alone and in a long ride in the vicinity. The world is beautiful enough for anyone who has the means to enjoy it! I rode for a while with Lady Ellenborough,[1] one of the prettiest women in England, who likes me quite well. But all this is of no use, and as for anything that can help, either I cannot attain it or cannot find anything to my liking.

[1] If Pückler had not been so distracted, he might have found in the beautiful, clever Lady Ellenborough a woman after his own heart. She was divorced from Ellenborough by Act of Parliament in 1830, due to her *liaison* with Prince von Schwarzenberg whom she followed to Paris in 1829. She later married the sheikh of a Bedouin tribe and lived in a camp near Damascus for many years. She died of dysentery whilst contemplating elopement with her dragoman.

June 9th

Today's ride was even longer than yesterday's. I ate in a village twenty miles from London, in splendid surroundings, saw two beautiful parks and only got home again at ten o'clock. I then had to make a rapid toilet as I was expected at the concert at Prince Leopold's where, with beating heart, I once more saw the lovely Henrietta whom I had carefully avoided for a long time.[1] She was pale and miserable; the ghastly strain of the eternal singing and the unfavourable climate have so pulled her down. I did not stay long but went to a *conversazione* at Lady Jersey's, where Count Redern gave me a letter from you with which I quickly hurried home.

June 11th

About your plan to go to Branitz, I do not know what I should say. When I marry, that is if I do, you must live at Muskau. I see no reason why we should not share the castle, but if that is not practicable, the offices could be made very pretty for you. Against this is the fact, which unfortunately cannot be denied, that you cannot live any longer in Muskau if I am to have any chance of getting an heiress. However, do not think of Branitz as a dwelling for more than a very short time. The main thing is to spread it abroad in Berlin and everywhere else that you, having got my affairs in order and on a more secure footing in my absence, are now leaving Muskau. This is enough for the world and, as soon as we no longer need this disgusting monster, we will do what we wish.

I myself am not going back to Muskau where I can play only a mediocre role or no role at all. As soon as I have wound up a few affairs which still offer hope, let us meet somewhere and strengthen ourselves with a little life together for the next stage of the future. If

[1] Pückler's brief *liaison* with Henrietta Sontag came to an abrupt end when he discovered that she was secretly engaged, perhaps even already married to Count Rossi. This episode provided further fuel to the campaign led by Lord Clanwilliam and the Duke of Cumberland to which Pückler alluded in his letter of May 11th: the spreading of damaging rumours about his character, private life and 'scandalous' divorce, which certainly contributed to his decision to leave London.

it is necessary I shall for a time willingly and from my heart surrender everything which requires expense and live just as well and pleasantly with the bare necessities, but still seize the first opportunity to embark again on the plan – which in the end is the only one which can help – that of the rich wife. Otherwise, I do not see how we can manage in the entirely unfavourable position in which we find ourselves; and considering your and my characters, which is always a principal factor in these matters, it would be absolutely foolish to say that you must do this or that if you are so made that you cannot do it. Will and faith may be able to accomplish anything, but it is a complete error to think that a person can give himself one or the other if he does not possess it. The genius who as a child painted all the walls, will never become a mechanic when he grows up even if his parents and everyone about him wish to make him one.

June 18th

I repeat that, if the goal is to be attained, the world must believe that our interests are now separated or no other woman will bring herself to marry me. Since, however, it is impossible that two other people could be as sure of each other as we, what we seem to be doing is a matter of total indifference to us; I could marry fifty women and fall in love with fifty – Schnucke would calmly keep her place over and beside them. Neither absence nor the strongest passion in love have been able to alter this one iota – and to live in peace and joy with you in Muskau, which is still for me the palace the knights in the fairytales seek, remains the goal of all my dearest castles in the air; and strangely enough, despite all the weakness of my hopes, it is as if an inner voice were calling: 'It will come true.' How? God alone knows that.

[June 25th

I have now so disposed of my affairs that I shall be able to leave England in a month at the latest to make a longer tour of Wales and, especially, Ireland, which excites my interest even more than Scotland. I am sorry that illness first and then the distractions of the metropolis robbed me of a sight of that country. It is an omission I must enter in my book of sins which – alas! – contains so many under the same heading of Indolence.]

Your Lou

TWENTY-SECOND LETTER

Cheltenham, July 12th, 1828

My dear,

At two in the morning I left London, this time really sick and in a bad mood – in harmony with the weather, which entirely *à l'anglaise* raged like a storm at sea and poured as if from a big jug. However, the heavens cleared at about eight o'clock and I got a little sleep, lulled by the soft rolling of the carriage. Refreshed by the rain, everything shone emerald green and a lovely scent from the meadows and the flowers blew in through the carriage windows. Then was your care-oppressed, peevish friend once more an innocent child, rejoicing in God and the beautiful world. Travelling in England is, indeed, extremely enjoyable – if I could only see your joy in it my own would be redoubled in your company. To travel here with you, without cares and unfettered by business, would be the sweetest of pleasures for me – I must really love you deeply, my darling, for if things are going badly with me I always find consolation in the fact that you, at least, are being spared the moment; yet, at the same time, if I see something that delights me I always feel as a reproach the pain of enjoying it without you.

What with us is called prosperity is here looked upon as mere sufficiency, and this extends through all classes. Down to the smallest detail, there exists a striving for adornment, a careful elegance and cleanliness; in a word: a striving towards the beautiful and the useful which, as yet, is entirely unknown in our lower classes.

July 13th

The weather is now unhappily disagreeable, cold and stormy, after what was for England a long heatwave. However it is not too bad

193

for travelling, and so I feel myself far more cheerful than in London. I am looking forward to the beautiful country in Wales, towards which I am journeying. So at least be with me in thought, and let our spirits glide hand in hand over land and sea, looking down from the mountains together and enjoying the silent intimacy of the valleys; for certainly spirits enjoy the beauty of God's magnificent Nature through all the world in forms as infinitely different as infinity itself is boundless.

I lead you first to the seven springs of the Thames, which rise an hour's drive away from Cheltenham. I had undertaken this excursion in a fly (a little sort of landau, drawn by a single horse), on whose covering I sat so as to enjoy the beautiful prospects from a higher viewpoint. After a long climb across a lonely mountain meadow, you finally see among a few alders a swampy group of little springs which, as far as the eye can follow them, trickle out as an unimportant little brook. This is the modest beginning of the proud Thames. I was entirely seized by a poetic mood, as I thought to myself that, only a few hours before and only a few miles away, I had seen the same water covered with a thousand ships; that the same glorious stream probably carries on its back more ships, more treasure and more men throughout the year than any of its colossal brothers; that the capital of the world lies on its banks and from them its all powerful trade rules the four corners of the world! With respectful admiration I gazed at the splashing pearls of water and compared them with Napoleon who, born incognito in Ajaccio, made all the thrones of the earth quake; I then thought of the avalanche, which launches itself under the claw of a starling and five minutes later buries a village – and of Rothschild, whose father sold ribbons, and without whom no power in Europe today seems able to make war.

Since there is little society for me and little new acquaintance, I left Cheltenham early in the morning. The country remains utterly lovely, full of meadowlands and deep green groups of trees, with ever clearer views of the mountains bounding the horizon. At almost every stage there is a considerable town, which is never without its towering Gothic church. The situation of the town of Tewkesbury is especially charming. Nothing could be more peaceful, more idyllic, and yet all these blossoming meadows were bloody battlefields at the time of the English Civil War, from which they also derive their names – grown so unsuitable in the course of the centuries – the Slaughters, Mordiford, Boneacre and so on.

Worcester, the capital of the county, affords nothing very remarkable apart from its magnificent cathedral.

Llangollen, July 15th

I travelled all through the night. The most beautiful effect awaited me this morning in Wales. The clouds seemed to herald the splendour of the valley of Llangollen, a locality which, to my mind, far surpasses all the beauties of the Rhineland and moreover displays a complete originality in the peaks and steep precipices of its mountains. A rushing river, the Dee, winds in a thousand fantastic bends through the meadowland, shadowed by the thickest woods. Steep mountains rise on both sides, now covered with ancient ruins, now with modern country houses, occasionally with manufacturing villages whose towering chimneys belch forth thick smoke, and sometimes with grotesque, lonely groups of rocks. The vegetation is rich, and mountain and valley are full of tall trees whose manifold shades of colour add infinitely to the grace and picturesqueness of the landscape. In the midst of this luxuriant Nature there rises a single long, black, bald mountain wall, covered only with thick, dark heather, which stretches for a considerable distance beside the road.

This splendid road, from London to Holyhead (200 miles), is as smooth as parquet, and here follows all the bends and turns of the chain of mountains so that at almost every minute the view completely changes. Without moving from your seat you can overlook the valley, now in front of you, now beside you, now behind you. At one place an aqueduct, of twenty-five slender arches – a work which would have done honour to the Romans – runs down the middle of the valley and over the Dee, making a second river 120 feet above the other. The mountain village of Llangollen contains only one delightful stopping place, and is rightly much visited because of its lovely surroundings. Half an hour ago, I climbed upon a gravestone in the churchyard beside the guest house, and, with heartfelt piety, happily enjoyed the beautiful view.

Permit me now to move from the romantic to the perhaps less exalted but still by no means despicable, and to turn myself *inwards*, that is to the room where my appetite, uncommonly increased by the mountain air, saw with no little pleasure upon a beautiful, flowered, Irish damask cloth: steaming coffee, fresh guinea fowl eggs, dark yellow mountain butter, thick cream, toast, muffins, and finally two freshly caught trout with charming rosy spots – a breakfast than which that great painter of human necessities, Walter Scott, could not have placed a better before his heroes in *Highlands*.

Bangor, evening

The rain which has accompanied me constantly from London today remained faithful, but the weather seemed to wish to improve. The variety of the landscape is extraordinary: sometimes you are ringed about with a jumble of mountains of all forms; then, gazing out over the land, you think that you are back on the plain again, until you are confined anew in a dark, narrow woodland path. Further on the river calmly drives a peaceful mill, and immediately afterwards foams down over blocks of stone and forms a splendid waterfall at the bottom – beyond that, after you have travelled for half an hour over an almost insignificant plain, you find yourself suddenly, not far from the *Cernioge mawr* Inn, at the holy of holies – an incredible view!

Gigantic black rocks constitute the noblest of amphitheatres, and their torn and jagged peaks seem to swim among the clouds. Under a rocky wall the river itself goes its arduous way, dashing down from precipice to precipice and dropping some eight hundred feet. Before us lay a seemingly endless perspective of mountains, winding one over the other. I was so entranced that I had to relieve myself by actually shouting aloud. By the way, I cannot sufficiently praise this splendid road which, never rising or sinking steeply, allows one to contemplate all the *belles horreurs* of this mountain world at such leisure. Where not guarded by rocks, it is completely shut in by low walls, in whose niches the stones for road repairs are piled up, which looks much neater than the haphazard heaps of stones on our high roads.

The mountain country of Wales has a very individual character which I find hard to compare with anything else. Its height is about that of the Riesengebirge, but it appears infinitely more grandiose and is far richer in mountain peaks. Also, the vegetation is manifold in its types of plant, though not so numerous in trees, and it has rivers and lakes which are entirely missing in the Riesengebirge. It may lack the latter's majestic, enclosed woods, but the higher region, from Capel Curig to within a few miles of Bangor, is as wild and precipitous as one could wish. Broad stretches of red and yellow blooming heather, as well as ferns and other plants which in our harsher climate do not thrive, grow in the cracks in the rocks and compensate for the trees, which do not grow at this height. The greatest variety in this picture, however, is provided by the wild, strange, colossal forms of the mountains themselves. Some look more like clouds than solid masses. The peak of Tryfan is covered with such strangely formed basalt columns that all travellers are convinced that they can see people up there, who have just climbed the mountain and are now gazing at the wide view – whereas they are in fact only the mountain spirits that Merlin banished thither in former ages.

I found it very tasteful that all the houses on the high road are kept in the character of the district, built of rough, reddish, quarry stone, roofed with slate, of a simple, heavy architectural form and provided with iron gates whose grilles imitate the crossing rays of two suns. The post boy showed me the remains of an old Druid castle to which, as I verified in my book, Caractacus betook himself after his defeat near Caer Caradoc. The Welsh language sounds rather like the cawing of crows. Almost all names begin with C, which is pronounced with a croak which a foreign throat cannot imitate. This ruin is now transformed into two or three inhabited huts, and their site is not even indicated. Further on there was a remarkable rock which resembled a bishop, with crozier and mitre, climbing out of a cave to preach Christianity to the astonished heathen. Why is it that, when Nature plays these games, it can make a noble impression, but when art imitates Nature, it always appears ridiculous?

July 16th

I have had a splendid sleep, and am now sitting in the guest house by the sea, quite rested from my journey, and enjoying the ships which are sailing on all sides through a clear flood. On the land side, a castle of black marble looms above a wood of ancient oaks. I shall begin my excursion with this castle and here, where I am very well lodged, I shall set up my headquarters.

Caernarvon, July 20th

After I had given the packet for you to Mr S., and most carefully recommended it, I left Bangor for the time being as quickly as four post horses could carry me. On the way I inspected several iron foundries, which I shall pass over since I saw nothing noteworthy in them. I began to feel somewhat unwell as I arrived at the inn in Caernarvon, where an extremely pretty girl with long black hair, the daughter of the landlord who was absent, very gracefully did the *honneurs*.

The next morning, at nine o'clock, I set out in fairly promising weather on a charabanc, drawn by two native horses and driven by a little boy who did not understand a word of English. We raced madly *en train de chasse* over the narrow hill paths of the region. All my cries were in vain, and seemed to be understood by him entirely in the opposite sense, so that we covered the nine miles to the lake of Llanberis, over stick and stone, in less than half an hour. Even now, I can hardly understand how the carriage and horse held out. At the fishermen's huts, which lie scattered and lonely in these parts, a softer form of conveyance awaited me, that is, a neat boat in which I embarked with two sturdy mountaineers. Snowdon now lay before us, but had unfortunately, as the local people say, pulled his nightcap over his head, whilst the lower mountains around him were bathed in brightest sunshine. The mountain is only four thousand feet high, but looks much more because its whole height rises with no foothills from the lake shore, whilst other mountains in these ranges generally lift their peaks from an already elevated base.

The crossing to the little guest house at the foot of Snowdon is three miles long and, since the wind blew strongly, we made very slow and uneven progress. The lake water is as black as ink, the mountains bald and studded with stones alternating with green alpine creepers. Here and there you see a few stunted trees, but the whole is wild and gloomy. Not far from the little church of Llanberis is the so-called Holy Well, inhabited by a single gigantic trout which has been shown to visitors for centuries. The trout does not often allow itself to be coaxed out and it is taken as a lucky sign if you catch a glimpse of it. As a foil to all oracles, I left it unvisited.

At the inn I quickly provided myself with a guide and a pony and hastened to be on my way, hoping all the time that the threatening clouds would break after midday. Unfortunately, however, the opposite happened – it became darker and darker, and before I had been half an hour upon my pony, which the guide was leading by the bridle, a dark mantle had enveloped mountains, valleys and ourselves, and heavy rain was streaming down on us against which my umbrella did not long protect me. We fled finally into the ruins of an old castle where I wearily climbed a ruined spiral staircase. I reached the remains of a balcony and found a good shelter under branches of ivy. But everything about me looked melancholy. The crumbling walls, through which the wind wailed, the monotonous fall of the rain and disappointed hope all made me quite sad; nothing, I thought, sighing, not even the smallest thing fell out as I wished but rather assumed the aspect of the unseasonable and the eccentric, so that what others could accomplish in sunshine, I must muddle through in rain and storm.

Impatiently I left the old walls and steered once more for the mountain. But the weather was now so frightening and the rising storm so dangerous, that we again had to seek shelter in a miserable ruined hut. The guide earnestly advised me to turn back, which was without doubt the most sensible thing to do, especially as we had not covered a third of our journey. But since I had earlier sworn to myself to drink your health, dear Lucie, on the summit of Snowdon, in champagne which I had for this purpose brought from Caernarvon, it seemed to me an evil omen to give up. So with the cheerfulness engendered of a firm determination in large and small matters, I said laughingly to the guide: 'If it were raining stones instead of water, I would not turn back until I had seen the peak of Snowdon,' and with that mounted my pony.

The path had become extremely difficult, since it now led over loose, smooth stones washed down by the rain, or extremely slippery grass. I admired how my doughty little animal kept going, shod only with smooth English shoes without studs.

In the meantime, it had become so cuttingly cold that I was wet through and could no longer go on riding. Since I have done so little climbing of late fatigue almost overmastered me, but I kept listening to the maa-maa of the mountain lambs plaintively ringing out. They graze here by the hundred on the meagre patches of grass. I never stopped thinking of the dear lamb at home, and strode on sturdily until I had completely recovered and begun to feel fresher than when I set out. I did not bother about views, since everything was entirely enveloped in cloud and I could hardly see twenty paces in front of me. In this secret *clair obscur* I finally reached the longed-for summit, which you come to over a narrow ridge of rock. A heap of stones, in the midst of which stands a wooden column, is erected as a landmark. I scratched my name beside a thousand others on a large stone, and then seized the cow horn which the innkeeper had given me as a drinking vessel and ordered my guide to uncork the champagne. It must have contained uncommonly bubbly air, for the cork flew up higher than the column under which we stood. Without borrowing anything from Münchhausen,[1] you can with a clear conscience declare that when I drank your health, on July 17th, the champagne cork flew almost 4,000 feet above sea level. As the cow horn was filled to overflowing, I shouted with stentorian voice into the darkness: 'Long live Lucie, with nine times nine,' according to the English custom. Then I emptied the glass three times and being truly thirsty and exhausted, as I had reason to be, champagne has never in my life tasted better.

And look! a charming lamb came climbing towards us through the veil of cloud, the mist parted and before us lay the golden earth in twinkling sunshine, yet all too soon the curtain closed again – a picture of my fate! The beautiful and desirable appear only by flashes, like will- o'-the-wisps before me – as soon as I seek to seize them, they vanish like a dream.

Since there was no further hope that the weather would clear today in the highest regions, we set out on our homeward way. I found myself so strengthened that I not only felt no more fatigue but even rediscovered a sensation I had not known for many years: that walking and running, instead of being a bore, gives an elastic pleasure. A picture of my former youth, I leapt so quickly down the rocks and wet slopes of rushes that I covered in a few minutes a part of the way that would earlier have taken me half an hour. I finally came out of the surrounding clouds once more and, even if the view

---

[1] Famous German teller of tall stories.

was less splendid than it had been on the summit, it still provided great enjoyment. Three and a half thousand feet below, the sea stretched boundlessly before me. In its bosom I could see the island of Anglesey, as in a relief, and in the nearby mountain gorges I counted twenty little lakes, many dark, many shining so brightly in the sun that the eye could hardly endure their mirror brilliance. In the meantime the guide too had climbed down; as I could judge the terrain quite well now for myself and still felt no fatigue, I dismissed him and his intelligent little pony to wander home by myself. The evening was beautiful and I decided to seek out the loveliest spots *et bien m'en prit* – because since Switzerland, I can remember no more charming walk.

I then decided to get down in the straightest possible line to the hut, where I had earlier tarried for an instant. Not far from it a girl was milking her cow, whose fresh milk was very welcome to me. There too I again met my guide. I was thankful to make use of him once more and do the rest of the way wrapped in my cloak, in much needed comfort on the back of my sure-footed pony. After I had changed my clothes at the inn, a precaution you should not neglect when travelling in the mountains, I embarked once more on the lake, magnificent now in the evening's red glow. The air had grown mild and warm, fish were jumping merrily and herons flying in delightful swoops round the reed beds, whilst here and there a fire in the mountains flickered up and the dull thunder of dynamited rocks from the distant quarries rolled over all.

The sickle of the moon had long been standing in the dark heaven when my black-haired Hebe once more welcomed me in Caernarvon.

Bangor, July 22nd

Bangor is a bathing resort too, that is everyone is free to dive at will into the sea. The artificial arrangement is, however, confined to the privately owned tubs of an old woman, who dwells by the shore in a miserable hut and, if an appointment has been made an hour in advance, warms sea water in pots on her hearth; at the bath itself she herself, *sans façon*, undresses the visitor, dries him off and, if he had not brought a servant for this purpose, dresses him again. After I had taken such a bath, *pour la rareté du fait*, I rented a little boat and had myself rowed over the narrow arm of the sea which separates Anglesey and Wales, to Beaumaris. *Sur cela n'ayant plus rien à dire*, I close my report and wish you, my dear Lucie, all the happiness and blessing you deserve, *et c'est beaucoup dire*.

Always your faithful Lou

TWENTY-THIRD LETTER

August 1st, 1828

This morning I received from you letters which made me sad! Indeed you are quite right – it was a hard trial of Fate's to disturb the most cheerful and peaceful happiness, the most complete understanding and, of all the minds in the world, to tear apart the two best suited to each other – just as the storm whips up the peaceful sea, condemning one to restless wandering and the other to comfortless solitude and both to sorrow, care, pain and longing!

But what if the storm was an unavoidable necessity for the sea dwellers, what if ever-peaceful air was harmful to them? Let us not then grieve overmuch; let us not regret the past, but rather struggle forward towards the better, and not lose each other even if the worst does befall! How often, too, are imaginary evils the hardest to bear. What burning pain is caused by injured vanity, and what shameful ideas of false honour! But I am no less guilty, and indeed would often almost wish for Falstaff's philosophy[1] on this score.

For all this, Nature has given me one precious gift which I would consider myself happy to be able to share with you. In almost every situation I find the good side rapidly and almost instinctively, and enjoy this with a freshness of feeling, with a childish Christmas joy in trifles, which will certainly never grow old in me. And in the long run, when did good not prevail over evil?

K. Park, August 4th

I am very well off in St Asaph. You live comfortably here, the society is likeable, and as everywhere in the country there is complete freedom. Yesterday I took a very pleasant ride of some twenty miles on a tireless horse of my host's, for distances disappear with good horses and roads.

---

[1] *Henry IV* (Part I, Act 5, scene i).

This morning, while everyone else was still asleep, I went walking in the park with the lovely little Fanny, the youngest daughter of the house, and she showed me her dairy and her aviary.

Instead of being dedicated to golden pheasants and exotic birds, the aviary was entirely of a domestic nature, exclusively given over to hens, geese, peacocks, doves and ducks. Yet because of its extraordinary cleanliness and efficiency, it offered a very pleasant spectacle. German housewives, hear and be amazed! Twice a day the dovecotes and broody houses are scrubbed out, and the straw beds of the hens were so dainty, the perches on which they roosted so smooth and bright, the duck ponds lined with ash laths such bright basins, the large grained barley and the cooked rice so appetizing that you would think you were in a birds' paradise. Also, the birds were all free for none had its wings clipped, and a little wood of high trees abutting immediately on their dwelling served them as a graceful pleasure ground. Most of them were rocking comfortably on their swaying tops as we arrived; but scarcely did they catch sight of little rosy Fanny, like a beneficent fairy with titbits in her apron, than they hurried down in noisy clouds and landed, pecking and strutting, at her feet. I felt myself idyllically soothed and drove home to allay the fires of my excitement before breakfast.

The afternoon saw me again on horseback. I sought for myself untrammelled ways in the wildest mountain regions inland, several times crossing the raging river without the benefit of a bridge, and often revelling in the most surprising and beautiful views. From time to time I met a country girl at her work, strikingly pretty in her unusual costume which displays the figure and the bosom very freely. Despite this they are as shy as fawns and virtuous as vestal virgins. Everything shows its mountain nature, as does my horse. Tireless as a machine of steel and iron, it gallops over the stones, up hill and down dale; jumps, with undisturbed calm, over the gates in the hedges and is soon excessively tired.

Today I finished up in a park where wooden statues, striped with white paint, contrasted strangely with the nobility of Nature. There was no one to be seen, except hundreds of rabbits sticking their heads out of the mountain slope, which was riddled with holes, or running wildly across the path. Best of all was a black pine wood surrounding a ring of brightly hued mallows, and everywhere reigned the same solitude.

Bangor, August 8th

I should have stayed a few weeks at K. Park, but you know my fickleness – monotony soon oppresses me, even if it is good – so I took leave of my pleasant friends, visited another estate where I had been invited for a few hours instead of days, saw a sunset from the ruins of Conway and arrived again at my headquarters, which I am now leaving forever.

Dublin, August 11th

No one can withstand an unfavourable sea voyage! For ten hours I was tossed about, sick to death. The heat, the disgusting smell of the boilers, above all the sickness – it was a frightful night, a true picture of human misery. On a longer sea voyage one finally recovers and many kinds of pleasure outweigh the deprivations, but short crossings, which only show the dark side, are my great antipathy. God be praised it is over, and I feel firm earth once more under me, although at times it seems to me that Ireland is swaying a little.

This kingdom is more like Germany than England. Here is none of England's almost over-refined industry and culture, nor, unhappily, her cleanliness. Houses and streets have a grubby appearance, although Dublin is adorned by a number of palaces and broad streets. The common people go about in rags, the people of the educated classes one meets lack English elegance; on the other hand the crowds of glittering uniforms, which one never sees in the streets of London, are reminiscent of the continent. Moreover, the surroundings of the town have none of the freshness I have become accustomed to; the earth is neglected, grass and trees more spindly. But the great features of the landscape – the bay, the far mountains of Wicklow, the foothills of Howth, the houses grouped like amphitheatres, the quays, the harbour – are beautiful. At least, that is my first impression. By the way, I find myself less comfortable in the best inn of the capital than in the little village of Bangor.

Since I had nothing else to do – for all the notable dwellings of this land are in the country – I inspected a number of *show places*. First the castle, where the viceroy resides when he is here; its miserable state apartments, with their rough boards, have little to offer that is attractive. More beautiful was a modern Gothic chapel the exterior of which exactly imitates the greatness of antiquity; within, it is adorned with splendid Italian stained glass and tastefully and richly adorned with wood-carving.

In the evening I visited the theatre, a very pretty house with a smaller and rougher audience than in London. The actors were not bad, but did not rise above mediocrity. Many uniforms mingled with ladies, almost filling all the lower boxes, which looked very elegant. The upper ranks of society, from what I hear, seldom visit the theatre.

Since I have now seen enough of the town, I began my rides today in the surrounding countryside, which reveals itself to be much more beautiful than I, arriving on the unfavourable side, could have imagined. A road offered me charming views, first over the gulf, cut through by a three-mile-long mole and closed by the lighthouses of Dublin and Howth, like two towers; then of the wooded hills of Wicklow, which rise like sugar loaves high above the others. Finally it led me through an avenue of ancient elms alongside the canal to Phoenix Park, the Prater of Dublin, which is in no way inferior to the Prater of Vienna either in beautiful grass tracts for riding, long alleys for driving or shady walks. On the whole I found the Park pretty empty, in contrast with the streets of the town through which I made my way home, which were considerably enlivened by wheeling and dealing. The grime, the poverty and the ragged garments of the common people often passed all belief. Yet they seemed good-humoured, and sometimes indulged on the open street in fits of cheerfulness bordering on madness. You can usually blame whisky for this; I saw a half-naked youth executing the national dance with the greatest energy on the market place for so long that, like a Mohammedan dervish, he was completely exhausted and at last fell unconscious among the cheers of the people.

A crowd of beggar boys also fills the streets, humming about like flies and unceasingly offering their services. They are the best brought-up and most cheerful street boys in the world. Anyone of them will run like a regular runner for many hours beside the horse, hold it when you dismount, take care of every commission, and be not only content but full of gratitude for the few pence he is given, and express it with Irish hyperbole. The Irish seem more patient than their neighbours, due to long slavery, but also somewhat oppressed. I was one of several witnesses when a young person, who had wrongly pasted up a theatrical notice, had his ears boxed and was ill-treated on the open street by the stage director without offering the least resistance. Any Englishman would have immediately engaged in reprisals.

August 15th

Although my chest is constantly painful and the doctor occasionally looks thoughtful, I still go out on most of my expeditions which are all that give me real pleasure. I feel much better with unadorned Nature than among men in their masks.

I had been gazing with longing for some time upon a mountain, about four or five miles distant, which displays on its peak three single standing rocks, for this reason called 'the Three Rocks'. The view from there had to be very beautiful – so I got up earlier than usual in order to be upon the summit at the right time. I frequently asked in the villages through which I passed about the best route, but could never get precise answers. Finally, I was assured, in a house which lay at the foot of the mountain, that you could only *walk* up but not ride. The first method, because of the condition of my chest, would not have been practicable; and since I had become acquainted with what impossibility means among these people, I took the direction pointed out to me quite comforted, knowing that I could entirely rely on my sturdy little mare, for Irish horses scramble over walls and rocks like cats. For a while I followed a fairly narrow footpath and, when this gave out, the dry bed of a mountain stream. For about three quarters of an hour, this led me upwards without any special difficulty. I now found myself on a great, bald plateau and saw the Three Rocks about a thousand paces away, stretching up their heads like witches' stones. The whole area looked like nothing but a wide, impassable bog. I probed very carefully, and soon found that eight or ten inches under the peat lay a pebbly bed which bore my weight.

After a little while I reached firm earth and stood on the highest point. There at last was the longed-for view – Ireland, laid out like a map before me. Dublin, like a smoking lime-kiln in the green plain (for the coal smoke prevents recognition of even one building), the bay with its lighthouses, the prominent foothills of Howth, and on the other side the mountains of Wicklow, stretching to the horizon – all were shining in the sun, so that I felt myself more than compensated for the little exertion.

The scene was further enlivened by a charming young woman, whom I discovered in these wastes engaged in the modest occupation of haymaking. The natural grace of Irish peasant women, who are often real beauties, is just as surprising as their costume or rather lack of costume; although it was very cold on these mountains, the sum of the young woman's clothing was a broad, very coarse, straw hat, and *literally* two or three folds of the roughest material, which a girdle held together under the breast. Her conversation, as with others I had met, was cheerful, bantering, even witty and entirely unconstrained; but a man would be much mistaken if, on this account, he thought she was flighty. On the contrary, this class in Ireland is almost entirely chaste and distinctly uninterested, so that if one or two sometimes stray from the path of virtue, it is seldom from the unnatural and base motive of self-interest.

After I had climbed down the mountain by another way, now leading my horse at its own pace, and reached a great country road, I passed on open park gate. As Ireland also resembles the continent in this respect, whereby the owner of such a property from king to country nobleman finds his own pleasure increased by the public's enjoyment, I rode in. However I soon gave up the inspection when I beheld two gigantic painted cut-outs of Capuchin monks, standing at the cross roads, each holding before him a great book on which was written in enormous letters: 'To the pheasantery', 'To the Abbey'. However, this bad taste is quite rare here.

Adieu, may Heaven give you cheer, and all the words of my letters echo true love back to you till death.

Your Lou

TWENTY-FOURTH LETTER

Dear and kind one,

The last few days have been passed by me in bed, in pain and fever, and only today can I answer your letters. The writing of the intelligent V has certainly flattered me, although the enthusiastic idea that my little effusions have influenced him exists only in his poet's soul. Do not long for my return before it is possible, and believe me; when a person is absent, he is desired, but when present, he is soon superfluous.

I rode out today for the first time to see the fair at Donnybrook, a few miles from Dublin, which is a kind of folk festival. Nothing, in fact, could be more national! The poverty, the dirt and the raging noise were just as entertaining as the gaiety and high spirits and cheap pleasures. I saw food and drink swallowed down with such gusto that I was forced to turn away quickly in order to conquer my disgust. Heat and dust, noise and stink made a longer stay almost unbearable. However, this did not trouble the natives. Many hundreds of tents had been set up, all ragged like most of the people, and hung with bright rags instead of flags. One even had a half-rotten dead cat set upon the top as a crest. Some of the lowest kind of buffoons were pushed among them on a rolling stage and, in worn-out tinsel clothes, danced and grimaced to the point of exhaustion. A third of the people lay or tumbled about drunk; others ate, screamed or fought. The women rode about, very often two or three to a single donkey, comfortably smoking cigars and encouraging their lovers. By far the most ridiculous sight was two beggars whose horse, which they rode saddleless and guided with a string, was so miserable that it should have been begging itself.

As I was leaving the market, a drunken pair of lovers overtook me. I rejoiced to see their behaviour. Both were as ugly as could be, but treated each other with great tenderness and affection. Nothing could be more gallant, and at the same time more worthy, than the lover's repeated precautions to save his fair one from falling, although he had not a little difficulty in keeping his own balance. From his gracious demonstrations and her merry laughter, I gathered that he was trying to entertain her properly and, notwithstanding her own exalted condition, her answers were made with a coquetry and confidence which, in a prettier woman, would certainly have appeared most attractive.

In the interests of truth, I must testify that there is no trace of English brutality to be detected in the demeanour of these Irish people; indeed they are more like the French, with just as much cheerfulness but more humour, which is the national characteristic helped by copious amounts of potheen (the best brandy, distilled in an unlawful fashion). I have myself to blame for the miserable picture I am placing before you, which is no more nearly related to Nature than are the thickly painted wax dolls of our salons.

B—m, September 14th

Yesterday I was a little hypochondriacal, and my soul was dull, *mais j'ai pris médecine, elle a operé*, and my soul is again cured. I am once more cheerful, and therefore much more a lover of mankind. Virtuous moreover, *faute d'occasion de pécher*, and gay in so far as I am laughing at myself, *faute de trouver quelque chose de plus ridicule.*

I have enlisted several farmers for my colonization plan; they are all eager to emigrate, but unfortunately have not a farthing with which to do it. It is not hard to persuade them that everything will be better than it is here. The most prosperous live in buildings which our farmers would think too bad for stables. I visited such a place and found it made of walls of boulders stopped with moss, and a roof of poles which was covered half with straw and half with turf. The floor was made of bare earth, and there was no ceiling under the aforesaid half-transparent roof. A chimney also seems an unnecessary luxury. The smoke went from the hearth on the floor out of the window holes, where it was hindered by no panes of glass. A low partition to the right cut off the sleeping quarters of the family, who all take their rest together; another, to the left, fenced in pig and cow. The hut stood in the middle of a field, without a garden or any kind of comfort, and was described by everyone as a splendid dwelling.

Glengariff, September 26th

Best Lucie, to write to you today is indeed an effort which deserves a reward, since I am excessively tired and have had to keep drinking coffee to stay awake.

At nine in the morning, I left Killarney in a cart of the worst construction, and followed the new highway which leads along the middle and upper lakes of the Bay of Kenmare. This road reveals more beauties than you find on the lakes themselves, since these have the great drawback of only offering a picturesque view on one side, the other being completely flat land. Eight miles from Killarney you reach the highest point of the road, where there is a solitary inn. Here you stand before the wide mountain gorge which harbours the greater part of the three lakes in its bosom, so that you can see them all at a single glance. From there on the road sinks again, through treeless but boldly formed mountains, down to the sea.

The famous O'Connell now resides about thirty miles from here, in the most deserted region of Ireland. Since I have long wished to get to know him, I sent a request with the necessary inquiries to him from here, and decided that while waiting for the answer to arrive, I would make an excursion to Glengariff Bay, whither I set out immediately after eating.

The road has entirely given out, from now on you can proceed only by mountain pony or on foot. Such a pony carried my luggage, the driver and I went alongside, and if either of us was tired the good pony had to carry him as well. The sun had set but the moon shone bright. The region was not without interest, but the path was dreadful, often leading through rocks and rushing streams without bridge or stepping stones. It grew difficult beyond all expectation after six to eight miles, when we had to climb an almost perpendicular mountain, treading only on loose, jagged rubble so that, at every instant, you slipped down half as far as you had just climbed up. It was almost worse on the other side, going down, especially when a mountain in front extinguished the moon. I was too fatigued to go further, and from then on rode the pony. This animal displayed real human intelligence. Going uphill he helped himself with his nose and his teeth, like a fifth leg, and going downhill he span himself out with the agility of a spider. If we came to a bog in which there were only a few odd rocks instead of regular stepping stones, he crept through it with the slowness of a sloth, always testing with his foot first to see whether the stone was able to bear him and his burden.

The whole scene was extremely strange. Single lights twinkled at the bottom of the valley, and a gentle wind stirred the tops of lofty oaks, ashes and birches, mingled with beautiful holly, whose deep red berries were visible even in the moonlight. The splendid bay shimmered, interwoven with the quivering rays of the moon, and I felt myself to be truly in Paradise when I reached her shore shortly afterwards, and found that I had arrived at the door of the friendliest of inns.

However cheerful this place might have seemed, in it there was still sorrow. Host and hostess, very polite people, came to meet me clad in deepest mourning. The wife's sister, she told me when I asked her, a lovely girl in Kerry, only eighteen years old and up till now the picture of health had, only yesterday, died from a brain fever, or more probably from the ignorance of the village doctor. In the eight-day sickness, the poor woman added, weeping, she had aged forty years, so that no one could recognize the body of the blooming girl nor those beautiful features which, such a short time ago, were the pride of her parents and the admiration of all the young men of the district. She reposes by my bedroom, dear Lucie, separated from me only by a wooden partition. Four steps from her stands the table on which I am writing to you. Such is the world! Life and death, joy and sorrow, hold out their hands to each other.

Your Lou

TWENTY-FIFTH LETTER

Derrinane Abbey, September 29th

Beloved friend,

Yesterday evening I sent off a messenger to Mr O'Connell, but having rashly paid him in advance, found him back at the inn soon afterwards with no answer and a broken collarbone. As soon as he had felt money in his pocket he had been unable to resist the whiskey, as a result of which he and his horse had fallen down a rock in the dark. He had, however, had the sensible inspiration to send a good friend on ahead and, when I woke up, I was happy to find a very polite invitation from the great agitator.

I have already said that I set out on my way at three o'clock; and although I had to ride for seven hours in heavy rain, with the wind in my face, and in this desert where not once was the shelter of a tree to be found and after the first half-hour not a thread of my clothing remained dry, yet I would not tear this very trying day from the book of my life for anything.

The start of my journey was difficult in every way. At first I could not get a horse. At last an old black carthorse appeared, which had been ordered for me, and a cat-like little animal which the guide rode. My toilet was also in disarray – one escaped galosh could not be found and the umbrella had been loosened from its ribs on Witches' Mountain. I replaced the first with a huge slipper of my host's, and tied the second together as well as I could. Then, holding it before me as a shield, my cloth cap covered with a piece of waxed linen on my head, I galloped off – not unlike Don Quixote, and moreover furnished with a real Sancho Panza – to new adventures.

Only a quarter-hour from the town the destructive gusts of wind brought the umbrella, once the ornament of New Bond Street and the bearer of so many hardships with me, to a lamentable end. All its ribs came loose and left only a torn piece of taffeta and a bundle of fishbones in my hand. I gave the remains to the guide, and thenceforth esteemed the weather without care, bearing that which could not be changed in the best of moods.

As long as we were in the neighbourhood of the Bay of Kenmare we rode as quickly as possible, for the path was quite passable. Soon, however, it became more difficult. The entrance to the rugged mountains was signalled by a picturesque bridge 100 feet high, called the Black Water Bridge. Here was a gorge planted with oaks, the last trees I saw from then on. I noticed that my portmanteau, which the guide had tied before him on his horse, was becoming wet through, and I therefore instructed the man to get a cover or mat from a neighbouring hut to spread over it. Later on I had occasion to rue this foresight, for apparently the whiskey also got hold of him there and I was only to see him again shortly before the end of the journey, although I often waited for him to catch up with me.

The path, which was gradually deteriorating, led for the most part beside the sea. All around me the storm was raging in splendour, now over the deserted moors, now through gorges and deep abysses or wild, chaotic tracts, where the rocks were piled so fantastically one upon another that one could only believe that it was here that the giants stormed Heaven. Here and there a petrified cloud formation presented figures like men and animals. Only rarely did I meet a ragged wanderer, and could not avoid thinking how easy it would be for someone to fall on me and rob me in such a place, without a single person knowing of it – for all my travelling money lay in the breast pocket of my overcoat, as I was travelling *omnia mea* with me, in the Grecian fashion. But far from any thought of robbery, the poor, good-natured people always greeted me respectfully, although my costume was less than impressive and in England would have proclaimed me no gentleman.

Many times I was in great uncertainty as to which of the almost invisible stepping stones I should alight upon, but each time I chose fortunately, always keeping as close as possible to the sea, never on the wrong path even if not always on the shortest. Meanwhile time was passing, and when, between long intervals, I met a human being and asked him: 'How far still to Mr O'Connell's?' he never failed to bless the purpose of this visit with: 'God bless your honour!' – but the number of miles seemed to increase rather than to decrease. I only understood this when I realized that I had missed a short cut of several miles, and so had suffered a needless loss of time.

Just as it began to grow dark, I reached a part of the coast which is beyond compare. The Quest for the Romantic would certainly be as unsuitable at this time as it was for Quixote himself, though I was quite pensive as I drove my tired horse at as good a pace as possible. It stumbled at every moment over the loose stones, and I finally brought it to a painful trot with great difficulty. My anxiety was increased when I remembered O'Connell's letter, in which he had written that the proper entrance to his property was to be found on the Killarney side, which carriages could only reach by water, but that the way from Kenmare was the most difficult, and I should therefore have engaged a more reliable guide if I were to avoid any mishap. Also there came back to me, as often happens when one is following a train of thought, a folk story of Croker's I had read recently in which it says: 'No country is better than the coast of Iveragh for drowning at sea or, if you prefer, breaking your neck on land'. I was still thinking of this when my horse suddenly shied and pulled round, with a leap I could scarcely credit from the old mare. I found myself in a narrow gorge; it was still light enough to see several paces before me and I could not understand the reason for this panic of my nag's. At last, it went forward reluctantly, but after a few paces I saw with astonishment that the fairly narrow path ended in the middle of the sea, and the bridle almost slipped from my hand as a foaming wave raced over me like a monster and splashed far up the narrow gully with its white foam. Good advice would have been invaluable here! Impassable cliffs stared at me from every side, before me roared the lake . . . only the way back was open to me.

I was at a loss as to what to decide. If I rode back, I could not count on coming across my guide again, and where then was I to pass the night? Apart from O'Connell's old rocky castle, which I could not find, I could not expect any sort of shelter for twenty miles; I was already feverish from wet and cold, my constitution certainly would not stand up to a bivouac on such a night – I had every reason to be disturbed. But all this reflection was of no use; I had to get back, that much was clear, and as quickly as possible.

My horse seemed to have come to the same conclusions for, as if endowed with new strength, it bore me away almost at a gallop. However, would you believe it, once more I was destined to be saved by a sable apparition. At that moment I saw a black form, like a vague shadow, glide across the path and lose itself among the rocks. My cries, my pleas, my promises were in vain – was it one of the smugglers who conduct their affairs on these coasts, or a superstitious peasant who took me, poor wretch, for a ghost? Anyway, he did not seem inclined to venture out, and I had almost despaired of the help I had hoped for when his head suddenly popped out of a split in the stone beside me. I soon succeeded in calming him, and he solved for me the riddle of the path which ended in the sea. It had been constructed only for low tide. 'At this time,' he said, 'the half-tide is already in, a quarter of an hour later it will be impossible to pass. I will try to lead you over it now, for a good tip, but we have not a moment to lose.' With these words he was, with one bound, on the horse behind me, and we rushed towards the sea which swelled higher at every moment. We had to force our way through the white waves and the rocks, which rose like ghosts in the dim twilight, and had the greatest difficulty with the horse. But the man knew the terrain in such detail that, although soaked in salt water up to the armpits, we reached the opposite shore safely.

Unfortunately here the terrified animal shied once more at a jutting cliff, and broke both bit and saddle girth clean in two. As the damage could not be repaired on the spot, apart from all my other difficulties, I now had the unpleasant prospect of riding the last six miles balancing on a loose saddle. The man had certainly given me excellent directions for the continuation of my journey, but it soon became so dark that you could no longer see any landmarks. The path seemed to lead across a wide moor and was, at first, quite level. After half an hour's bumpy trot, jamming my knees together as much as possible so as not to lose the saddle between my legs, I noticed that the path was again turning right into the higher mountains, for the climb was becoming ever steeper and more difficult to negotiate. Here I found a woman passing the night with her pigs or goats. The path divided into two arms, and I asked which I must take to get to Derrinane. 'Oh, both take you there,' she said, 'but the left is two miles shorter.' Naturally I took the left, but soon found to my chagrin that it was only passable for goats. I cursed the old witch and her deceptive information; in vain the horse exhausted itself scrambling through the blocks of stone and at last, half stumbling, half falling, threw saddle and me off altogether. It was impossible to hold the saddle on by myself, it kept slipping off, and I had to be content with laying it on my shoulders and leading the horse.

Until then I had kept myself in pretty good spirits, and even now the spirit was willing, but the flesh began to weaken. The man from the sea had said: 'Another six miles and you are there', and after I had ridden smartly for half an hour, I remembered that the woman I had questioned had said it was still six miles by the shortest way to Derrinane. I began to fear that this ghostly mountain castle could never be reached, and one goblin would only throw me to the others. Entirely useless, good for nothing, shuddering with both heat and cold, I had sat myself down on a stone when, like the consoling voice of an angel in the desert, a call from my guide rang out and soon after I heard the hoofbeat of his horse. He had taken an entirely different route through the inner mountains, avoiding the sea passage, and, fortunately, had learned from the woman which direction I had taken. In the precious feeling of renewed safety I forgot all abuse, loaded the rescuing angel with my saddle and wet cloak, handed over to him the naked horse and, seating myself on his, pressed forward as fast as possible.

We had another five miles to ride, the guide told me, through a mountain pass hemmed in by precipices. I can report nothing more of the rest of the journey. The darkness was so great that I could only follow the figure of the man before me, like a dim shadow, with the utmost difficulty. At last a bright shimmer of light broke through the dark, the path became smoother, the outline of hedges became visible, and in a few minutes we drew rein before an old building that stood upon the rocky shore, its friendly, golden lights streaming through the night. Eleven o'clock was just striking from the tower, and I confess that I began to be anxious about my dinner when the only living soul I saw was a man in a nightshirt at an upper window.

Soon, however, there was a bustle in the house, an elegant servant appeared with a silver candlestick and opened a side door for me. Inside, I saw with wonder a company of fifteen to twenty people sitting at a long table, at wine and dessert. A tall, handsome man of kindly appearance came towards me, excused himself that he had not expected me at so late an hour, regretted my journey in such terrible weather, presented me for the time being to his family, who constituted more than half the company, and then led me to my bedroom. This was the great O'Connell. A short toilet quickly restored me, while downstairs they were taking care of everything for me, and providing a much needed meal after such a journey.

As I came into the hall, I found the greater part of the company still assembled. They entertained me very well, and it would be ungrateful not to praise Mr O'Connell's old wine which in truth was splendid. After the ladies had left us he sat down beside me, and Ireland could not fail to be the subject of discussion. 'Have you seen many of its remarkable things yet?' he asked. 'Have you been to the North, to admire the Giant's Causeway?' 'Oh no,' I rejoined smiling, 'before I visit Ireland's Giant's Causeway, I wish to see Ireland's giants.' And thereupon I drank off a glass of his good claret, to him and his great cause. Daniel O'Connell is indeed no common man, though he is a man of the people. His power in Ireland is so great that, at this moment, he could single-handedly raise the banner of revolt from one end of the island to the other, if he were not much too clear-sighted, and much too sure of his success by far less dangerous means. By legal, openly publicized methods, cleverly using the moment and mood of the nation, he has created this power over the people which, without army or weapons, is yet like that of a king. Indeed in many respects it is actually greater – it is hard to imagine His Majesty King George IV keeping forty thousand of his loyal Irish subjects from drinking whiskey for three days, as O'Connell was able to do at the memorable election for Clare.[1]

The other day I had even more opportunity to observe O'Connell. In everything he surpasses my expectation. The outward man is charming and the expression of intelligent kindness in his countenance, joined with resolution and shrewdness, exceedingly winning. He has perhaps more suavity than true, magnanimous eloquence, and you often notice too much premeditation in his speeches, but apart from that you cannot help but follow the strength of his arguments with interest, and often laugh at his wit. Certain it is that he looks far more like a general of Napoleon's regime than a Dublin lawyer. This resemblance is the more striking because he speaks French excellently, for he was educated at the Jesuit colleges of Douai and St Omer. His family is old and was once

---

[1] Daniel O'Connell's election as MP for County Clare in 1828 was a major factor in the campaign for Catholic Emancipation; as a Catholic he was debarred from taking his seat, which sparked off a great clamour in Ireland.

apparently very important in the land. His friends even maintain that he is descended from the former kings of Kerry, and this undoubtedly increases his standing with the people. He himself told me, not entirely without pretension, that one of his forefathers was Count O'Connell and Cordon Rouge in France, another a baron in Austria, a general and Imperial Chamberlain, but that he was head of the family.

As far as I could see, he is regarded by his colleagues with almost religious veneration. He is now about fifty years old and very youthful, although he wears a blond wig. Moreover, he has lived through a pretty turbulent youth. Among other things, a duel fought ten years ago made him fairly famous. As his talents were becoming dangerous to them, the Protestants set up against him a certain Desterre, a swordsman and bully by profession, who rode through all the lanes of Dublin with a hunting crop in order, as he said, to lay it once across the shoulders of the King of Kerry. The natural consequence was a meeting the next morning, at which O'Connell sent his bullet into Desterre's heart, whilst the latter's shot only made a hole in his hat. This was his first victory over the Orangemen, from which followed so much that was important and, we hope, more will come.

His ambition seems to me boundless, and if he should put through the Emancipation Bill, which I do not doubt that he will,[1] his career, far from being over, will then begin in earnest. Apparently the evil in Ireland and her rule by Great Britain lie too deep to be rooted out thoroughly by the Emancipation of the Catholics – but this would take me too far from my purpose. Coming back to O'Connell, I must also remark that nature has endowed him with that gift, so splendid in a party leader, of a great voice, together with good lungs and a strong constitution. His understanding is sharp and quick and his knowledge, even outside his profession, not inconsiderable. Moreover as I have already said, he has popular and winning manners, although something of the actor may be seen in

---

[1] And Pückler was right. The Catholic Relief Act of 1829 removed most of the civil disabilities against Catholics; but Wellington's government surrendered only reluctantly to the popular demand for this bill, and tried to limit its effects by disenfranchising the '40-shilling freeholders' of Ireland – the very people who had voted for O'Connell – and by refusing to let O'Connell take his seat on the grounds that he had been elected before the Act was passed. He therefore stood again in County Clare, and won.

them along with a little of what the English call 'vulgarity'; but when was there ever a picture quite without shadows?

Since O'Connell was busy, I made a morning promenade with the friar to an uninhabited island, striding dry shod over the smooth sea sands emptied by the ebb tide. Here stand the very ruins of the old abbey of Derrinane. These will one day be restored by the family, presumably when certain hopes are fulfilled. When we came back we found O'Connell, like a chieftain, on the castle terrace, surrounded by his vassals and other local groups, who were receiving instructions or to whom he was laying down the law; since he is a jurist and advocate this comes easily to him. No one, moreover, would dare to appeal against his judgements – O'Connell and the Pope are here alike infallible. There are never lawsuits in his domain and this extends, I believe, not only over his own tenants but over the whole district.

Kenmare, September 30th

Although I was invited with real Irish hospitality to stay another week for a great feast which was being prepared, and to which many guests were invited, I believed that this should not be taken entirely *à la lettre*, and also longed too sorely for Glengariff to remain longer than was necessary for my purpose. I therefore took leave of the family this morning with sincere thanks for their kind reception. O'Connell accompanied me to the boundary of his domain, riding a beautiful, big grey on which he looked even more military than in his house. Although quite devoid of vegetation, the rough path still offered many noble views, partly over the rocks inland, partly over the sea full of reefs and islands, several of which, quite isolated, rose like high, pointed mountains out of the water.

Mr O'Connell bade me remark one of these islands and told me that, several years before, he had shipped an ox over there and set it loose, so that it might feed on the good and untouched meadows undisturbed. However after several days this animal took such thorough possession of the island that it raged at anyone who attempted to land there, and attacked and chased off the fishermen trying to spread their nets on the shore. It was often to be seen, like Jupiter in the form of a bull with raised tail and fire-darting eyes, rushing wildly round his domain, looking to see if anyone dared come too near him. The emancipated ox was at last so troublesome and dangerous that they had to shoot it. This seemed to me an excellent satire on the love of freedom, by which desire for power commonly becomes desire for dominion, and against my will the association of ideas immediately awakened comical pictures in my mind. By a ruinous bridge, beside a swollen mountain stream, O'Connell halted to say his last farewell to me, and I could not go away without wishing this fighter for the rights of his fellow citizens well. I expressed the hope that, when we saw each other again, the oppressive structure of English intolerance might be destroyed through the efforts of himself and his fellow workers, like decaying walls by a river in flood. So we parted.

I found the happy mood and good-humoured politeness of the people I met very taking. No people I know show more gratitude for the least friendly word bestowed on them by a gentleman, without any shadow of self-interest. Indeed, I know no country in which I would rather be a great landowner. With what I have done elsewhere (receiving in return only ingratitude and obstructions of every kind), I would undoubtedly not only have bound ten or twelve thousand workers to myself, body and soul, but would also have achieved infinitely greater results with far less cost and time; for everything here is attainable by nature and man, especially the practicable.

For all their crudity, these people combine probity with the poetic homeliness of the Germans and the mental quickness of the French, and possess to boot all the naturalness and submissiveness of the Italians. You can quite rightly say of them that they have others to thank for their faults, but for their virtues, only themselves.

October 3rd

Everything is beautiful here, even the air, which is renowned for its healthful properties – and until now no taxes have been levied upon it. No insects plague mankind, for the bay is so deep that the ebb tide scarcely bares the bottom, and the constant soft breeze from the valleys is not apparently harmful. The climate remains nearly always equable, neither too warm nor too cold, and the vegetation is so luxuriant that it needs only one thing more, and that a little one, to clothe the bald mountains and rocks with beautiful verdure – namely plants and goats. For the first, money must be spent in order to invest it with pleasure, while the second allows nothing to grow that is not protected by double walls. In former days these mountains must have been covered with lofty woods, but the English, who think only of making as much money as possible in Ireland, cut them all down to provide fuel for the iron works which have arisen since then.

Another advantage of this region, to my taste, is its isolation. A carriage can hardly reach it, and only a few curious travellers like myself make the difficult journey. The people living here are not gathered together in villages but scattered among the mountains and, unspoilt by the bustle of towns, lead a patriarchal life. It is also not as repulsively poor as other parts of the country. The needs of these people are modest; they have to bring in turf for the fire, grass for their cows, and the sea gives them fish for nourishment – more than they need. For the owner with a pleasure in creation there lies an inexhaustible field. If I were a capitalist, here would I lie down.

My kind host is providing for the despatch of this letter. Heaven grant that, as it was written in a happy mood, so it will arrive. Always remember my grandmother's motto – *coeur content, grand talent.*

Your faithful, devoted Lou

TWENTY-SIXTH LETTER

Macroom, October 5th, 1828

Beloved dear one,

You know that since the time of James II, when idolatry of the Sabbath began and soon developed into a raging party issue, English Protestants have laid upon this day the true stamp of death. Dancing, music and song are taboo – the really pious even cover the cages of canary birds so that no sound of singing may issue from them on the holy day. No bread may be baked, and no useful business transacted – but all other crimes seem to flourish more luxuriantly than on weekdays, for the streets are never more crowded with drunkards than on Sundays, and never, according to police reports, are certain houses more crowded with visitors. Many of the English hold it a much greater sin to dance on Sunday than to steal, and I even read in a printed history of Whitby that its once rich abbey might have been ruined because, though the monks permitted themselves every kind of crime including murder and rape, their wicked abbot had permitted work on the building of the cloister to continue on the Sabbath.

The good Mrs W. was also infected with this lunacy, and it was pretty hard for me to justify the heinous sin of starting a journey on a Sunday, on the grounds of pressing necessity. In order to mollify her, I first drove with the entire family over the bay to church at B., which was not far out of my way.

At seven o'clock I reached Cashel, where I found the inn in the most fearful hullaballoo, because of a meeting of the Liberal Club and the dinner which was to follow it. Hardly had I got to my room before the president *in propria persona*, together with a deputation, arrived to invite me to attend the dinner. I begged earnestly to be excused on the grounds of fatigue and a bad headache, but promised to appear with the dessert, because I was curious to see their proceedings at close quarters. The Club owes its foundation to a

223

very wise aim: it is composed of a mixture of Catholics and Protestants who have undertaken to work at the reconciliation of both parties and, at the same time, to strive with all their might for Emancipation. When I entered, I found about eighty to a hundred persons seated at a long table; all of them stood up while the president led me to the head of the table. I made them a little speech of thanks, whereupon my health was drunk and I drank theirs in return. Innumerable toasts followed, always accompanied by speeches. Their eloquence was however not outstanding, the same commonplaces being constantly repeated, only in different words. After half an hour I seized a favourable moment to take my leave. Please grant it to me too, for I am very tired.

B., October 17th

Since yesterday, I have been a guest in a pretty little Gothic castle at the foot of the mountains. From one window I can see fertile meadows, from the other woods, lake and rocks. The host is Mr O.R.'s brother, and in addition to his castle he possesses a very pretty wife to whom I am paying a little court, since the gentlemen hunt and drink too much for my taste. The family property should really have come to my amusing friend but, because he was always a dissolute fish who from his youth seems to have been addicted to whiskey punch and good living, his father made the property over to the younger son. However, the brothers are the best of friends, and the harmless, good-humoured nature of the elder finds absolutely no wormwood in the wine that he drinks at his brother's table. So it is on the other side; the younger respects misfortune and sees that his amusing senior, even if he gets drunk every evening, lacks for nothing. Such a relationship does honour to them both, the more so since, at their father's death, the lawyers thought the case ripe for the courts. They have acted cleverly and kindly in letting it drop, thereby keeping the oyster for themselves, instead of letting it be seized by the lawyers, as in the caricature, leaving only the two halves of the shell for them to eat.

At supper we ate oysters, which are magnificent on the west and south coasts of Ireland. A gentleman of the district, who is used to looking for oysters on his property, gave us some details about their treatment and natural history which were quite new to me. *Je vous les communique, même au risque de vous ennuyer.* First you must know that three-year-old oysters are the best for eating, for only then have they reached the appropriate size and corpulence; later they become tough. The skilled oyster breeder has banks of every age and, according to the nature of the ground, oysters of different taste and flavour. In their natural state they never reach their proper maturity. This is how man comes to their aid – you take the young ones, when they are no larger than a four groschen piece, and sow them like corn in a part of the sea not too far from the shore. The seabed should be soft mud, and the oysters no more than fourteen feet deep. After three years you fish them up again, and then sow others from the mother bank. Naturally you have several such mud banks in operation, so that every year you are able to empty a ripe one. It appears that the oysters have to be very old before they multiply, since no natural birth takes place in the artificial colonies I have described. The manner of these births is moreover strange, another example of the endless multifariousness of nature. Apparently the oyster is a hermaphrodite, and all it does is plant fifteen to sixteen little oysters like warts on the outside of the shell, and when they have reached the right consistency they fall off. The bringing forth of these sixteen children so draws upon the old Mamma Oyster that, if you open her up afterwards, you will find nothing but a little slimy water in her; indeed, immediately after the little ones have fallen off, she digs herself six or seven inches under the mud. Here she spends an entire year before she has recovered enough to think again of procreation. That is why it is quite easy to fish up the young ones without coming too near the old ones, who are quietly sleeping in the deep. Oyster fishing is done by means of an instrument rather like the one you use to take mud out of rivers; and at the time of sowing the oysters are thrown into a sailcloth and, as I have said, scattered like corn. Very old mothers finally become barren when their shell is so thick that love can no longer penetrate, just like the hearts of men.

October 22nd

Since Fitzpatrick, the piper whom I had ordered for yesterday, was still tarrying in the town today, I had him play for me privately in my room during breakfast, and in this way was able to have a closer look at his instrument. It is, as you already know, peculiar to Ireland, and a strange mingling of old and new is to be seen in it. The original, simple bagpipe has been united with the sounds of the flute, the oboe, the single organ and the bassoon. Together they present a strange but fairly complete concert. The elegant little windbag is fastened to the left arm by a silken ribbon; the communicating wind tube lies across the body, whilst the hands play on an upright pipe with holes like a flageolet, to which five or six shorter ones are tied, like a colossal Papageno flute. While it is being played the right arm moves incessantly to and from the body, to keep air in the windbag. The opening of a flap brings out a deep, humming tone, which works like the loud pedal of the piano.

Through the movement of his whole body as well as the aforementioned pipes, Fitzpatrick brought forth a sound which no other instrument possesses. The sight of the whole, which you must imagine for yourself, was truly very unusual. The beautiful old man had thick, white, curly hair, and his bagpipe was most splendidly adorned: the pipes of ebony mounted with silver, the ribbon richly embroidered and the bag hung with flame-coloured silk and silver fringes. I had him play the oldest Irish melodies to me, wild compositions which usually begin in a melancholy guise, like the songs of the Slavs, and end in a jig, the Irish national dance, or in warlike music. One of these melodies was the very convincing *facsimile* of a fox hunt, and another that I thought was borrowed from the hunting chorus in *Freischütz* was in fact five hundred years older.

After a while the piper left off, and said very politely: 'It must be known to you, sir, that when sober the Irish bagpipe has not a good sound. It needs evening or the silence of the night, gay company and the lovesome perfume of smoking whiskey punch. So now allow me to take my leave.' I richly rewarded the good old man, who will always stand for me as a real representative of the Irish nation.

With Fitzpatrick I also take my leave, dearest Lucie, in order to negotiate the long journey back to Dublin, from where I also expect to send off my next letter to you.

Your faithful Lou

TWENTY-SEVENTH LETTER

Dublin, October 29th, 1828

Dear, kind friend,

When one has been leading a half-wild life for so long, the tameness of the town appears quite strange. I can now almost understand the homesickness of the Indian, of whom even the best educated run back to their woods in the end! The charm of freedom is too great.

If I did not wish to indulge in tomfoolery, or to speak of things that have nothing to do with my journey and my present sojourn, life in the world would make my letters quite empty. I could have a printed form drawn up with a few things filled in – somewhat like this: 'Got up late and in a bad temper. Went visiting, rode or drove. Dinner at Lord or Mr . . .'s, good or bad. Conversation: commonplaces. In the evening, party, rout, ball or entirely dilettante concert, from which my ears are still suffering.' In London, you could set down once and for all: 'The crowd soon crushed me to death, and the heat was more oppressive than on the top bench of a Turkish bath. Today's physical exertions were 5 degrees (if you can so estimate a fox hunt). Spiritual gain – o. Result – *Diem perdidi.*'

Here it is not quite so trying. At this time of year, you will be no more exhausted than in a large German town, but will still get too many invitations to be able to decline conveniently.

November 20th

I had luncheon at Lady Morgan's. She told me many interesting details about the well-known Miss O'Neill whom, as you know, I consider the greatest dramatic talent I have ever had the opportunity of seeing. She said that this artist, although endowed from the beginning with noble genius, was long neglected in the local theatre where she played for some time, and was indeed regarded as quite negligible! This meant that she was so poor that, when she got home in the evening after an exhausting performance, she found nothing to revive her but a spoonful of potatoes and a wretched bed that she shared with three of her sisters. Lady M. visited her once and found the poor girl darning her two pairs of old stockings, which she washed every day so as to arrive in clean clothes at the theatre. After that Lady M. procured many articles of clothing for her, and concerned herself especially with her toilet, which up till then had been entirely neglected. As a result she got slightly more employment, but only a little applause.

At this time one of the directors of the London theatre chanced to come to Dublin, saw her and, being a better judge, immediately engaged her for the capital. Here, on her first performance, she caused a *furore*, and in an instant was transformed from a poor and unknown actress to the brightest star in the English theatrical firmament, shedding her rays over the whole land. I still remember with enchantment her performances in London. Since then, I have never been able to bear to see the role of Juliet played by another actress, even our best. They seem to me only manner, affectation, unnaturalness. You had to see for yourself the whole life of Shakespeare's Juliet unrolling before the audience in just a few hours. First you saw a child, innocent, young, joyous, unconstrainedly frolicsome; then, as love awakened, a new sun seemed to rise above her, all her movements were richer, her demeanour more radiant – she was the maiden giving herself utterly to love with all the fire of the South. So she opened in to the loveliest, richest bloom – but cares and misfortunes soon ripened the noble fruit. Noble dignity, utter tenderness for her husband, the most resolute determination in time of need took the place of the burning passion, of the mood of light enjoyment, and at the end how fearful, how heartrending, how true and how beautiful was her despair when all was lost.

In her acting she sometimes allowed herself to go to the outermost bounds, which no one else could have done without falling into the ridiculous. But with her the effect was like an electric shock. Her madness and death as Belvedera (in Otway's *Venice Preserved*)[1] had a physical truth so horrifying that one could hardly bear the sight of it. I remember well that after seeing that performance I could bear

[1] Translator's parenthesis.

no further emotional experience, and when I awoke the next morning I shed hot tears over Belvedera's fate. Of course I was very young at the time, but many shared my feelings, and it was striking that Germans as well as Frenchmen and Italians spoke enthusiastically of her. You could not call her exactly beautiful, although she had a noble form, splendid shoulders and arms and beautiful hair. But her visage possessed that undefinable, tragic expression which stirred the deepest feelings of the soul.

The Dubliners remained blind in the face of so much genius and talent. When the famous, fêted, idolized Miss O'Neill came back from London a year later, to play a few guest roles, the charm she exercised was so great that not only was the whole audience in a noisy tumult, but several ladies were carried out in a faint, unconscious; and one went quite mad at the sight of Belvedera's frenzy, and died in a lunatic asylum – undoubtedly a sacrifice to Nemesis for the former stupidity of the others.

Your ever faithful, Lou

TWENTY-EIGHTH LETTER

Holyhead, December 15th, 1828, evening

Beloved friend,

At eleven in the evening I left Dublin in a postchaise, in lovely bright moonlight, the breeze as warm as summer. You can imagine that I had material for various reflections – since only then did I truly realize that the sacrifice of two years of life, of a sorrowful parting and the expenditure of a great sum of money, have been in vain; these thoughts were indeed melancholy.

Nevertheless I did not allow myself to be quite bowed down by them. Did not Parry have to sail three times in vain to the North Pole, Napoleon heap victory on victory for twenty years only to pine away on St Helena, and how few people's wishes come true, just as they want? Every cloud has a silver lining, and I have profited much from these two years in other respects – I have become more clear-sighted and resolute, have gained many new memories, have become a more perfect gardener, and have learned to speak and write fairly fluent English. But my poor Schnucke has had to look after herself at home, and has had no other consolation than that she loves me very much. That is why her Lou is coming home exactly as he left – older, I fear, in appearance, but with just as young a heart as ever and, instead of being melancholy as he would have reason enough to be, the joy of seeing his Schnucke again makes him *au fond* happy and content.

On the ship I found people still busy loading a fine carriage, burdened with almost as many superfluities and comforts as I take when I journey in this way. The valet and the servants were assiduously and respectfully busied about it, while a little man with a blond, carefully curled head, dressed very elegantly all in black, of about twenty years old, strolled to and fro on the deck with all the indolence of an English fashionable, without taking the slightest notice of his property or of the efforts of his servants. As I later learnt he had just come into his inheritance in Ireland, with an income of £20,000 a year, and now had the notion of showing it off to everybody. He was hastening to Naples, and seemed in such a good mood that not even seasickness could dampen his spirits. Whilst I was talking to him, I thought to myself about the two of us: *voilà le commencement et la fin!* The world is sending forth one and saying to him – Enjoy me – and to the other, whom she is sending home – Ruminate on me. May Heaven preserve my good stomach for this! But this melancholy view arose only from the nausea caused by the boilers and seasickness and, after a little reflection, I rejoiced at the sight of this hopeful young man, as if it were myself still enjoying the illusions of my youth.

This evening I mean to continue with the mail coach, and hope that a good dinner will provide a cure for the nausea which the crossing has left behind.

Hereford, December 17th

It cannot be denied that, when one has been deprived of it for a time, it is always a pleasure to come back to English comfort. Variety is certainly the spice of life and gives everything a renewed value. The good inns, the cleanly served breakfasts and dinners, the spacious, carefully warmed beds, the polite and skilful waiters, struck me very pleasantly after the lack of them in Ireland, and soon reconciled me to the higher prices.

At ten in the morning I left Shrewsbury with the mail, and reached Hereford at ten in the evening. As it was not cold, I sat outside and gave my servant the place in the coach. Two or three unremarkable men and a pretty, lively boy of eleven years old made up my company on the *impériale*, where there was a great deal of political talk. The boy, who was the son of a prosperous landowner, was travelling the hundred miles from his school to be home for Christmas. This custom of trusting such young children to their own devices undoubtedly gives them increased self-reliance in later life, which gives the English an advantage over other nations, especially the Germans. The child's joy and lively restlessness, the nearer we drew to his father's house, touched and delighted me. There was something so natural and sincere in it that I involuntarily thought back to my own childhood years, that immeasurable happiness, unvalued at the time, that we can only recognize in retrospect!

Bristol, December 20th

I hope you are following me on the map, which will make my letters more intelligible to you, even if you cannot enjoy the beautiful views that go with it, though I am bringing back with me true pictures of them in my memory. At two o'clock I drove into Bristol on a very full stagecoach on the box of which, in spite of the heavy rain, I only managed with difficulty to get the last place. We crossed the river on a fine bridge, which gives the best standpoint for a view of the castle. Rising directly over the perpendicular cliffs which fall to the River Wye, it provides a particularly picturesque panorama.

The weather meanwhile was growing ever more dreadful, and at last degenerated into a real storm. It was at our backs, but the journey over the channel was most unpleasant. The four horses, all the luggage and the passengers were packed pell-mell into a little boat, so crowded that you could hardly move in it. Irresistibly driven by the storm, the boat lay right over on its side, and the waves sprayed us unceasingly and wet us through from head to foot. When we finally arrived, the landing was as difficult as it was dirty, and during it, to my great displeasure, I lost a part of the works of Lord Byron. They told me that, because of the many storms, the sandy bottom and the cliffs, this crossing often causes accidents. Six months previously, the ship with the mail was wrecked and many people lost their lives. This time we could not reach the usual landing place, and so had to disembark on the beach from which we went on foot, up a pathway of red and white striped marble, to the inn. Here we boarded another stagecoach, or landboat, which, overflowing with twenty people and slower than the mail, drove us to Bristol. Of this admirable place I took in today only clear gaslights and well-stocked, cheerful shops.

Bath, December 21st, evening

I have already told you that the surroundings of Bristol rightly have a high reputation. In richness, luxuriance of vegetation and fertility, it cannot be surpassed by any; in picturesque beauty, certainly not by many. *C'est comme la terre promise*; everything that you see, you sit down before as a gourmet; and everything that you enjoy is here in full perfection.

Bristol, a town with a hundred thousand inhabitants, lies in a deep valley; Clifton, which rises on the terraced mountain immediately above it, seems only another part of the same town. Out of the maze of houses of the old capital in the valley there rise three weathered, Gothic churches. In their feeling of ancient greatness, they seem like the proud remains of feudal and monastic rulers (since these went hand in hand like warring brothers), refusing to bow their grey heads amid the thickets that have shot up in these modern times.

In the evening I visited the theatre, and found the house as pretty as the play was bad. They were playing *Rienzi*, a miserable modern tragedy which, because of the exaggeration and clumsiness of the actors, aroused neither tears nor laughter, but only lack of sympathy and boredom. So I soon left that desecrated temple of Melpomene, (the Tragic Muse),[1] and called on the verger of the abbey, to ask permission to look at the church by moonlight. As soon as he had opened it for me I sent him away, and wandered about like a lonely shade among the pillars and graves for a long time. I let the sober tragedy of life arise before me, surrounded by the horror of the night and of death.

December 24th

The weather is still so bad and hangs such a veil over all distant things, that I can make no excursions, and have to confine myself to the town. This however lends itself to most interesting walks on account of the crowds and the variety of its prospects. I always begin with my favourite church, and always end with it – like the man whose life comes forth from death and ends with it. The architect who built this splendid place has gone far beyond the common in ornament and proportions. For instance, outside and near the portal, there rise two Jacob's ladders with angels climbing up them, right to the roof, where the little beings lose themselves behind the

[1] Translator's parenthesis.

gables. The busy little heaven-stormers are quite charming to see and, to my mind, entirely in keeping with the spirit of that fantastic architecture, which was able to combine the most naïve with the most noble, the most intricate decoration with the most grandiose, and all earthly nature with the giants of the woods, flowers with rocks and precious stones (in the bright windows), people and animals – and by these means was sure, at that time, to arouse the holiest feelings. To me this is when truly romantic, that is, truly German architecture emerged, springing out of our most individual mentality. Yet I believe that we are now remote from it, for it belongs to a more sentimental era. We can admire and love its details, but no longer create anything in the same genre without its bearing the deadening stamp of imitation. Steam engines and constitutional government contend with it now, better than any modern art. To every age its own.

Your Lou

TWENTY-NINTH LETTER

Salisbury, December 27th, 1828

Beloved friend,

Yesterday evening at seven o'clock I left Bath, again with the mail, for Salisbury.

The box of the mail has become my throne, from which I exercise my sway. Holding the reins over four extremely spirited steeds, I gaze proudly over the countryside, hastening forward (which not all rulers can boast of), and yet I often wish I had wings to be more quickly with you.

In London, I did nothing the whole morning but seek out a worthy consort for Francis, as you commanded, but the real Blenheim spaniels are desperately rare. What I did see was not suitable. The ears were either too long or too short, the legs too crooked or too bandy, the hair was too bright or not richly enough marked, the disposition too snappy or too lethargic; in short, I had soon to give up the fruitless search.

As I came into Canterbury, all the towers were flying flags for the New Year, but I celebrated it even more splendidly in the proudest and most beautiful of all English cathedrals. This romanesque building, which was begun by the Saxons, continued by the Normans and recently very tastefully restored, consists of three quite different but complementary churches, with many irregular side chapels and steps leading upwards and downwards; and a black and white chequered stone floor, with a forest of pillars in harmonious confusion. The yellowish colour of the sandstone is a great advantage, especially in the Norman part of the church, where it alternates with black marble columns. Here lies the effigy of the Black Prince, in brass, on his stone sarcophagus. Above him hangs a half-mouldered habergeon, next to the sword and shield of Poitiers. Apart from this, a crowd of other monuments adorns the church, among them those of Henry IV and Thomas à Becket, who was murdered in one of the stone chapels. A large number of the old, bright windows have been preserved and, with the uncommon beauty of the colours, some show real patterns and arabesques like transparent carpets, others look like the jewelwork of precious stones. There are a few historical paintings on show.

What gives this grandiose cathedral a special advantage over others in England is that there is no distracting rood screen in the middle, and you can see the whole extent of the nave, which is four to five hundred feet long, at a glance. The organ is placed in one of the curved upper galleries and thence its sound gives an enchanting effect. I was fortunate in that, just as I was about to leave, the singers and musicians held a practice hour, and their beautiful, invisible, heavenly choir filled the cathedral at the very moment when the last rays of the sun fired the windows in sapphire blue and ruby red. The Archbishop of Canterbury is the Primate of England and the only subject, apart from the blood royal, who has the rank of prince, but only in his archbishopric as far as I know. This protestant clergyman has £60,000 a year, and may marry. I do not know how else he differs from the Catholic princes of the Church.

Calais, January 2nd, 1829

At last I am once more in my beloved France! However few advantages it initially appears to offer, yet did I greet this half-native earth, the purer air, the spontaneous, friendly, confiding manners almost with the feeling of a prisoner returning home after a long confinement.

At three o'clock we were awakened in Dover, and climbed on to the packet boat in complete darkness. We were wandering up and down all prepared for half an hour, without there being any signs of setting sail. At one point the rumour spread that one of the boilers was damaged. The most fearful immediately rushed back on to the quay, the rest shrieked for the captain, but he was nowhere to be found. At last he sent someone to inform us that it would be dangerous to sail, and that the luggage would be taken on to a French steamer which left at eight o'clock. I used the intervening time to see the sun rise from the fort, which crowns the high, chalk cliffs over the town. The English, who have enough money to carry out any useful plan, have blasted a tunnel through the cliff, constituting a kind of funnel, in which two spiral staircases, 240 feet high, lead to the top. The view from there is extremely picturesque, and in an almost cloudless sky, the sun climbed up out of the sea over the wide prospect. In the ecstasy which I permitted myself, I could easily have missed the departure of the ship, which was weighing anchor at the moment of my arrival.

The strong wind wafted us over in two and a half hours. This time the seasickness was bearable, and a splendid dinner, such as no English inn provides, brought me into Calais in the best of condition. Incidentally, this hotel (the Bourbon), as far as the cooking is concerned, is one of the best in France.

January 3rd

The first morning walk in France provided some precious experiences. The constant sunshine, the clear sky which I had not seen for so long, and at last a town whose houses and roofs can be seen clearly in the air, unobscured by mist, fog or coal smoke – I simply gaped at everything. I felt I was home again and wandered down to the harbour to take a last farewell of the sea. There it lay before me, mirror smooth and blue, everywhere unbounded, except at the English coast whose presence was signalled by a black mountain of cloud, apparently the solidified fog of this island. I followed the jetty (a kind of wooden mole) which led over the sea for a good quarter of an hour, and soon found myself at the end of it, quite alone except for a water bird, which was swimming about with lightning swiftness in the silver flood, often diving under and then, minutes later, coming to the surface much further on. The bird continued this play for a long time, and was so clever and gay that you might have believed he was presenting his art expressly for me. I was just about to give way to all kinds of fancies concerning this spectacle when I heard behind me the steps and voices of an English family, and both of us flew quickly away, the bird and I.

When I returned to the town, I visited the famous Brummell. I see that you are opening the *Dictionnaire Historique et des Contemporains* in vain to find this famous name. Did he distinguish

237

himself in the Revolution or a counter-revolution, is he a warrior, a statesman? *Vous n'êtes pas*. He is much more and much less, depending on how you look at it. In a word, he is one of the most famous and, in his time, most powerful dandies London has ever known. Brummell once ruled an entire generation through the cut of his coat, and leather breeches went out of fashion because everyone despaired of being able to imitate his properly. When at last he turned his back on Great Britain, he left to his native land, as a parting gift, the imperishable secret of the starched neckband. The elegants of the capital had been so tormented by their inability to fathom it that, according to the *Literary Gazette*, one of them, a young duke, actually died miserably of a broken heart. The seeds of disease had, however, already been sown in him for, on one solemn occasion, he had shyly asked Brummell's opinion of the coat he was wearing. The latter had given him only a fleeting glance, and had asked in wonder, 'Do you call this thing a coat?' His self-respect had never recovered from this.

Although fashion nowadays is no longer set by clothes, it is only the means that are altered; the result remains unchanged. The influence which Brummell, without fortune or birth, without a fine figure or conspicuous intelligence, exerted for many years in London entirely through noble impudence, a droll originality, a pleasant sociability and a talent in dress, gives an excellent measure of the nature of that society; and since I have sufficiently described this to you in my earlier letters, you will now understand Brummell's position.

For a long time Brummell enjoyed the highest favour of the Prince of Wales, who first introduced him into the world of fashion, but later he treated this illustrious person with so little regard that it led to a breach. One day, he so far forgot himself as to call out to the Prince after dinner: 'Pray, George, will you ring the bell for me?' The Prince, deeply affronted by the indiscreet laughter of the company, as well as by the impertinent familiarity of the adventurer, stood up calmly and rang – but when the servant came in, he pointed his finger at Brummell and said: 'This person wants his carriage.' Brummell did not lose his composure, but replied: 'Capital, Georgie! By God, I quite forgot that the lovely Duchess is waiting for me. I am taking the joke in earnest and leaving you. So goodbye, your Royal Highness.' From that moment on, the Prince never allowed him in his house again. But this did him almost more harm in the fashionable world than it did to Brummell, who was able to turn the matter round as if it had been he who broke with the Prince. He was in the habit of saying to his intimate friends: 'That fellow first ruined me in champagne, then won my money, and now thinks he can cut me.' A few days later fate decreed that Brummell should meet the Prince in New Bond Street, with a few fashionable gentlemen. The Prince behaved as if he did not see him, but Brummell, full of ease and effrontery, approached Colonel P, one of the company and also one of the leaders of the elegant world, and whilst he was shaking his hand, took his quizzing-glass with all the impertinent condescension of which he was master and, fixing the Prince with it, whispered to the Colonel so that all could hear: 'Who the devil is your fat old friend, Colonel, whom you were just talking to?' With this he left the company, standing in consternation, mounted his horse and rode away laughing.

These anecdotes were relayed to me by an entirely reliable source, who had them from an eyewitness. I am less certain whether it is true that, on an earlier occasion, at a dinner where everyone had already drunk too much, the Prince reacted to a sarcastic remark of Brummell's, who was sitting beside him, by throwing a glass of wine in his face. Unable to perpetrate such an act against the person of the Prince, with great presence of mind Brummell at once seized his own glass and, pouring it over the coat of his neighbour, called out good-humouredly: 'The Prince has commanded that it should go round to the left.'

For some time after this Brummell continued to reign in London and to cast his great antagonist into the shade – indeed, this was the time when his genius took its highest flight. The Prince was famed for the inimitable knot in which he tied his neckband, and in order to wound him in his tenderest, most sensitive spot, Brummell invented the use of starch and isinglass for cravats. From this memorable moment on his victory was decisive and, as I have said, for years dandies tortured themselves in vain to wear neckbands as he did. The Prince was losing the game to force Brummell out of exclusive society, but at last it all came to an end; Brummell lost everything and had to flee – however, he left on his writing-desk a sealed packet. When they opened it, they found nothing but the following, written in large letters: 'My friends, starch is the thing'. And as great men live on in their works when they themselves are long since dust, so Brummell's starch remains visible at the neck of every fashionable, and proclaims his lofty genius. But he has himself been living since then in Calais, where he is safe from his creditors, and every bird of passage from the great world who bends his steps in this direction, dutifully pays his former patriarch the tribute of a visit, or of an invitation to dinner.

This I did, too, though under an assumed name. Unfortunately another stranger had been before me with the dinner invitation, so I have no means of judging how a coat should really look, or whether the long sojourn in Calais and the inroads of age have made the clothes of the former king of fashion less classic, for on my first visit I found him still at his second toilet (three are necessary for his morning) in a flowered dressing gown, a satin cap with gold tassels on his head, and Turkish slippers on his feet. He was shaving himself, and after that carefully cleaning his remaining teeth with his favourite piece of red root. The furniture surrounding him was fairly elegant, and indeed could still be called quite rich, though much cleaned, and I cannot deny that his whole demeanour seemed to me to be in keeping with it. Although forced from his former position, he still showed withal a sufficient fund of good humour. His manner was that of good society, simple and natural and of great urbanity, as the dandies of today are in a position to testify. Smiling, he showed me his Paris wig, which he proclaimed much better than all the English ones and called himself *le ci-devant jeune homme, qui passe sa vie entre Paris et Londres.* He seemed rather curious about me, questioned me about social relations in London without, however, infringing good manners in any way by the least importunity, and made it obvious that he was very well informed of all that goes on in the English fashionable and political worlds. '*Je suis au fait de tout,*' he said, '*mais à quoi cela me sert-il? On me laisse mourir de faim ici. J'espère pourtant que mon ancien ami, le Duc de W, enverra un beau jour le Consul d'ici à la Chine, et qu'ensuite il me nommera à sa place. Alors je suis sauvé.*' The English nation should do some little thing for the man who invented the starched neckband. How many did I see in London with substantial sinecures who have done far less for their native land?

As I was taking my leave and going down the stairs, he opened the door and called after me: '*J'espère que vous trouverez votre chemin, mon Suisse n'est pas là, je crains.'* Alas, thought I, no money, no Swiss.[1]

Not to leave you too long without news, I am sending off this letter from here. Perhaps I shall myself be following soon. In any case, I shall spend fourteen days in Paris and look after all your commissions there. Remember me in the meantime, always with the old love.

Your faithful, Lou

---

[1] In his later years Brummell became increasingly slovenly in his dress and personal habits, and died in the pauper lunatic asylum in Caen in 1840.

THIRTIETH LETTER

Paris, January 5th, 1829

My dear, beloved friend,

I could not write to you yesterday because the post coach from Calais to Paris took two days and a night, and only stopped for half an hour for eating every twelve hours. The journey is not the most pleasant, indeed something dead, something miserable and dirty strikes one about the whole country, as well as the capital, a striking contrast with the undulating bustle, splendour and neatness of England.

You could not sit worse, nor fare more uncomfortably and more slowly than I did here in my sky-high cabriolet; indeed, I have been without the most ordinary comforts for some time now. In spite of all this, never have my spirits nor my health been better than on this journey. I was uninterruptedly happy and content because I was entirely free. Oh, great gift of freedom, for how long have we not prized you highly enough! If every man was to get it clear in his mind what he as an individual needed for happiness and content, and then to choose unhesitatingly whatever led to that end and gladly threw away everything else, how many mistakes would be avoided, how much petty ambition would be done away with, how much true joy would be promoted? We would all find a great overflowing of wellbeing in life, instead of tormenting ourselves into the grave, joyless and discontented.

I would like to rest here for a few days and make my purchases. Then I shall fly to your arms, without seeing even *one* acquaintance, if I can help it, *car cela m'entraînerait trop*. So do not expect to hear anything new from me about the old Paris. A few scattered remarks in my diary will be all that I can offer you.

Mainz, January 31st

The sudden change from the English and French fireplaces to the German stoves did not have the best effect on me, *et me donne des pressentiments de migraine.* The dreadfully wet thaw has its own drawbacks. In a few hours we shall set out for Oppenheim *pour y tenter le passage*, since there seems no possibility here, although they say that a quarter of an hour is often enough to break the ice and set the river free. The frost had made my skin, no longer accustomed to it, crack so much that I am peeling like a caterpillar. So I can truly say that I am jumping out of my skin to get to Muskau.

Frankfurt, evening

Since it froze a little in the night, something I learnt only after I had written the above, we tried the crossing at Mainz. Half in barges, half on the cracking ice, we came over successfully, and found in the inn above the river a charming Rhine maiden from Bingen who would have beguiled me, had I been less pressed, to a longer stay here. We drove through three sovereign states to reach Frankfurt in four hours, and my first expedition here was to the post to inform myself as to the departure of the post-chaise. I learned that it goes only on Monday night – today is Saturday – and for me, my servants and my three hundred pounds in weight of effects, they asked three hundred taler for the forty miles to Leipzig. The Prussian post-chaise is indeed far dearer than the English, and two persons with their own carriage travel much more cheaply and faster. Since my fortune now consists of fifty talers, I went away quite crushed by this news, but outside ran into a man who was returning to Leipzig and persuaded my friend Annesley and a Frenchman named Ge'ard to club together with me to engage this coachman, who undertook to set us down in Leipzig on Thursday evening, whilst the post only gets there a day sooner. We each gave him twelve taler which, for me and my servant, still only made twenty-four instead of sixty. Admittedly we shall be five days on the way, and with the heavy glass coach and two horses we can only count on a vigorous walking pace, and a little trotting. All the same, the saving was necessary for me, and I have long ceased to be fastidious.

The worst is that we have to get up every day at five o'clock and spend the night in bad inns, but privation is always a gain in retrospect, and therefore a happiness in itself, especially if you are forced into it and do not have to struggle to it through painful reflection. I was never so practical a philosopher as now, Schnucke of my heart, *c'est que je me porte bien, et c'est la véritable cause de toute sorte de sagesse.*

Leipzig, February 5th

Best of all Schnuckes, I have not been able to write to you during the whole of our troublesome but cheerful journey, *et c'est dommage, car j'aurais pu vous donner des échantillons fort amusants de notre conversation, dont ma mauvaise mémoire m'a fait depuis oublier tous les détails.* But when you get up at five o'clock and go to your quarters at nine, there is not enough time left for eating and sleeping nor, without torturing yourself, for writing, and I only write to my Schnucke when it can be done comfortably and with pleasure. That this pleasure quite often comes my way I have demonstrated, even since your letter informed me that my letters now no longer interest you because you will soon have me in person.

We had continuing fine, cold weather; were jolly, laughed a lot and ate like wolves. It occurred to me that I had now traversed this same road three times, and in what different moods! The first time I travelled here and back to report to Barclai de Tolly's headquarters at Frankfurt, immediately after the last campaign with France, and before my diet. At that time I was in good financial circumstances, had just become a Prussian, but was tormented by ambition and plans and by miserable health, resulting in melancholy. The second time I travelled back to Muskau from Frankfurt, just before our wedding. My money situation was even better, I already had you, my old girl, but at that time I did not know how to appreciate you properly and had love, that rending madness, in my body. So I was feeling my oats – that is, I had so much, ten times more than I asked for; I was discontented, proud and high-handed, and thus, melancholy. Both times nothing went wrong for me. I travelled in an English carriage, with four horses, did what my mood dictated, and denied myself nothing.

Both times I was still young and pretty, *au moins je m'en flatte.* Now comes the third time, *et cette époque me retrouve vieux et ruiné.* Instead of the English carriage and the four horses flying along at a smart trot, I am sitting in an old cab, harnessed with two old nags which wearily drag themselves and their load like snails. I am sitting uncomfortably, because I have to share the carriage with three others, freeze intermittently and in the evening expect only bad refreshment and a bad bed. Still I am well, experience has made of me a practical philosopher who knows how to take the world as it comes, I am encumbered with no rank and social considerations, so I feel myself as free as a bird in the air; I am enjoying the company which surrounds me instead of finding them *corvée*, eat a bad dinner with appetite instead of getting indigestion from a good one, and the torments of ambition and confusion of a thousand plans are foreign to me, and the result is *contentement* and gaiety *par conséquence*.

Is not the world a comical thing, or rather are not we? And who can judge the good or bad fortune of others! The Frenchman was the most amiable of us three, and I repeat: I am sorry that I have forgotten the many funny anecdotes with which he refreshed us.

After I have paid the driver and my bill in advance, including tomorrow morning's breakfast, I shall have two gold Friedrichs left. I hope you received my letter from Mainz, dear Schnucke, and are sending me help to Dresden. If not, I shall pawn my watch there. My first outing tomorrow will be to the post. Good night.

The village of Luppe, February 6th

Schnucke, my heart, how both your letters rejoiced me, which I found lying on a big table in front of my door even before I went to the office – a pretty and efficient custom for letters lying in the *poste restante*. Kind heart, you are my real guardian angel, and I could not have wished for more than your loving care; the fifty talers, the fly, old Vivarais and the fur – *mais tout cela est délicieux! Vous avez donc le talent de me deviner, Schnucke, et de renchérir même sur ce que je désire.* When I was sitting in Dublin with sixty pounds, and indeed did not know where to turn, there fell, as if from a guardian angel, exactly *a tempo*, your five hundred; and today when *au bout de mon latin* I wanted to pawn my watch, and my letter asking for help had not reached you, your love has anticipated my wishes. A thousand thanks, dear kind Schnucke, *des attentions pareilles viennent du coeur, et vont au coeur.*

I immediately made an arrangement with another driver, who will take me to Meissen for six talers. He has a very good glass coach in which, all alone with my servant, I will find plenty of room, for my former travelling companions, who did not quite know what to make of me after I had diligently worn myself out in misleading them during the whole journey, took leave of me to journey to Berlin.

I am writing to you now from a village inn in which some half a dozen of the prettiest girls are lodged, *et j'avoue que c'est pour les beaux yeux d'une d'entre elles* that I am staying here for the night. The number of pretty girls in Saxony is really striking, and so is their light-heartedness and ease. I am sitting here in a window seat of the big, warm room, which is as full as a salon but only with the people of the inn: girls, boys, drivers and a few strangers, who are being served at different tables with an evening meal very rich and luxurious for their station in life. Near the stove sit four girls and a charming, half-naked child stripping feathers; singing and laughing opposite me is the loveliest, with white teeth and rosy lips, sewing and making very funny remarks in her Saxon dialect, whilst I am now answering her, now writing, now addressing an excellent fresh roast pork, stuck with gherkins, over which Big Hannah allows herself a few jokes. A rendezvous is arranged; she is so fresh, so *bien portante* – a country beauty with such obliging naiveté has not come my way in a long time.

At the Blue Star, Dresden, February 7th

Not far from Lommatsch I was awakened by sleighbells, and saw a very elegant basket sleigh with a new outfit drive past me and pull up at the nearby inn, where my coachman also wished to refresh his horses. The splendid sleighroad (for that is what I found from Paris to here), and the wish to drive to Schnucke in Muskau, led me to strike a bargain with the owner of the elegant vehicle, *fier du trésor qui m'attendait à Meissen*.

For twenty-five talers I purchased sleigh and covers and the owner undertook to drive me on to Meissen. When I arrived there and drove into the courtyard of the inn, the first thing on which my eyes fell was the good fly, *et je pleurais presque de plaisir en la revoyant*.

When I called, there appeared *souffre-douleur* Vivarais with the fur in his hand, behaving like pigskin himself *car il était furieuse-ment sale et je rougissais un peu quand il me traita d'Altesse.* Schnucke, if you had read my letter attentively, you would have found that I am not called Herr von Gablenz but von Groditz, *et je l'avoue, sans les moyens de faire paraître le prince décemment, j'aime ce nom de Groditz cent fois davantage.* Also Vivarais' recognition of my name would have had the unpleasant consequence that the hired coachman, who was behind me, would have learnt it and then told it in Dresden, so that I could not make my journey secretly as I wished. So as not to meet anyone, I alighted at the Blue Star. *Ceci tourna à mon avantage, car c'est une fort bonne auberge.*

Bautzen, February 8th

Now I am again in my dear incognito, and have it to thank for two amusing conversations. First, however, I must remark that our district can never be shown to greater advantage to a stranger than in winter in deep snow. The snow makes everything as clean as in England, even the houses look better, all the roads seem splendid highways, there is no more sand, and even the melancholy pines astonish the traveller like splendid evergreen woods on which precious stones sparkle in the sun.

I have apparently caught a desperate cough and cold from the fearfully hot room, after long being as well as a fish. However I do not complain. Your bays are behaving very well and simply dancing along with the fly, although the new sleigh, with three hundred-weight of luggage piled upon it, is tied on behind. I had lunch in Bischofswerda. Again there was a flock of pretty girls, especially the innkeeper's daughter, Marie. I ate at the table d'hôte which consisted of four people apart from me, and joked a great deal with Miss Marie. One of the guests was the dandy of the district, exaggeratedly dressed in an out-of-date style and extremely amusing. The conversation turned, by chance, upon my humble self and was no light test of my self-control, but at the same time showed me how foolish one is to bother about public gossip because, for one thing, one is much less interesting to the public than one imagines, and for another the public is for the most part wrongly informed. Listen to the following conversation and laugh.

The dandy, in a blue, extravagantly-cut coat adorned with steel buttons, with a bright yellow neckband, a white waistcoat with disastrous collar, a great stick-pin of Bohemian diamonds, crookedly creased cossack trousers and spurs – for, as he informed us at table, he had had to ride on a shaft so as to drive the lady of his heart on a sleigh – this Bischofswerder elegant was also the owner of a recently-founded spinning factory and spoke of the Muskau alum mines with great praise. 'To whom do these alum mines belong?' I asked. 'Now to the Princess Pückler, whose husband recently died.' 'God forbid,' cried another (the companion of the fashionable, as I later learned), 'he is not dead, they have only made a friendly separation, because the Princess and he simply do not suit each other. One can only live happily in quietude and in the country, the other must always be in great cities and travelling about in the world. So the Princess has now taken over all the property and the Prince has settled down in London and also married there.' 'No, no, you have been misinformed there,' cried the host. 'He was engaged to the Empress of Otahaiti, but it fell through. A gentleman who was passing through here last summer on his way back from the Muskau baths, told me all this in detail.' 'Is there a bath there too?' I asked, pinching myself so as not to burst out laughing. 'Yes, a very fine one. An immense amount of money was spent on it to make something green grow on the sandy soil; it must indeed be a little paradise – as far as it goes – but it is not much visited since we have too much of this kind here in the neighbourhood. The doctors all recommend Teplitz or Marienbad.' 'Is the Prince still a young man?' I asked. 'Oh, no,' answered the dandy, 'he already has a long grown-up son, the Count Pückler who has joined the Saxon bodyguard. He has become a wild fellow!' Now, out came several of the old, exaggerated half-true stories and I had another question on the tip of my tongue. But in came Vivarais, the donkey, and shouted: 'Your Highness, the carriage is harnessed!' Everyone looked at me open-mouthed – I had represented myself as a draper from England – and, leaving my servant to pay, I fled hastily into the carriage. In Bautzen, I could not bring myself to put up at the sad Eagle, where we took leave of each other, but betook myself to the Crown – why I have chosen this particular way, I shall recount to you in person.

That I have been trying, since Leipzig, to think how I can mislead and surprise you goes without saying, for I love my

Schnucke much too dearly not to relish teasing her a bit. Although you have anxiously warned me to handle you very tenderly – it can't be helped, you will simply have to be teased, and you have also richly earned it by your outrage in believing that I could possibly pass through Leipzig without asking for your letters at the post. So Heaven, I hope, will support me in misleading you. I am going tomorrow to the hunting lodge, dining there, and only arriving at Muskau when you will be least expecting me.

Schnucke, Lou is coming home just as he went away; with not a hair altered, always a great libertine, a great fool and a great child. Nothing of this detracts from the philosopher who, like a mighty eagle, hovers in the blue vault above this clown.

Schnucke, you see that I must joke with you in Bautzen as in London – it has become second nature to me, *et partout je trouve de quoi – tant bien que mal.* What is enlivening me here, though perhaps making me a little too long-winded, is that I have no more post to pay, *car cette lettre je l'apporte moi-même, et ce n'est que le lendemain de mon arrivée qu'on vous la remettra*, indeed the last article will be written in Muskau itself. *En attendant bonne nuit.*

Muskau, February 10th, morning

Good morning, Schnucke! What a happy feeling to be able to say this to you myself in a few minutes, and how different it sounds from three hundred miles away! So, for the last time, I make my daily report, *et l'impatience de te parler, chère Schnucke, m'enlève l'envie d'écrire.*

So only as a chronicle do I report that yesterday morning I swung into Bautzen to await Ziethen. In bright sunshine and under a blue sky, I finally drove into Muskau at about one o'clock. In Nieder-Gurig there was a funeral on the road in the snow, and twenty mourners were singing around it. This cheered my Irish friend, who thought he saw an Irish wake in this ceremony, and only missed the drinking. In Borberg, where Vivarais was baiting the horses, I had young Mienchen Ziethen make me coffee, smoked an Eisenach farmer's pipe, and fed my fancy on the coming surprise scene. But nothing came of it, old Schnucke was too excited and moved and, indeed, I caught it from her, and when we came to we were both on our knees like two children, embracing each other, crying, laughing and weeping. Then, indeed, did I get all kinds of scolding, but was very good and treated Schnucke very lovingly. At five o'clock I squeezed myself into my truckle bed, got up in a fever at half-past seven, arranged Schnucke's presents, kissed her tenderly in imagination, and wrote these lines.

With them ends the famous correspondence, begotten of the inclination of a Lou and a Schnucke for each other, which finds its greatest ease in these green meadows.

INDEX